rati...
also written
books, on Engl...
tages, and he lives in
his wife and three children.

'Apart from giving fascinating informa-
tion on the history of building materials
and methods, thereby explaining
regional variations, he shows us the
place of typical farmhouses as centres
of economic and social life' *Sunday
Telegraph*

R.J. Brown

ENGLISH
FARMHOUSES

Hamlyn Paperbacks

A Hamlyn Paperback
Published by Arrow Books Limited
17-21 Conway Street, London W1P 6JD

A division of the Hutchinson Publishing Group

London Melbourne Sydney Auckland
Johannesburg and agencies throughout
the world

First published in Great Britain 1982 by Robert
Hale Ltd
Hamlyn Paperbacks edition 1985

Printed and bound in Great Britain by
Cox & Wyman Ltd, Reading

ISBN 0 09 935380 6

Contents

Illustrations

Acknowledgements

In the preparation of this book I am greatly indebted to all the writers mentioned in the Bibliography whose research over numerous years makes a book like mine possible, and in addition to all those other authors of books and articles too numerous to mention who have assisted in some way in the production of *English Farmhouses*. In particular I would like to acknowledge the help given by the works of R.W. Brunskill whose book *Illustrated Handbook of Vernacular Architecture* has done so much to stimulate not only mine but many others' interest in traditional buildings, to Alex Clifton-Taylor's book *The Pattern of English Building Materials,* now a standard work, to Eric Mercer's book *English Vernacular Houses* for assistance on house plans, to M.W. Barley's book *The English Farmhouse and Cottage,* to the books and numerous articles by Cecil Hewett on timber joints, and to the important regional and technical reports by R.W. Brunskill, N.W. Alcock, R.T. Mason, J.M. Fletcher, J.W. Tonkin, J.T. Smith and R.B. Wood-Jones.

Also, I would like to express my appreciation for the help and co-operation I have received from the staff of the following public libraries: Aylesbury, Birmingham, Bedford, Brighton, Colchester, Chester, Exeter, Hereford, Lincoln, Liverpool, Manchester, Norwich and Shrewsbury.

In addition I would like to thank my wife for her encouragement and assistance throughout and in particular for typing the draft, my son David from whose photographs the drawings were made, and Katherine and Peter for their help.

R.J.B.

Glossary

Abacus	The top member of the capital of a column immediately below the architrave of the entablature.
Arcade	The structural members – posts and braces – which form the lateral division between the main span and its aisles.
Arcade-plate	A horizontal member supported by the arcade posts tying them together and carrying the feet of the rafters of both the main and aisle roofs.
Arcade-post	A vertical member, forming part of the arcade and supporting the arcade-plate.
Architrave	The lowest member of an entablature often adopted as a moulding around an opening in a wall such as a door, window etc.
Architrave, shouldered	An architrave in which the moulding turns away from the opening, near the top, rises and then returns across the top.
Baluster	A vertical member supporting the handrail.
Barge-board	A timber board, sometimes carved, fixed at the gable end and following the slope of the roof to mask the ends of the horizontal roof timbers.
Batten	A small strip of wood used horizontally to hang or attach tiles, slates etc.
Bolection moulding	A raised moulding of bold outline of double curvature.
Bond	The regular arrangement of bricks or stones in order to avoid a continuous vertical joint and so increasing the strength of the wall.
Boss	A projecting ornament either square or round covering the intersection of the ribs in a panelled ceiling or roof.

Bower	The women's apartment in a medieval house.
Brace	A diagonal timber, either straight or curved, to strengthen framework.
Cames	Grooved bars of lead for joining small pieces of glass into a larger sheet.
Canopy	The projecting curved timber hood at the upper end of the medieval open hall.
Cap, Capital	The ornamental expanded top of a post or pillar designed to receive an arched superstructure as in a crown-post.
Casement	A window, of either metal or wood, which is hinged on one side, so opening inwards or outwards.
Catslide roof	A roof having the main slope extending uninterruptedly over an extension.
Chamfer	A splay, usually forty-five degrees, formed when the arris is cut away.
Cladding	A material covering the external face of the building but which is not structural.
Closer	A small brick – a half header – used to complete the bonding pattern at the return of the wall or at a jamb.
Collar, collar beam	A horizontal timber placed above wall-plate level spanning between and tying together a pair of rafters.
Console	A decorative bracket usually in the form of an 'S'.
Corbel	A projection of stone or timber from the face of the wall for the support of a superincumbent weight.
Cove	A concave surface set at an angle generally between vertical and horizontal surfaces.
Cross-wing	A range at the end of and set at right angles to the main range of a house.
Cusp	The projecting points separating the foils in tracery.

Damp-proof course	A horizontal layer of impervious material inserted in a wall to prevent rising damp.
Dentils	Small projecting rectangular blocks to give tooth-like appearance used as decoration on cornices.
Diaper	An all-over pattern of diamond, square or lozenge shapes generally used in brickwork and formed with bricks of two colours.
Dormer	A window projecting vertically from a sloping roof and having a roof of its own.
Dripstone	See *Hood-mould*.
Eaves	The horizontal overhang of a roof projecting beyond the face of a wall.
Entablature	In Classical architecture the horizontal part generally consisting of architrave, frieze and cornice supported on columns or pilasters.
Fascia	A horizontal board to conceal the ends of floor joists in jetty construction and end of rafters etc at roof level.
Fenestration	The arrangement of wndows on the elevation of the external wall.
Fielded panel	A panel with recessed and bevelled margins.
Firehood	A canopy of stone or timber and plaster over a fireplace to lead the smoke to the flue.
Foiled	In Gothic architecture cut into circles which may be grouped together in threes (trefoiled), fours (quatrefoiled), fives (cinquefoiled) etc.
Gable	The vertical triangular wall at the end of the roof, also applied to the wall at the end of a ridged roof.
Galleting	The use of pebbles or chips of stone inserted into the mortar courses generally for decoration but sometimes, when the mortar joints are large, for strength.
Gauge	The part of a roofing slate or tile which is exposed to view.

Header	A brick or stone so laid that only its end appears on the wall-face.
Heck	A short internal wall carrying the firehood, often with an entrance beside it.
Herring-bone	Stones, bricks or tiles laid diagonally and sloping in opposite directions to form a zigzag pattern.
Hip	The sloping external intersection of two inclined roof surfaces.
Hood-mould	A projecting moulding over a door, window or other opening.
Inglenook	The area under a large chimney or firehood.
Jamb	The vertical side of an opening for a door or window in a wall.
Jetty	The projection of an upper floor beyond the storey below on a timber-framed house.
Joist	One of several horizontal parallel timbers laid between walls or beams to carry flooring.
Jowl	The enlarged head of a timber post to carry a tie-beam.
Keystone	The central stone of an arch.
Kneeler	A corbel stone at the bottom of a gable parapet or coping.
Lath	A thin, narrow strip of wood used to provide a backing for plaster.
Light	The vertical opening of a window framed by mullions and/or jambs.
Lintel	A horizontal timber, stone or concrete beam spanning an opening.
Mortar	The material used in bedding, jointing and pointing brick or stone with another.
Mortice	A socket cut in a piece of wood to receive a tenon.
Mullion	A vertical structural member sub-dividing a window.

Newel stair	A spiral stair with steps framed into a central vertical post.
Nogging	Brick used in the filling of panels between timber studwork.
Outshut	An extension of a building under a lean-to roof.
Ovolo moulding	A moulding of Classical origin forming a quarter-round or semi-ellipse in section.
Pediment	A gable of low pitch, straight sided or curved above a door, window etc.
Pilaster	A shallow pier attached to the wall, usually having a base, shaft and capital to comply with one of the Classical orders.
Platband	A horizontal plain projecting band of masonry or brickwork as distinct from a moulded string course.
Plinth	The projecting base of a wall often with a splayed top.
Pointing	The exposed face of the joint of brickwork or stonework which is smoothed with the point of a trowel.
Purlin	In roof construction, a longitudinal horizontal timber supporting the common rafters.
Quoin	Dressed stones or distinctive brickwork at the external angle of a wall.
Rafter	One of several inclined timbers supporting the roof covering.
Random	Not laid in courses.
Rendering	Cement or lime-plaster covering to external face of a wall.
Reredos	A stone wall at the back of a timber and plaster firehood.
Reveal	The side wall of an opening or recess which is at right angles to the face of the main wall.
Ridge	The apex of a roof, the ridge-piece being the horizontal longitudinal timber supporting the tops of the rafters.

Riser	Of a staircase, the vertical member of a step.
Rubble	Unsquared and undressed stone.
Sash	A glazed wooden window which slides up and down by means of a pulley.
Shutters	Timber boards between which semi-liquid material can be poured for building a wall.
Soffit	The underside of a lintel, beam or arch.
Solar	The principal chamber, usually at the upper end of the hall, in a medieval house.
Spandrel	The space between the curved or shaped head of an opening and a rectangular outer frame; the space between the curved brace and a tie-beam.
Spere	A wall usually at the lower end of the open hall and projecting from one or both sides of the hall to screen the entrances.
Spere-truss	A roof truss, with below the tie-beam two speres leaving a wide central opening into the hall from the cross-passage.
Stop	The feature at the end of a moulding or chamfer to transfer the batten to a square section.
Strapwork	Flat interlaced decoration derived from strips of cut leather, popular in Tudor period.
Stretcher	A brick or stone so laid that only its long side appears on the wall-face.
String	Of a staircase, the raking side member carrying the treads and risers; closed string in which the treads and risers are housed, the open string in which the string is cut to the profile of the treads and risers.
String-course	A projecting horizontal band or moulding on the external face of a wall.
Strut	In roof construction, a vertical or diagonal timber which does not support a longitudinal member.

Studs	The vertical members of a timber-framed house between the main posts.
Swag	An ornamental festoon of foliage etc which is fastened up at both ends and hangs down in the centre.
Tenon	The end of a piece of wood reduced in width in order to fit into a mortice of another piece of wood thus making a joint.
Tie-beam	In roof construction, the main horizontal timber of a truss joining together the feet of the principal rafter at the wall-plate.
Torching	The filling-in with lime and hair mortar of the uneven space between the underside of tiles or slates on an unboarded or unfelted roof.
Tracery	The decorative pattern at the head of a Gothic window or opening, generally formed by the interlacing extension of the mullions.
Transom	A horizontal structural member sub-dividing a window.
Tread	Of a staircase, the horizontal member of a step.
Truss	A rigid framework spanning the building used to support the ridge, purlins etc that carries the common rafters.
Underbuilt	A wall added beneath a jetty.
Valley	The sloping internal junction of two inclined roof surfaces.
Venetian window	A window with three openings, the centre one arched and wider than the others.
Wall-plate	A horizontal timber member at the top of the wall to receive the ends of the rafters, tie-beams etc.
Windbrace	A timber member often curved and set diagonally between the principal rafters and the side purlins to increase resistance to wind pressure and stiffen the roof structure longitudinally.
Winder stair	A stair turning continuously.

Yoke   A short horizontal timber joining the rafters together near the apex of the roof often supporting a ridge.

English Farmhouses –
An Introduction

England has a rich inheritance of old houses, each varying enormously in age, style, status and construction, of which the farmhouse represents a significant proportion. Precisely how many farmhouses or former farmhouses still survive is difficult to estimate, but W. G. Hoskins has claimed that in Devon alone some twelve thousand still exist. Many also survive in other areas where pastoral farming predominated and farms were small or where there was an early enclosure of the land such as in parts of the South-east, like the Weald, and in East Anglia and Essex, or where partible inheritance (gavelkind) was practised, in which the members of the family were left equal shares in a property which led to the establishment of many small farms.

Most farmhouses are essentially vernacular buildings – traditional buildings, built of local materials in a limited variety of house types which evolved over the centuries to suit the farming and social needs of the various communities. At the lower end of these vernacular buildings are the two-roomed farmhouses, many of which are today classified as cottages but which originated as small farms or smallholdings. In fact it is probable that the majority of detached houses, except those of the rural craftsmen, built prior to the eighteenth century are or at least were originally farmhouses which, although in most cases the land associated with them was small, have lost their lands due to the effects of enclosures. Even in the eighteenth and nineteenth centuries one- and two-roomed farmhouses were being built in many of the upland regions, with the continuing encroachment and enclosures of the moorland and mountain slopes. At the upper end of these vernacular buildings are the larger farmhouses with three, four or more ground-floor rooms. Often these were small manor houses, many of which were little more than working farms.

It is this variety in shape, size and age of these old farmhouses that is one of the delights of rural England, built as they are out of local materials which harmonize in their natural environment. This great diversity has been brought about by a number of factors – geological, climatic, social and economic – all of which have influenced to some degree the various plans, method of construction and materials used.

The geology of England is such that the country can be split into two

21

zones – the highland zone which contains the moors and mountainous regions of the South-west, the West and much of the North and the lowland zone which comprises mainly the low-lying land of the South, the South-east and the East. Clearly the building materials which these two greatly contrasting regions yielded dictated the overall appearance of the house. The building material of the highland zone at the vernacular level was generally stone, the major exceptions being the cob buildings of Devon and other parts of the South-west, the timber-framed houses of the West Midlands and Welsh Marches and the brick houses of Yorkshire along the coastal strip. The major building material used in the lowland zone was timber, being replaced at the end of the seventeenth century by brick.

Up until the eighteenth century farmhouses were invariably built of materials that came most readily to hand, though the similarity did not always influence the style, as can be seen in the remarkable differences in say the timber-framed houses of the South-east, eastern England and the West Midlands. Similarly, farmhouses of the great stone-bearing regions differed greatly. The limestone belt which stretches from Dorset into Humberside produced in the main a stone which could be easily worked and a style of house that incorporated many refinements generally associated with larger buildings. Elsewhere over much of northern England, as well as in the South-west, the stones available were the harder limestones, granite, slates and shales, all of which, because of their intractable nature, imposed limitations and attributed much to the simple, rugged design of the houses built but which like all vernacular buildings blend in so happily with the bleak and exposed nature of the regions in which these stones are found.

In addition this natural division greatly affected the social and economic development of England, for from the earliest times soil and terrain have both dictated the pattern of agriculture. In the North and South-west of England, because the lands are mainly dominated by the moors and mountains, much of it over eight hundred feet above sea-level, the soils are generally thin and poor, the climate damp and, in the North, cold as well. In the main, except for some exceptional areas – along the coastal plains of Durham and Cumberland, in the Lancashire and Cheshire plain, and in Devon and Somerset in the coastlands and in the larger vales – the land was generally only suitable for the rearing of livestock which formed the bulk of the agriculture. In contrast the South-east and eastern England in both landscape and climate are very different. Here the landscape comprises generally gently undulating land with, apart from the chalk downs, few hills, producing in the main a much deeper, richer soil. Add to this the drier climate, and one has the ideal condition for arable farming. Between these two, in most of the Midlands, is the area of mixed farming where the farmer had a choice between arable or pasture, often combining the two, the proportion varying in accordance with the condition of his land and the demand for his various produces.

In parts of the highland zone the combination of soil and climate made them inexorably poor, and this is obviously reflected in the housing. In some parts of the highland zone houses of one or two ground-floor rooms were a common feature in the eighteenth and nineteenth centuries built on the edges of the moors and the upper slopes of the valleys, many of them being abandoned, particularly during the agricultural depression in the latter half of the nineteenth century. This is not to say, however, that all the highland zone was poor, for within these areas the richer lands produced sufficient wealth to enable farmers to build houses of better quality, as many of the farmhouses of Devon and Cumbria indicate. In these areas the houses built were not inferior to those built in many parts of the lowland zone, but many of the old concepts, such as the cross-passage and the access to the parlour only obtained from the hall, were often preserved. Likewise not all the lowland was rich; there were poor areas, but since they were relatively small and not highly populated, they could be more readily absorbed into the larger, richer areas in which they lay.

In the thirteenth and fourteenth centuries a large proportion of the country was farmed in the open-field system. In much of the lowland zone and in particular in the Midland counties from the Pennines to the Chilterns, and also in addition in parts of the highland zone, this comprised two, three or four large arable strips with, depending on the number of fields, either one or two being fallow while the others were being cultivated. Each field was divided into strips, divided by unploughed baulks and distributed amongst the villagers, with each man working two, three or more strips depending on his individual status in different parts of each field. Surrounding these arable fields were the common pastures on which the animals grazed, and beyond these was the waste.

In these areas where this system of farming predominated, there was a high degree of peasant co-operation, relying on each other for their continuing survival. Consequently the houses of the community grew up in the nucleated village, along the village street and in the lanes that ran into the open fields beyond. The sites of the buildings were invariably long and narrow, and at first the houses were built parallel to the main street with the houses occupying the entire width of the site, apart perhaps from an access to the yard at the rear flanked by farm buildings. The site, complete with a croft or enclosed pasture, held in severalty, probably completed the holding, and these strips of land would stretch out to the open fields that surrounded the village.

The early dwellings of the peasant farmers were of frail

construction, and in the sixteenth and seventeenth centuries many of the dwellings within the village were replaced with more substantial dwellings of timber and stone and in some parts brick. These new houses, together with those provided to accommodate the increase in population, were all contained within the old village, for the open fields were too valuable to allow encroachment. In many cases these new dwellings were built on the old site, but because of the narrowness of many sites and the inadequate frontage for the new larger dwellings, it often necessitated their rebuilding with the gables facing the street.

Enclosures had a great effect on these nucleated villages. These enclosures of the open fields took place at various times in various parts of the country. In some parts the enclosure of the open fields occurred at a very early date, and in Kent there is little evidence of the open-field system ever being employed. Following the depletion of the population by the Black Death in the fourteenth century there was shortage of labour, and the old feudal system began to break down. The Black Death unwittingly laid the foundation of the future wealth and prosperity of the country. Because of the decline in the population and consequently the decreasing demand for food, new ways of utilizing the land were sought. Much arable land disappeared to be replaced with pasture on which sheep grazed, and this continued throughout the fifteenth and sixteenth centuries. Although many of these enclosures caused concern, there were many others, often devised by mutual consent between two or more farmers, which encouraged better use of the arable land remaining. At the end of the sixteenth century, with the increase in population which forced up prices of foodstuffs, there was an increasing desire for many arable farmers to increase their holdings. Up to this time much enclosure had been effected, at first chiefly for purposes of sheep-farming, but by the beginning of the eighteenth century about half the arable land of the country still remained open. This was soon to change. Enclosures continued spasmodically throughout the country, but during the second half and the first decade of the following century the number increased rapidly. This impetus was caused by the great increase in the population of the manufacturing towns brought about by the Industrial Revolution which opened up fresh and large markets for the farmers' products. These Parliamentary enclosures of the eighteenth and nineteenth centuries – from the 1720s to 1870 or so – and those of the Tudor period caused great hardship to many, and there was in all those areas where they occurred the continuing dispossession of the smallholder, his land being acquired by the larger farmers.

During the latter half of the eighteenth century in many parts of the country about a third of the farms disappeared. With this increased size of farms, larger farmhouses, with more rooms to deal with and the storage of the resulting increase in agricultural produces, were necessary. Consequently the farmhouses within the village were inconvenient and were frequently abandoned for new farmhouses built on their new holdings, with the former farmhouses being divided into tenements for the new landless class who were required to work on the new enlarged farms. Therefore, in many parts of the country where the open-field system of agriculture was practised, many of the houses within the village are former farmhouses belonging either to former farmers who have moved out of the village or to former husbandmen or smallholders who have been dispossessed.

Most farmhouses located today in the villages are only a few of the survivors of the many, both large and small, which at one time made up the community. They are to be found mainly in the Midland counties where the open-field system was particularly strong and where there was a late enclosure of the land. Even about 1800 over most of the Midlands it was still unusual to see a farm or cottage outside a village complex. In those areas where open fields still survived, villages were compact and isolated farms absent. Even after enclosures had occurred, the scattered pattern of some holdings spread over a large area, still encouraging the farm complex to continue to be located within the village.

In contrast to the lowlands, in the uplands the pasture was ample and was the mainstay of the agriculture, while the arable fields, which were more often than not small and often varying greatly in number from one to seven and more, were subsidiary, supplying only the immediate needs of the community. In all these areas where there was a plentiful supply of pasture, there was, unlike areas with the open-field system, little pressure on the pasture by increasing the arable land. Consequently most of the pastoral areas of highland England were enclosed either from the beginning or from an early date, and even in those areas where there was some kind of communal cultivation of the arable land, this did not restrict the carrying-out of enclosures of the pastures by common consent. Transhumance, the seasonal migration of pastoral people with their herds from winter settlements to summer hill pastures on other parts of the moors, was a feature of upland life in the Middle Ages and still survived in a few areas in northern England in the sixteenth and seventeenth centuries. In the North the herdsmen were housed in small temporary buildings known as 'sheilings', the remains of which can still be seen in Cumbria and Northumberland.

In most of these areas where pastoral farming predominated, the farmhouses and their buildings were located in small, isolated settlements or hamlets. By the beginning of the nineteenth century in the South-west, westwards of the Cotswolds into Devon and Cornwall, hamlets, consisting of three or four farmhouses with their yards and perhaps a cottage or two, were a feature of the landscape, all linked by narrow, winding tracks and lanes. Even where compact villages existed, unlike those of the Midlands, they were surrounded by dispersed hamlets and isolated farms. These isolated settlements can still be seen today, some of the best being on Dartmoor, where Lettaford is a typical example of an unaltered moorland hamlet formerly comprising three farmhouses, all of the longhouse plan, and numerous farm buildings, with a chapel and a cottage added later. In the Lake District too, as well as most of the Pennine upland, few settlements had more than twenty dwellings, the majority having no more than a few farmsteads and cottages. These isolated settlements are still a feature of the Lake District and other parts of the North, with villages being found only in the more fertile valleys and coastal plains.

Hamlets were not only a feature of the highlands but can also be found in many parts of the lowlands too, where there was an early tradition of small-scale individual enclosures. In parts of Essex and Suffolk where, during the fourteenth, fifteenth and sixteenth centuries, pastoral farming was practised, hamlets or small villages, their scattered buildings loosely grouped around a spacious common, were a feature. In other parts too, in those formerly wooded districts such as in the Chilterns, Cannock Chase in Charnwood, the Arden district of Warwickshire and the Forest of Dean, hamlets predominated. In the South-east in formerly well-wooded areas, particularly in the Weald and elsewhere in Kent where the very early enclosure of the open field and the custom of partible inheritance existed, hamlets were the characteristic settlement prior to the nineteenth century.

The majority of farmsteads are located neither in villages nor in hamlets but are isolated farmsteads which have come about for a number of reasons. The earliest of these isolated farms were formed by assarting – the colonization of the woodland for farming – or the occupation of the uncultivated moorland. Assarts may not be easy to identify for not all early enclosures were by this means, for many of the hedged medieval fields were formed by mutual agreement to exchange their strips to create more compact land holdings. However, many of the isolated farmsteads in Essex, Suffolk, Kent and Sussex, as well as further west in such places as the Arden in Warwickshire, were formed by the late-medieval colonization of the woodland and waste. These early settlements are further complicated by the number of medieval moated manorial farmsteads of the fourteenth century that are to be found in these areas. This provision of moats continued to no small extent throughout the sixteenth century, although in many instances where there is a moated farmhouse of the Tudor or later period, these often replaced an earlier house on the same site. At small farmhouses these moats are often dry and in some cases fragmented. In Essex the Royal Commission on Historical Monuments includes some 280 moated sites in 400 or so parishes, while N. Scarfe has identified some 300 moated farmsteads, or farmsteads with remains of moats, most in the north-western half of the county. Similarly there are numerous moated farmsteads in the heavy clay districts of Suffolk, as there are in parts of Norfolk, Cambridgeshire and Hertfordshire. These isolated moated farmsteads can also be found in other parts of the country, for instance in Kent, Sussex, Hereford and Worcester and parts of the West Midlands. In medieval times these moats were undoubtedly for defence, but later they served to enclose cattle at night and in the winter. The occupation of uncultivated moorland is to be found in many parts of upland England, where, although there are many farmsteads situated in small settlements, many isolated farmsteads, some of medieval origin, can be found. The encroachment and continuing colonization of the valley slopes continued throughout the seventeenth and eighteenth centuries when many old farms were enlarged and new ones built.

Isolated farmsteads were also formed from the decay or destruction of former nucleated villages or hamlets. This may be the result of plague, which, although reaching its peak in the fourteenth century, continued to break out spasmodically until well into the seventeenth century, depopulating many villages and hamlets. The main cause of the destruction of these settlements was undoubtedly the effect of enclosures, particularly in Tudor times when villages and hamlets were swept away to provide sheep-runs, leaving only the manor farm standing. The effects of enclosures continued, and the final phase was often the ultimate blow for a hamlet, converting it into a single farmstead.

The most numerous of these isolated farmsteads, however, are the result of the enclosure of the open fields and commons. Early isolated farmsteads appear in both highland and lowland England in all those areas where the early enclosure of the land was a feature, but it is not until Tudor times, with the sudden increase in agreed enclosures, that they began to appear in any great number. At this time the main distinction in the lowland zone was between the enclosed wooded countryside with dispersed settlements on the one hand and the open-field countryside with nucleated villages on the other. William Harrison in 1577 noted that in the open-field country the houses 'stood altogether by streets and joining one to another', whereas in the 'woodland countries' they were dispersed 'here and there'. Enclosures continued throughout the seventeenth century, the number increasing dramatically with the Parliamentary enclosures during the second half of the eighteenth century. These affected in the main the Midlands, transforming the appearance of the landscape, and the distinction previously made between enclosed and open-field regions was largely obliterated. In all these areas new farmhouses of brick and stone began to appear outside the villages in their new consolidated fields which, unlike the small irregular-shaped fields of earlier enclosures, were larger, squarer fields often bounded by straight hedges or with straight stone walls. The enclosure of the arable fields continued, although greatly reduced in number, throughout the nineteenth century, finally enclosing those remaining open fields that had survived amid the largely enclosed landscape. New farmsteads also appeared sometime after the initial enclosure as large allotments were gradually re-organized in new compact units. In the highland zone too there are many isolated farmsteads due to these Parliamentary enclosures throughout the eighteenth century, and these continued well into the nineteenth century, for the enclosure and improvement of the moors remained far from complete. New farmsteads in the nineteenth century began to appear on the moors and higher up the valley sides in places that had not long before been uninhabited moorland and waste.

Throughout the centuries two main factors in the evolution of the farmhouse, as with all housing, were the continuing desires for more comfort and greater privacy. To these can be added the influences that seek to protect and proclaim a family's status, requiring it to live in a house which befits its place in society.

The early peasant medieval houses provided little comfort for their inhabitants. Generally these dwellings had low walls with a steeply pitched thatched roof with an open hall generally filled with smoke from the central open hearth; windows were small holes kept to a minimum, for they were a source of draught and damp, with the doors covered with ox-hide or coarse fabric. The household effects were generally limited to a few pieces of furniture, a bed or two and a few cooking implements.

Few domestic houses survive from before the fifteenth century, and those that do are former manor houses either of the first-floor hall type of the twelfth and thirteenth centuries or the later ground-floor open-hall type of aisled construction in which the emphasis was on the hall, the home of the lord where the manorial court was held. In contrast to these, most of the peasant houses of the period, being frail structures, have not survived the ravages of time. Most were constructed of either thin timbers, earth, turf or chalk and, from the thirteenth century onwards in almost all stone-producing areas, of stone. All these materials were to be found close to hand and from the evidence of excavations required little, if any, skilled labour in their erection.

From the archaeological evidence so far, these peasant houses can be divided into three main types, the one-roomed or slightly larger two-roomed cot, the longhouse and the farm complex. The cot was at the lower end of the social scale and was the hut of the cotter or border who had no land of his own. The longhouses probably belonged to medieval villeins and generally comprised at one end the living quarters, often divided into two rooms, and at the other the byre, usually separated from the living quarters by a cross-walk or cross-passage but always with access between the two. These early longhouses appeared to vary greatly in size, some being little bigger than the average two-roomed cot, some thirty feet by twelve, while others were over seventy-five feet long. Most, however, were about forty-five feet long. The distribution of these longhouses was widespread, and evidence of their existence has been found over a large area of England with the exception of East Anglia, Kent and parts of the central Midlands. The largest of the three medieval house types was the farm complex in which the byre and/or barn was separated from the farmhouse, with the farm buildings usually set at right angles to it to form the basis of a courtyard. This would be the farm of the most prosperous of the villagers, probably emerging yeoman farmers who were in many parts acquiring their freeholds. In many cases there is evidence of former longhouses being rebuilt to form the larger farm complex. The frail nature of these medieval dwellings necessitated their repair or rebuilding about once a generation, often on a completely new foundation and to a new alignment.

Not all farmhouses were of frail construction, and from the end of the fourteenth century onwards substantial but relatively small houses of timber-framed construction began to appear in the South-east, particularly the Weald, and in Essex, Suffolk and the adjoining parts of Hertfordshire and Cambridgeshire. Many were undoubtedly manor houses, but some at least were being built for the new emerging class of yeoman farmers, who, because perhaps of early enclosures with the gradual acquisition of land and the custom of partible inheritance common in Kent and Norfolk and parts of Essex, Suffolk and Cambridgeshire, had begun to build up large farms with secure tenures. Although aisled construction had by then been abandoned, the open hall with central hearth was retained, with either a service bay at one end or a service bay at one end and a solar bay at the other.

Throughout the fourteenth and fifteenth centuries poorly constructed buildings still survived in most parts of the country and were a feature of most rural settlements. Towards the end of the sixteenth century, however, these older dwellings were swept away in what W. G. Hoskins has termed the 'rebuilding of rural England'. Over much of the country the period of this rebuilding dates from 1570 to 1640, and this is evident from the number of Elizabethan and Jacobean farmhouses that survive today. Further north, in Cumbria, Northumberland and Durham, this occurred somewhat later, although there are some examples, particularly in Cumbria, built for the new statesman class who had obtained the right to bequeath their land by Will and paid only a small monetary rent. Many of the farmsteads of the Cotswolds and throughout the limestone belt, from eastern Somerset through Gloucestershire and Northamptonshire into Leicestershire and Lincolnshire, built or re-built in local stone date from this period, as do many of the timber-framed farmhouses of the West Midlands, while there is evidence that in Devon the prosperous yeoman farmers were rebuilding their houses. In the South-east too, particularly the Weald, many buildings were built or re-built in timber, and J.L.M. Gulley has claimed that during this period more houses were built in the Weald than at any time before or since. Similar evidence is to be found in eastern England; in Essex this wave of rebuilding was at its height between 1590 and 1640, and this applies similarly to Cambridgeshire and Suffolk. In fact it is clear that, apart from Cumbria, Northumberland and Durham, the evidence for this great rebuilding between 1570 and 1640 is abundant. During this period most of the old and more substantial farmhouses, especially the timber-framed ones of the Weald as well as in Essex, Cambridgeshire, Hertfordshire and East Anglia, incorporated considerable structural alterations. These normally took the form of the insertion of a ceiling into the medieval open hall and the construction of a smoke bay or chimney to replace the open earth.

In the main all this building, rebuilding and reconstruction was undertaken by lesser gentry, yeomen and husbandmen with the accumulation of wealth derived from the continuing and widening gap between fixed expenses, such as wages and rents, and the rapid increase in the price obtained for farm produce demanded by the increasing population. This increase in the general prosperity of the farmer is also evident from the many minor comforts that were now being provided within the house. William Harrison, writing in about 1580, noted that glass was replacing unglazed windows made of timber lattice work or horn, that feather beds were replacing straw pallets, that pillows were being used instead of wooden head-rests and that platters and spoons were being made out of metal instead of wood. This is confirmed by details of the household inventories which revealed a substantial increase in the domestic effects of all kinds in the average farmhouse, with the possible exception of those in the far north, providing a higher level of domestic comfort than ever before.

This general rebuilding was brought to a sudden end with the outbreak of the Civil War in 1642, and even after 1649 the building of

new farmhouses was slow to resume. It was not until the 1660s that
the rebuilding continued, as can be seen by the numerous dated
examples throughout the country, of both stone and brick. Even in
Cumbria, an area not greatly affected by the rebuilding earlier in the
century, there is much evidence of rebuilding between the years 1670
and 1710, particularly for the statesmen. In the South-east and East
the old timber-framed houses of previous centuries began to be
modernized to provide the inhabitants with greater comfort. Many
began to be clad with plaster, brick, tiles and weatherboarding to
provide a warmer and less draughty and damp house. The new
fashionable sash windows and panelled doors often completed the
modernization. In addition many old houses of one or one-and-a-half
storeys were raised to provide accommodation of two full storeys and
bays, wings or outshuts added to provide additional accommodation
for either domestic or agricultural purposes. New houses, whether of
timber, stone or brick, incorporated these refinements, if they could
be afforded, from the start. New plans also developed, providing a
better and more compact house. The former house types popular
during the sixteenth and seventeenth centuries began to be displaced
with houses which reproduced the styles of the fashionable
Renaissance. From the end of the seventeenth century farmhouses too
were being influenced by the new style, giving rise to more
symmetrical designs. The most marked change was that the hall, that
essential feature of the farmhouse for so long, was losing its status with
the increasing number of living-rooms. The impact of the fashionable
styles varied from class to class and from region to region, but sooner
or later the earlier house types were abandoned. The most drastic
changes came in all those areas where the regional styles had developed
out of the medieval tradition of the open hall, the cross-passage and
cross-wing plans.

By the beginning of the eighteenth century large five-bay
farmhouses with a symmetrical façade, with the doorway flanked by
two tall windows on either side, with five windows to the first floor
built in the new two-room-deep double-pile plan, with the living-
rooms to the front and the service rooms at the rear, began to appear.
By the 1730s smaller farmhouses with a balanced façade of three bays –
central doorway flanked by a window on either side – became popular
despite the minor agricultural recession, in some regions, during the
second quarter of the eighteenth century. The building of these new
symmetrical houses gained additional impetus at the end of the
eighteenth century with the final enclosures of the open fields. No
longer were long, rectangular and inconvenient houses built with
inter-communicating rooms and low ceilings, but spacious, well-
planned ones which for the first time were designed for the comforts

and requirements of the family rather than those of the farm.

This continuing development and improvement to the farmhouse was a gradual process, for old concepts, developed over the centuries, were often retained. Many of the new concepts in housing originated in the South-east, for not only was it favoured with its climate and soil which made it one of the richer parts of the country and its close proximity to London provided an easy outlet for farm products, but its close proximity and trading connections with the Continent also brought in new ideas in both designs and comfort. These new ideas spread only slowly northwards and westwards, not reaching the extreme North until a hundred years or so later.

So the history of the English farmhouse is one of continuing change. Today is no exception. The number of farms is falling with the re-organization of agriculture and the frequent amalgamation of small farms into larger units, resulting in the selling-off of the farmhouse to new owners not connected with farming and adopting them to their needs. The remaining farmhouses, too, often have little connection with the farm, for it is no longer necessary for the farmer to be tied to the farmstead as in days gone by. There are, however, many ancient farmhouses built from the fifteenth century to the end of the eighteenth century still to be found throughout the country. These remaining farmhouses built in the vernacular tradition are essential components of the English landscape, showing clearly the influence of the continuing changing values, yet retaining many of the local traditions which have occurred over the centuries.

PART ONE

Types and Plans

Introduction

The social and agricultural needs of farmers and their families can often be seen in the design of their houses. As with other houses at the vernacular level, most farmhouses can be classified into two main groups, 'divided' or 'undivided' houses. Divided houses are those which have a through-passage, in the form of either a cross-passage or a screens-passage, which divided the living quarters from the service rooms. This group includes the open-hall house in its various forms and the cross-passage farmhouse which includes the longhouse. The undivided houses have no through-passage and are of a later form than the divided houses, the service rooms being incorporated within the house. To this group belong the lobby-entry farmhouse, the direct-entry farmhouse and the later double-pile farmhouse.

Until the double-pile house became established in the middle of the eighteenth century, in the vernacular house, with the exception of some subsidiary rooms which occupied only part of the depth of the building, all main rooms were one room deep, the overall depth depending on the length of timber available for roof construction. Most houses were therefore rectangular in plan, and the irregular shapes seen today are adaptations of the original plan either in the form of a single-storey outshut at the rear or on larger houses a transverse wing at one or sometimes both ends. The houses are often divided into two parts, the upper end which contains the private rooms or withdrawing-rooms, and the lower end, often referred to as the low house or nether house, which contains the kitchen and service rooms or, in the case of the longhouse, the byre.

Except for a few which were originally designed for first-floor living, the majority of farmhouses were designed for ground-floor living. In the days of the open hall the main rooms, including the principal bedrooms, were on the ground floor, and it was not until these were chambered over to provide a floor over the whole house that the upper floor could have become the bedroom floor. Even then in many farmhouses the principal bedroom remained on the ground floor, with the upper floor being little more than an ill-lit attic. It was not until the adoption of the dormer window and finally the raising of the roof to allow two full storey-height floors that the first floor became universally adopted as the bedroom floor.

In studying the various house plans, it is useful to remember the two zones first defined by Sir Cyril Fox and which have now been largely accepted. They are based on geological divisions, with the highland zone coinciding with the hardstone areas – those areas to the north and west of the limestone belt which runs from Dorset in the south to Yorkshire in the north – and the lowland zone – the area to the south and east of the limestone belt which includes the plains of Humberside. These two zones also generally correspond with the mainly arable-dominated farming of the South and East and the mainly pastoral-dominated farming of the North and West, and it will be seen later that the traditional farmhouse is more closely related to agricultural than to social development. The line however between both zones is difficult to define, for the agrarian regions do not correspond with the geological ones.

The names of the various rooms used in the following chapters often differ from their meaning in today's houses. The principal room would be the hall, the room most used by the household in which the family ate and generally lived and where, when there was no separate kitchen, the meals were cooked. In the North the hall was often referred to as the house or hall-house, or less often as homesbody, homestead or simply dwelling house. In those houses in which one room was used for both living and cooking it became widespread practice, from the middle of the seventeenth century onwards, to downgrade the room to that of a kitchen. Next in importance to the hall was the parlour, which was originally a combined bedroom and workroom for use by the female members of the family – a survival of the medieval bower. In many farmhouses in the South it was not until the seventeenth century and much later in the North that the main bedroom was one of the chambered rooms upstairs and the parlour given its present-day connotation. Later, at much the same time as the downgrading of the hall into the kitchen, the parlour was often referred to as the sitting-room, and the hall became merely the entrance lobby. Even the smallest of farmhouses had one service room, generally known as the buttery, a room used for the storage of provisions and in particular drink. Less commonly this room was called the pantry, which in medieval times was also used to store flour and other provisions. In larger farmhouses there were two service rooms; in the highland zone the second was often the dairy and was generally agricultural rather than domestic, while in the lowland zone it was generally the milkhouse. Larger farmhouses often had as many as five service rooms, and in addition to the buttery, dairy and milkhouse, there might have been a kitchen, a brewhouse, a quernhouse (a room where malt was ground), a bakehouse and a boulting, although some of these may have been housed in separate buildings away from the main house.

Very few farmhouses today remain unaltered, and the insertion of the upper floors in the open hall, the replacement of the open hearth with a chimney stack, the adaptation of the service rooms into living accommodation, the blocking-up and forming of new door openings, the removal of partitions and screens and the building of new ones and the extensions to the sides and rear have, in many cases, made it difficult to discern the original design. In some cases the farmhouses mentioned in the following chapters relate to their original design rather than their existing plan.

The size of a house, as with other buildings, is and always was classified by the number of bays, and so in many legal and other documents houses were often described as having two, three or four bays, much as today when houses are described as having two, three or four bedrooms. In box-frame and cruck construction these bays are the internal compartments of a house defined by the structural divisions in the side walls which generally support the roof trusses and roof. These bays did, however, have a close relationship to the room, for usually the partitions were placed on the same line, and so a room would be either one, two or three bays long. The length of these bays varied greatly, from less than four feet to as much as eighteen feet, and even in the same house were rarely the same. In the standard two-bay hall open to the roof the central truss denoting the bay was rarely placed in the centre, and the end solar and service bays were generally of different lengths depending on the social needs of the inhabitants. It was not unusual to have an additional small bay for the screens-passage, smoke bay or chimney stack. In stone and brick buildings where there is no structural division the bays are defined by the external division of the building by fenestration.

The follow abbreviations have been used in the house plans: B – Buttery, BH – Backhouse, BN – Barn, BY – Byre, CP – Cross-passage, C/S – Cart shed, D – Dairy, DH – Downhouse, D/R – Dining-room, H – Hall, HM – Hay mew, K – Kitchen, O/H – Open hall, P – Parlour, Pan – Pantry, S – Solar, S/R – Service room, St – Stable.

The First-floor Hall
Farmhouse

Most houses were always designed for ground-floor living, but there were some which for some reason, usually defensive, were built for first-floor living, the lower floor, with the exception of the bastle-houses which accommodated animals, being used only for storage. At the vernacular level there were two types, the first-floor hall house (1) and the tower house.

First-floor halls, features of many private houses built during the thirteenth century, are Norman in origin. Other than the occasional town house they are manorial or religious in origin. The basic plan was simple. On the first floor was the hall, usually of two bays and at one end a single-bay solar, both open to the roof. Access to the hall was obtained by means of a door reached by an external staircase. The hall was heated by a fireplace located on either the rear or side wall, but the solar was rarely heated. The ground floor was generally an open space with an external door and only small windows for ventilation.

One of the most complete examples is perhaps Boothby Pagnell Manor House, Lincolnshire, a small manor house built about 1200. The house, which had as its only defence a moat, is rectangular in plan and has a wall about four feet thick at the base and above this some two feet thick built of stone rubble with ashlar dressings. The ground floor is vaulted – the undercroft under the hall of two bays with quadripartite rib-vaulting and under the solar a tunnel-vault set at right angles to the front – and above this reached by an external stone stair are the hall and solar. The external door, which formerly led directly into the hall, has a typical Norman rounded head with chamfered jambs. The hall was originally lit by two small arched windows, one to the right of the external entrance door and the other in the end wall of the hall, each divided by a polygonal colonnette or shaft with a simple capital. The window to the front elevation was replaced in the fifteenth century by a larger four-light window, and the original window was reset in the end wall of the hall alongside the other original window. The solar too had two twelfth-century windows similar to those in the hall, but the one in the end wall of the solar has been blocked in. The ground floor still retains its original doorway with a lintel with a quarter-circle corbel at each end, but the windows have been altered and are of a later date. A lintel similar to that on the

38

Elevation

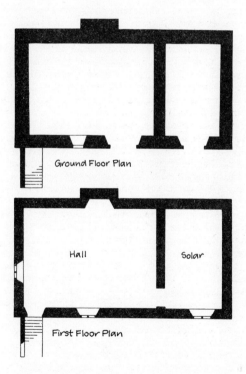

Ground Floor Plan

Hall   Solar

First Floor Plan

1. Typical twelfth-century first-floor house.

ground floor is to be found to the doorway between the hall and solar. Within the hall the fireplace with its projecting hood is the most notable feature.

Although the manor house at Boothby Pagnell is one of the most complete examples to have survived, there are others, all possibly of slightly later date, which are of great interest. At Hoad Farm, Acrise, Kent, at one end of the fourteenth-century flint-built house there projects a narrower part, which at high level still retains the lancet windows, in which must have been the first-floor hall of the original thirteenth-century house. Another flint-built house is Manor Farm, Hambledon, Hampshire. All these have been altered, and most have been incorporated into larger houses.

Another which has in recent years been discovered is Manor Farm, Little Chesterford, Essex (2), where alterations to the stone wing, which was built about 1200, have revealed two existing doorways in the larger of the two first-floor rooms; one doorway is Tudor, but the other is older and seems likely to have been the original entrance reached by an external stairway. This doorway, together with the fact it was built in the thirteenth century, probably establishes that this was originally a first-floor hall house. In layout, this wing is similar to that of Boothby Pagnell Manor House; it is rectangular in plan and measures $38\frac{1}{2}$ feet long and nineteen feet wide internally with the walls to the ground floor some three feet thick reducing to about two feet at first-floor level. There is no evidence of the ground floor being divided at this time, and there remain two original small stone windows with semicircular rere-arches. The two doorways, with two-centred arches, from this wing into the screens-passage of the later aisled hall are probably of a later build. The first floor has a timber-lodged floor with a large bridging-joist running the full length of the building supported at or near the centre with a samson-post, this again indicating that the ground floor was originally open. The first floor is divided into two – the hall and solar – and apart from the two surviving doorways there are the remains of the moulded shaft of a thirteenth-century window. This wing was extensively modernized in the sixteenth century, and most of the windows were replaced, internal partitions provided to divide the ground floor and a new staircase put in and the roof renewed.

Most known examples of upper-hall type houses are constructed of stone, built from about 1150 until around 1300, but there are a number of houses similar to them and of contemporary date built of timber. A number have later open-hall ranges built alongside, and it is often suggested that these earlier buildings were solar cross-wings to former ground-floor hall ranges which for some reason have disappeared. This theory cannot, of course, be disproved and in some cases may well be true, but the general arrangement and the high architectural standard of some of these upper rooms, often with provision of a first-floor fireplace built at the same time as the house, coupled with the fact that there is generally no evidence of the existence of a former ground-floor hall, perhaps indicate that this is unlikely. It is equally unlikely that, at a time when such stone-built first-floor hall houses were being built (such as Temple Manor, Strood, the Old Rectory, Ickham and the manor house at Sandwich, all in Kent, and the Old Clergy House, West Dean, and Lodsworth Manor, both in Sussex, and many more), none were being built in timber.

There are a few timber-framed buildings which survive from the end of the thirteenth century which are in arrangement similar to those first-floor hall houses built of stone. J.M. Fletcher cites two examples in Harwell, Oxfordshire. The southern range at Middle Farm which was built about 1280 is of three bays, the upper floor being divided into a two-bay room to the front with a single-bay room at the rear. The height of the ground-floor room is at present about eight feet, but Mr Fletcher indicates that the original floor was probably less than six feet from the ground. Of slightly later date is the cross-wing at Wellshead Farm, a former parsonage and, like the south range at Middle Farm, originally three bays long, although now part of the end bay has been demolished. From the evidence of the mortices in the posts it seems that the original height of the first floor above ground level was about $5\frac{1}{2}$ feet. In both these cases the ceiling height of the ground floor would have made them unsuitable for habitation, and they were probably used only for storage or as service rooms. There are other houses similar in many respects to these two in the region.

Houses similar in design but later in date are to be found in the West Midlands. Middle Beanhall Farm, Bradley, Hereford and Worcester (3), was an upper-floor hall type house when built in about 1500, receiving its present appearance in 1635 when the four attic gables, originally with continuous windows similar to those at Mere Hall, Hanbury, were introduced in an attempt to copy the then fashionable long gallery. In nearby Himbleton, Shell Manor Farm has a solar wing which may well have been a first-floor hall house. This wing, built in the middle of the fifteenth century, is earlier than the remainder of the house – the hall and service wing – which is of late sixteenth-century date. It has a comparatively low three-bay ground floor with the heavy joists grooved for a wattle ceiling, and above this a two-bay room with a single-bay chamber at one end, both open to the roof. There is a stone fireplace and stack on the external wall to the second bay, which is undoubtedly contemporary with the wing. In all respects the arrangement of the upper floor conforms with that of the standard stone-built first-floor hall house. Nearby is Huddington Court, a

2. Manor Farm, Little Chesterford, Essex. This former manor house originated as a stone-built first-floor hall house in about 1200. Later, between 1315 and 1330, an aisled hall was added and the stone wing converted to a service wing. In the fifteenth century the timber-framed solar wing was added.

3. Middle Beanhall Farm, Bradley, Hereford and Worcester. This old farmhouse was built in about 1500 as an upper-floor hall type receiving its present appearance in 1635 when the four attic gables, originally with a continuous window, were introduced to copy the then fashionable long gallery.

similar but larger house containing four bays instead of the usual three, with the hall on the upper floor occupying the centre two bays. This and the old wing at Shell Manor may, as has been suggested elsewhere, have been the solar wings of older, larger houses.

There is another type of first-floor hall house which evolved to satisfy a particular need and which is a product of that part of England close to the Scottish border. These are the bastle-houses (4), defensible farmhouses in which cattle and other animals were housed on the ground floor, with human beings on the floor above, a house type which, with only a few exceptions, is unique in England. They are nearly all to be found within twenty-five miles of the border with Scotland and were at one time numerous. The Royal Commission on Historical Monuments lists some ninety and states that there are probably many others, and many more that have long since disappeared, and they cite the *Gilsland Survey* of 1603 for Cumberland which lists some forty-five, of which only two can now be identified. Most are today derelict or at best used as a farm building or store, such as at White House Farm, Glassonby, Cumbria, Hole, in Bellingham (5), Ottercops, in Elsdon, and Low Fairnley, in Rothley, all in Northumberland; only a few, among them Denton Foot, in Nether, and Peel O'Hill, in Bewcastle, both in Cumbria, and in Northumberland Little Ryle, in Alnham, and Falstone Farm, Falstone, are still lived in, though all have been considerably extended and altered.

Nearly all these farmhouses were built from about 1550 until 1650, and the earlier ones were built without doubt to be defended. The walls are extremely thick, generally about 4 feet although they vary from 3½ up to 5 feet on the ground floor, reducing slightly on the floor above. Access to the ground floor was by a simple splayed doorway set in the centre of one of the gable walls with a door hung on harr-hinges and barricaded from the inside by drawbars which could be drawn out from a slot in the wall. There were no windows on this floor, only narrow ventilation slits, usually two or three placed in the longitudinal walls. Entry to the floor above was achieved by means of a door located towards one end of the longitudinal wall and must originally have been reached from the outside by means of a retrievable ladder, for all the external stone stairs which survive today appear to be of a later build, for none are bonded to the main wall. This floor had two or three small windows, each with iron bars, two of which were always placed on each side of the door. On the gable wall furthest away from the door was probably a timber and plaster firehood, for all the fireplaces are of a later date. The first floor was constructed either of timber with the joists spanning the width of the building or as a stone barrel-vault. In both cases internal access was needed between the ground and upper

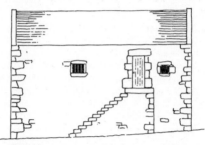

Elevation

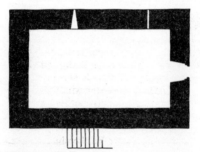

Ground Floor Plan

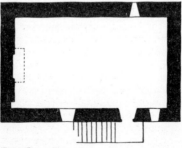

First Floor Plan

4. Typical bastle-house of late sixteenth- or early seventeenth-century date.

floor so that the person securing the ground-floor door was not left among the animals. In most cases, as is evident from those bastles with the vaulted floor, this was achieved by means of a narrow opening in the floor reached from the ground floor by a ladder which could be drawn up. Only occasionally, as at the ruined bastle at Crag, Hepple, Northumberland, is there evidence of an internal stone stair.

The size of these bastle-houses varies greatly, but generally they are between 30 and 40 feet long and 20 and 25 feet wide externally, providing in some cases very limited accommodation in one single room. However, there are others which are much larger, such as the derelict but relatively complete one at Akeld, Northumberland, which is 63 feet long externally and which is also unusual in that access to the upper floor is from a two-way external stairway at the gable end, and one at Little Ryle, Alnham, Northumberland, which is some 56 feet long and 27 feet wide and has been enlarged and altered to form a substantial farmhouse.

Although the need for defensible houses along the Scottish border had disappeared by the middle of the seventeenth century, some farmhouses in the area continued to be built in the traditional way with a byre below and living accommodation above. In size they were much the same as earlier bastle-houses, but as they no longer required to be a stronghold, the thickness of the walls was reduced to about two feet and the number and overall size of the windows to the upper floor were increased. A few examples still exist, although all are now derelict or used as farm buildings, among them Windy Hall, Alston with Garrigill, Cumbria, and Wester Old Town and West Side, both in Allendale, Northumberland. At Bunkershill, a derelict farmstead at Alston with Garrigill, Cumbria, the house was built into the slope of the ground so that access to the upper floor could be obtained directly from the ground and the external stairway done away with.

In County Durham too there are houses, such as Baal Hill House, near Wolsingham, and Old Hall Farm, High Coniscliffe, which were designed for first-floor living. They are similar to the bastle-houses further north but are generally superior in both accommodation – usually two rooms on the first floor – and the quality of their architectural details. They appear to be older than bastle-houses and more in the tradition of the first-floor hall houses in the south. The height of the barrel-vaulted ground floor was low, and it is more likely to have been used for storage than as a byre. However, farmhouses not of a defensible character but having the living accommodation over a byre remained popular in the North-east, especially with smallholders, well into the nineteenth century. Why this arrangement continued so long after the original need had declined is not clear, but it has been suggested that the warmth generated by the animals below contributed

5. Hole bastle-house, Bellingham, Northumberland.

towards the heating of the accommodation above and helped to perpetuate the practice.

Elsewhere in the country this arrangement is virtually unknown, but among the farm buildings at Neadon, Manaton, Devon, there stands a remarkable and to date a unique example in that county. The living accommodation is on the first floor, and the traceried windows in one gable end indicate that the house was built in the latter part of the fifteenth century. The upper floor was clearly divided into two rooms, each with a fireplace, and one with the remains of a garderobe which discharged via a buttressed shaft to the outside. As in the later bastle-house, the upper floor was reached by an external stone stairway, but this has been removed and the former house part converted into a hay loft with the ground floor still being used, as it always was, as a byre.

Another type of defensible house was the tower house, known also in the North, where most were built, as a pele-tower, a term which often incorporates all defensive houses in the region including the bastles. These tower houses differ from all other first-floor hall houses in that, instead of the accommodation being confined to the first floor, there is a second and occasionally a third floor. In addition the ground-floor space was less, for unlike the bastle-house which was needed to house the animals in times of attack, the pele-tower was not, for it stood within a barmkin – an enclosure surrounded by a wall – in which the animals and local population took refuge when under attack. The ground floor was therefore used solely for storage or perhaps as a service area. Access to this area was from the outside by means of a stout door capable of being barred from the inside. Above this was the main living-room or hall, with the solar occupying the floor above and, in some cases, a further chamber above this. Unlike other first-floor hall houses there was no external stairway, and access between the floor was by a stone staircase, either spiral stairs placed in one corner or in a projecting turret or a straight flight incorporated within the thickness of the wall. In some pele-towers the staircase between the ground floor and first floor was omitted, and access was gained by means of a ladder which could be pulled up. Access was also possible onto the roof, where the parapet walls were often corbelled and battlemented, leaving a walkway around the gabled roof.

The earliest pele-towers dated from the fourteenth century and continued to be built until the late sixteenth century along the Scottish border and as far south as North Yorkshire. Although many have been abandoned and have disappeared or become derelict, a good number still survive incorporated within later buildings. These pele-towers varied greatly in size according to the status of the owner, and there are many examples such as Sizergh Castle and Muncaster Castle, both in

Cumbria, Langley Castle, Haydon Bridge, Haughton Castle, Humshaugh, Belsay Castle and Chipchase Castle, all in Northumberland, which are all large and impressive.

There were others that were relatively small which must have originally been little more than small manor houses or large farmhouses and have remained so until today. The small derelict fourteenth-century pele-tower built of rubble which stands beside the former fifteenth-century farmhouse at Kentmere Hall, Cumbria, is typical. Similar is Cocklaw, Chollerton, Northumberland, where the present farmhouse is built alongside a well-preserved but ruinous fifteenth-century pele-tower. The pele-tower at Wraysholme, Flookburgh, is slightly later, probably late fifteenth century, and attached to it is a farmhouse dated 1848. The pele-tower is rectangular, some 40 feet by 28 feet, and was originally three storeys high and had a garderobe projecting from one corner. Brackenhill Tower, near Longtown, Cumbria, dates from 1586 and now stands within a farmstead enclosed with other buildings of the seventeenth and eighteenth centuries. The tower is almost square, measuring 35 feet by 39 feet, and is some 40 feet high with walls 5 feet thick. The ground floor has the customary vaulted ceiling with newel stairs to the upper floor. The tower is no longer occupied. At Howgill Farm, near Dufton, Cumbria, the pele-tower is now almost unrecognizable, being incorporated into a later house all under one roof.

Outside northern England tower houses are rare but are to be found occasionally, in particular in those counties adjacent to Wales. One such example is Upper Millichope Farm, Millichope, a tower house built at the beginning of the fourteenth century. It follows the basic plan with the entrance on the ground floor, and to the right of this in the corner is a spiral staircase leading to the former hall above. In this room there are two slender, two-light windows each with a slender shaft and seats in the reveals. These two floors are all that remain of the original house, for above this the house has been rebuilt, probably in the sixteenth century, in timber with brick infilling.

The Open-hall Farmhouse

The common feature of nearly all medieval houses in England was the open hall, and it remained so up until the sixteenth century. It was always the largest room in the house, open from the ground floor to the apex of the roof, in which in early times the owner, his family, his guests and his servants or retainers all dined, slept and lived when indoors and where the manorial court was held. In or near the centre of the open hall was the open hearth, the smoke escaping as best it could through the small gablets at the junction of the hips and ridge or else through a louvre in the roof. Beyond the hearth was the 'upper end', which was occupied by the family and contained the high table and bench for meals. At the other end, the 'lower end', the servants and retainers lived. In the open hall the social division between the family and the servants was marked by the central open truss. Even in the smallest farmhouse this division between the upper and lower ends is noticeable, with superior architectural details to all those parts not only in but also visible from the upper end.

The earliest farmhouses with an open hall are those of aisled construction and are almost certainly of manorial status. These halls, which were larger than those in comparable later houses, had two large bays, both approximately equal and each about 16 feet in length.

There is evidence, based on Fyfield Hall, Essex, to indicate that a two-bay aisled hall without any other rooms was the simplest type of house and persisted as late as the end of the thirteenth century. To this was added, at the lower end, a two-storey extension built either in series with the house or else as a projecting cross-wing containing on the ground floor the buttery and pantry, each with its own door into the hall, and above these a chamber, probably the 'solar', for the private use of the family. Further up the social scale were the houses with an extension or cross-wing at both ends. The lower end adjacent to the entrance still contained on the ground floor the service rooms, while above the chamber was used according to circumstances, for guests, servants or the adult sons of the family. At the upper end, the ground-floor room was the parlour, used by the daughters of the family or as a withdrawing-room after meals. From the often rough and rude square ceiling joists of the parlour in nearly all medieval houses, it is clear that this was not regarded as the 'best room' as it later was. The architectural details bestowed on the hall were not carried on into the parlour and service rooms, the ceiling joists and underside of the floor boards receiving nothing more than a coat of limewash. Above the parlour was the solar.

Elevation

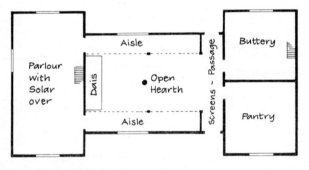

Ground Floor Plan

6. Typical aisled house with two cross-wings.

Sometimes, when the cross-wings were provided, they were of two bays, but more commonly they were of three, the third bay containing a small ante-room and staircase. In both cases the solar or chamber would be open to the roof with a central open truss. Although partitioned off from the open hall, the partitions to these upper rooms often stopped some two or three feet from the top so that the smoke from the open hearth could pass across both chambers and out through the gable end. With hipped roofs the gablets at the apex were sometimes positioned above the division wall of the hall, and so this was avoided. According to the social status of the household, there were one or two service rooms, either a combined buttery and pantry with a single doorway into the hall or a separate buttery and pantry each with their own doorway. In some of the larger houses there was a third door which gave access to the chamber above or in a few cases to an outside kitchen. The main entrance to the house was situated at the lower end of the hall, well away from the central open hearth, and it became structurally defined by a spere-truss and screens which formed a cross-passage known as a 'screens-passage'. These screens were framed between the arcade posts and the external walls, leaving a wide opening known as the spere-opening in the centre, leading to the hall in which another screen, originally movable, was fitted. The spere-truss became almost a standard part of farmhouse design long after the decline of aisled construction and was still being built in Lancashire and Cheshire as late as the early part of the sixteenth century.

7. Purton Green Farmhouse, Stansfield, Suffolk. This old house dates from around the middle of the thirteenth century and in 1969 was purchased by the Landmark Trust and restored from near-dereliction.

There are a number of aisled farmhouses which still survive, although all have been considerably altered. One of the earliest and most interesting is Purton Green Farmhouse, Stansfield, Suffolk (7), which dates from around the middle of the thirteenth century. It is a house of modest size consisting originally of a two-bay hall with a service bay and solar over at the lower end and built in series with the hall. There is no evidence of a screens-passage, the arcade posts at the lower end being incorporated in the partition between the hall and service rooms. Although the upper end of the hall was rebuilt and extended in the sixteenth century to provide a new jettied solar block, there is no evidence of the existence of an earlier solar block at this end. In 1969 the old farmhouse, which had been converted into tenements, was purchased by the Landmark Trust and restored from near dereliction. The former hall was opened up, and the floor and chimney, which were inserted at the time the new solar block was built, were removed. Very similar in plan is Edgar's Farm, Stowmarket, Suffolk, which has now been erected at the Museum of Rural Life at Stowmarket. Built about 1300, it had a two-bay hall divided by a cross-frame and at the lower end a service bay with a chamber over. Others of similar size are Bedingfield Hall Farm, Suffolk, of late thirteenth- or early fourteenth-century date, Manor Farm, Bourn, Cambridgeshire (8), built about 1260, and Capon's Farm, Cowfold, Sussex, probably built between 1300 and 1330.

A little larger than those mentioned above is Stanton's Farm, Black Notley, Essex, which, when originally built at the beginning of the fourteenth century, comprised a two-bay hall, with an oriel window built in the upper bay and with service bay and chamber over at one end, and a parlour bay and solar at the other end all built in series. The solar has since been destroyed and a cross-wing added to the end of the service bay together with several other extensions and additions to the hall. The arcade posts, below roof level, have been either removed or buried in later brickwork. Next in size are houses with an aisled hall, a cross-wing and an end bay. Lampett's Farm, Fyfield, Essex, a manor house built early in the fourteenth century, was, when built, of this type although today there is some doubt about the lower-end bay.

The largest of these aisled halls were those with two cross-wings. The finest example is probably St Clere's Hall, St Osyth, Essex, a manor house built in the fourteenth century. An interesting farmhouse which over a period of years developed into this form is Manor Farm, Little Chesterford, Essex (2), with an aisled hall which was built between 1315 and 1330 onto a stone cross-wing attributed to the first part of the thirteenth century with, at the upper end, a timber-framed solar wing possibly of later date.

Outside the South-east and East Anglia, the other county in which

8. Manor Farm, Bourn, Cambridgeshire. This aisled-hall manor house was built about 1260 and later extended and altered.

aisled farmhouses were once built is West Yorkshire, along the western edge of the southern Pennines. Although these too had a large open hall with two two-storeyed bays at each end, they were of much later date, being generally constructed at the end of the fifteenth and beginning of the sixteenth century. Being of later construction than those further south, the open hearth had been abandoned, and they had at the lower end a stone reredos against which the fire was laid beneath a firehood. Most appear to have been built of timber and partly rebuilt and clad in stone in the seventeenth century, making it difficult to know the number and extent of the aisles. One notable example was Woodhouse Farm, Shelley Woodhouse, Kirkburton, a farmhouse built in the fifteenth century; when threatened with demolition, the frame and rafters were dismantled and removed to the Avoncroft Museum of Buildings at Bromsgrove. This single-aisled house consisted of a service bay, a two-bay hall and a solar bay which had been almost entirely replaced in the seventeenth century by a stone cross-wing probably at the same time as the house was clad in stone. The remains of the screen survived, and evidence was found of the coved canopy to the dais flanked by a low side screen on the aisle side.

By the middle of the fourteenth century the aisled hall in East Anglia and the South-east had generally been abandoned, for the arcade posts, which restricted the clear floor area, proved to be inconvenient. Elsewhere in the country quasi-aisled construction in the form of a base-cruck continued to be used in order to obtain a large span without the inconvenience of arcade posts, for the inward incline of the crucks enabled the arcade plates to be supported from the external walls, thus obtaining a large, uninterrupted span.

The general arrangement of these base-cruck houses followed those constructed with aisles. The simplest surviving example is at Manor Farm, Wasperton, Warwickshire, which when originally built comprised a single rectangular block with a two-bay hall and a narrow bay at one end occupied by the screens-passage and divided from the hall by the spere-truss. As arcade posts were no longer used, two stout spere-posts were introduced to support the truss and a screen formed between these posts and the external walls. Slightly larger is Hyde Farm, Stoke Bliss, Hereford and Worcester, which originally consisted of a hall range with a small two-bay solar wing at one end. Chennell's Brook Farm, Horsham, Sussex, was a little larger, for it had a two-bay hall, a screens-passage and a small service bay in one range with a three-bay solar cross-wing at the upper end. Superior houses had a three-bay hall range comprising a two-bay hall and a screens-passage with a two-storey cross-wing at each end with the upper floors open to the roof. The solar wing was generally of three bays, a two-bay parlour with a small unheated ante-room, as at Amberley Court, Marden, Hereford and Worcester, although at Middle Farm, Oxfordshire (9), there is a four-bay range with each bay of differing lengths totalling some forty-seven feet. This range, together with the hall range, was built onto the earlier, possibly first-floor hall house, previously described, which was at this time converted into the service wing. In addition to these main ranges additional accommodation was probably provided in detached buildings, and this must have been true at Manor Farm, Wasperton, with such limited accommodation. External kitchens were always a feature, and one still survives at Swanstone Court, Dilwyn, Hereford and Worcester, facing the rear door of the screens-passage now linked to the house by a passage. At Rectory Farm, Grafton Flyford, there is a detached solar wing which, although medieval in date, is of a later build than the hall.

The span obtained by these base-crucks compared favourably but was generally less than those obtained with aisled construction. At Chennell's Brook Farm, the span is 22 feet, while at Middle Farm, Amberley Court, and Manor Farm, Wasperton, this span is some 24

9. Middle Farm, Harwell, Oxfordshire. A base-cruck farmhouse built in the
fourteenth century.

feet, compared with 27 feet at Manor Farm, Little Chesterford – 17
feet between arcade posts with 5 feet-wide aisles – and 26 feet at
Stanton's Farm, Black Notley – 14 feet between arcade posts with 6
feet-wide aisles.

Most base-cruck farmhouses date from about 1300, although a date
of 1250 has been given to Hyde Farm and dates of around 1300 have
been ascribed to Chennell's Brook Farm and Rectory Farm. Others,
such as Middle Farm, Harwell, Oxfordshire (9), Swanstone Court,
Wellbrook Manor, Peterchurch, Lower Brockhampton Manor and
Pegg's Farm, Wellington Heath, all in Hereford and Worcester, Hook
Farm, Lower Woodcott, Hampshire, and Priory Farm, Balscott,
Oxfordshire, are all of mid or late fourteenth-century date, while
Court Farm, Preston Wynne, and Amberley Court are probably of
early fifteenth-century date.

Nearly all of these old base-cruck farmhouses have been greatly
altered and extended. At Manor Farm, Wasperton, the hall was

reduced in size in the second half of the fifteenth century when a new solar wing was built and one of the base-crucks removed. Both the base-crucks at Chennell's Brook Farm have been largely removed and the rest greatly mutilated, as is Rectory Farm, although it still retains its central truss. The roof at Swanstone Court was replaced in the eighteenth century, while Court Farm, Preston Wynne, Hereford and Worcester, was extended in the seventeenth century and dormer windows inserted into the hall, although the base-cruck and spere-truss and posts still survive. At Wellbrook Manor the service wing has been destroyed but the solar wing remains, while at Lower Brockhampton Manor, the two-storey solar cross-wing has been removed but there still remains a two-bay hall open to the roof, a spere-truss and screen, a screens-passage, with a gallery above, and a large service cross-wing. Some, such as Hyde Farm, Wellbrook Manor, Chennell's Brook Farm, Manor Farm, Wasperton, and Rectory Farm, have been clad in stone or brickwork and have lost much of their character and are unrecognizable from the outside, although both Hyde Farm and Wellbrook Manor still retain much of their timberwork including the base-cruck dividing the two bays of the hall and the spere-truss intact. In nearly all cases, except for Lower Brockhampton Manor, the hall has had a floor inserted. At Pegg's Farm this was carried out early in the sixteenth century, and in recent years the roof trusses and spere-truss have been exposed.

The distribution of the base-cruck farmhouse was much greater than that of aisled construction, spreading from Sussex into the Midlands and down into the West Country, with the main concentration in Hereford and Worcester. It has not as yet been discovered in eastern England where this uninterrupted floor space was achieved by other means. At Tiptofts Manor, Wimbish, Essex, a house constructed early in the fourteenth century, an elementary form of hammer-beam was used to support the arcade plate. Slightly more common was the use of the raised aisle. It was used at Gatehouse Farm, Felsted, Essex (10), a small farmhouse built in about the first quarter of the fourteenth century on the usual medieval plan of a two-bay hall originally flanked at both ends by projecting cross-wings, but the solar wing has in recent years been destroyed. The hall is of modest size compared with those of aisled construction, being only 23 feet long, yet it spans 20 feet, which is greater than most later single-span houses. Similar construction is to be found at a disused hall at Church Farm, Fressington, Suffolk, only part of the hall survives, one gable end, a spere-type hall frame and 1½ bays of the hall. The building dates from about 1330 and has many elaborate details, but its purpose is unknown, and it is now used as a store. These raised aisles were also used at Wymondley Bury, Little Wymondley, Hertfordshire, a house

10. Gatehouse Farmhouse, Felsted, Essex. A remarkable farmhouse built in the first quarter of the fourteenth century. Unlike other farmhouses of about this time in eastern England the aisle posts had been removed and replaced with raised aisles.

probably built in the early fourteenth century with a two-bay open hall, a two-storeyed bay at one end and a non-projecting two-storeyed cross-wing at the other.

With the decline of the manorial system the importance of the hall also declined, and by the fifteenth century aisled and quasi-aisled construction had been generally abandoned for dwellings. Yet the medieval house plan with the hall still open to the roof and flanked at one or both ends by a two-storey bay remained the standard house type in the South-east and in eastern England. The simplest open-hall house was that of two bays, one containing the hall and the other containing the service room below and solar above (11A). One such example is Winkhurst Farm, which formerly stood at Bough Beech, Chiddingstone, and has been recently re-erected in its original condition in the Weald and Downland Open Air Museum at Singleton, West Sussex. Slightly larger was the three-bay house with a

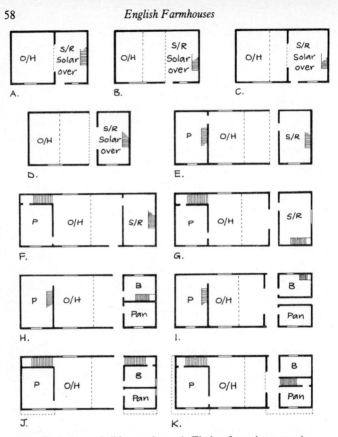

11. Typical open-hall house plans – 1. Timber-framed construction.

two-bay open hall and the bay containing the service room below and solar above (11B, C and D). There were several variations to this house type; in some cases there was no partition between the open hall and service area (11B), although there was probably some form of removable screen, and in some cases there were opposed entrances with the solar overshot (11D). Next in size was the three-bay house with a single-bay open hall and a single-bay service room at one end with chamber above and a single-bay parlour with solar above at the other end. By far the most common to survive today are the houses of four bays containing a two-bay open hall flanked at each end by a two-storey bay (11E). Entry to the hall was either in the form of a direct entry at the lower end of the hall (11F) or more commonly by way of a screens-passage (11E). The screens-passage could be situated either within the hall or within the service room with the upper floor overshot. This four-bay house plan could be extended at either the parlour or the service end by an additional bay.

The layout of the basic four-bay house was similar to that of the earlier aisled construction. The parlour with solar above abuts the upper end of the hall and the service rooms with a chamber over the lower end. There was either a single door at the upper end which gave access to the parlour with a stair leading to the solar above (11E, H and I) or in the larger house two doors, one at both ends of the partition, giving access to the parlour and to the stairs to the solar above (11F, G, J and K). These doors were sometimes flanked by short projecting screens shielding the doorways from the dais. At the lower end of the hall there were one, two or three doors, one door clearly indicating a combined buttery – pantry (11E, F and G), while two doors indicated a separate buttery and pantry (11H). When a third door was provided, this gave access either to the chamber stair (11J and K) or less commonly to an outside kitchen (11I). When no separate stair access was provided, a stair was located in one of the service rooms.

Unlike houses of aisled construction, the later hall houses of eastern England and the South-east rarely have cross-wings projecting beyond the face of the hall, and those that do are generally of the high vernacular status.

They are to be found occasionally, particularly in eastern England (12A and C). One such example is Moat Farm, Combs, Suffolk, a timber-framed house built in the fifteenth century with a two-bay open hall, a two-storeyed service bay and a two-storeyed four-bay cross-wing solar end. Another is Malton Farm, Orwell, Cambridgeshire, which has a cross-wing at both ends. There are also many, however, in which these cross-wings are not contemporary with the building to which they are attached.

Generally these open-hall houses were rectangular in plan with a solar bay, hall and service bay built in line, and though one finds examples, such as Boyley's Farm, East Grinstead, and Hurter's Farm, East Chiltington, both in Sussex, Bird's Farm, Barton, Cambridgeshire, and Blue Gates Farm, Great Bromley, Essex, in which the upper floors to the end bays are built flush with the wall below, they are rare in comparison with those in which the end bays are jettied. This jettying is generally at the front only, sometimes at the rear as well and even on occasions to the side.

In eastern England these jettied upper storeys were given their own ridged roofs set at right-angles to that of the roof to the hall and so in

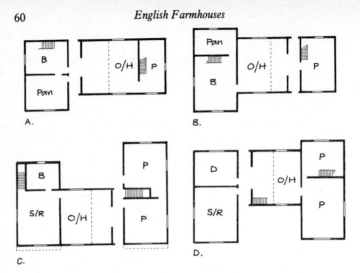

12. Typical open-hall house plans – 2. Timber-framed construction.

effect formed a 'cross-wing' (13). Occasionally these cross-wings are extended at the rear beyond the face of the hall. This can occur at either the solar or the service end but rarely at both ends to form a "U"-shaped house. Examples of houses with jettied cross-wings are not uncommon in eastern England, and though many have been greatly altered, several notable examples still exist. These cross-wings can occur at one end, as at Walnut Tree Farm, Luffenhall, Hertfordshire (14), and Gatehouse Farm, Ardleigh, Essex, but more commonly they are at both ends, as at Abbotts Hall Farm, Stanway (15), Baytree Farm, Great Horkesley, Appleton's Farm, Bulphan, and Bream's Farm, Great Leighs, all in Essex, and Cromer Farm, Cromer, Hertfordshire. All these houses are of fifteenth-century date. In some cases the eaves to the hall still remain lower than the eaves of the cross-wings but, owing to the abandonment of the aisle, not so low as those of preceding centuries.

In the South-east and particularly in the Weald another house type evolved known as the Wealden house (16). The basic house plan remained the same as elsewhere, although in nearly all cases the screens-passage is clearly defined, often by a separate narrow bay, usually about seven feet wide, between the hall and service rooms, and there was often a wide spered opening into the hall. In addition, instead of being roofed in three separate parts with three ridge lines,

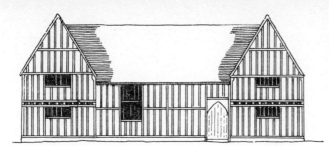

ELEVATION

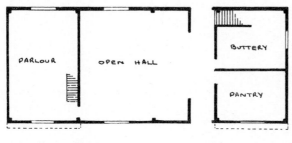

PARLOUR

OPEN HALL

BUTTERY

PANTRY

GROUND FLOOR PLAN

13. Typical fifteenth-century open-hall farmhouse in eastern England.

14. Walnut Tree Farm, Luffenhall, near Ardeley, Hertfordshire, an excellent example of a medieval open-hall house with jettied cross-wing to one end and a service bay at the other end.

15. Abbotts Hall Farm, Stanway, Essex, a fifteenth-century hall house.

the complete house was covered under a single steeply pitched hipped roof with one ridge line. Jettied end chambers continued to be used, but the front line of the eaves continued across the front of the halls to produce extra deep projecting eaves. Generally the eaves were coved and carried by means of curved brackets at each end and in the centre of the main tie beam of the hall roof.

The origin of the Wealden house is obscure, but it appears at some date around 1400, reaching its peak about eighty years later, and continued to be built for about another fifty years. The high standard of these houses can clearly be seen by the moulded partition beams and cornices and the moulded fascias to the jetties and also the elaborate

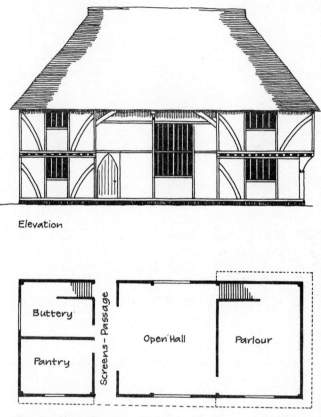

Elevation

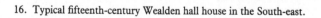

Ground Floor Plan

16. Typical fifteenth-century Wealden hall house in the South-east.

17. Old Bell Farm, Harrietsham, Kent. This farmhouse built late in the fifteenth century is probably one of the finest Wealden houses to be seen in Kent still retaining many of its original features.

18. Brewerstreet Farm, Bletchingley, Surrey, a fifteenth-century Wealden hall house which unlike other Wealden houses in the South-east has gabled end bays. The roof is of Horsham slate like many of the older houses in the region.

glazed oriel windows with moulded jambs, mullions and transoms at a time when most farmhouses would have had simple mullioned and shuttered windows without glass. These Wealden houses are to be found mainly in Sussex, Surrey and Kent and in particular in the Weald and to the east of Maidstone. Old Bell Farm, Harrietsham, Kent (17), is one of the finest remaining examples. Built in the late fifteenth century, it still contains its original front entrance door and four-centred arch, three doors in the screens-passage, its crown-post roof and one of its solid block stairs. The centre recess is coved, the bressummers to the jettied wings moulded, and there is a two-storey bay window to the hall which was probably glazed at one time for its full height. Other notable and generally unrestored examples are Westhoy Farm, Smarden, Hawkenbury Farm, Staplehurst, Link Farm, Egerton, Sands Farm, Warnham, Shirley Farm, Woodchurch, and Batchelors Farm, Limpsfield. Another impressive Wealden house is Brewerstreet Farmhouse, Bletchingley, Surrey (18), a farmhouse built in the fifteenth century with a central hall flanked at each end by a two-storey bay in the usual way, but instead of there being a fully hipped roof as in most other Wealden houses of the South-east, the roofs above the jettied end bays are gabled.

Although most of the Wealden type farmhouses survive in the Weald of Kent, Surrey and East Sussex, and to a certain extent elsewhere in these counties, particularly Kent, occasionally they are to be found further afield, for example Charity Farm, Edlesborough, Buckinghamshire, Studhall Hall Farm, Bedfordshire, Paradise Farmhouse, Barton Mills (19), and Stonewall Farm, Hemingstone, both in Suffolk and both built about 1500. In all these farmhouses the roofs were gabled and not hipped as in the South-east. The Wealden house type is in no way solely confined to farmhouses, and they are in fact more numerous in towns and villages.

In some Wealden farmhouses there is only a jettied bay at one end, and although there must be some that had one end bay removed at some time, as at Pullens Farm, Horsmonden, Kent, there are too many examples for this to be always the case. When Bayleaf Farmhouse (20), a fifteenth-century Wealden house which formerly stood at Bough Beech, Chiddingstone, Kent, was reconstructed at the Weald and Downland Open Air Museum, the evidence was clear that the solar bay was built at a later date than the remainder of the house. Also the chamber over the service rooms is of such a high standard that it seems likely that this end of the house was for a time at least used as a combined solar-service wing. In addition, the solar wing has many details which differ from the remainder of the house, clearly indicating a different building date. There are a number of incomplete or two-third Wealdens such as Rose Farm, Broomfield, and Harts Heath

19. Paradise Farmhouse, formerly Street Farmhouse, Barton Mills, Suffolk. This is a typical late fifteenth-century Wealden hall house found in East Anglia.

20. Bayleaf Farmhouse. A fifteenth-century Wealden hall house, formerly situated at Bough Beech, Chiddingstone, Kent and moved and rebuilt at the Weald and Downland Open Air Museum, Singleton, West Sussex in its original state.

Farm, Staplehurst, both in Kent, which were perhaps planned to be extended at a later date and were for some reason never in fact completed.

Unlike the aisled house, in the later open-hall house the central open truss was rarely placed centrally; one bay – sometimes the upper bay, sometimes the lower one – was always longer than the other. Often the difference in length was only a foot or so, but at Hurter's Farm, East Chiltington, Sussex, they measured 9 feet 3 inches and 3 feet 9 inches respectively, although the smaller bay situated at the lower end also contained opposed entrances, and perhaps this was a one-bay hall with some form of cross-passage. The overall length of the open hall obviously varied; at Hurter's Farm the overall length including the possible cross-passage is only some 13 feet, as is Pullens Farm, Horsmonden, Kent (21), which has only a single-bay hall. However, most two-bay open halls vary between 23 and 26 feet in length.

The type of central truss spanning the hall also differed greatly in various parts of the country. In the East and South-east the crown-post and collar purlin form of construction was almost universally adopted, while in the West it was the arch-braced collar beam. Both these types, and especially the arch-braced collar-beam roof, which was probably the most ornamental type of roof, were given special decorative treatment. In the North the roofs were of the king-post construction, probably due to the fact that the open hearth was never a feature in northern England and that the firehood, situated at the lower end of the hall, drew the occupants away from the centre of the hall.

Although many farmhouses with halls originally open to the roof survive today, in eastern England and the South-east very few retain their open halls. Two examples are Sparling's Farm and Bridgehouse Farm both in Felsted, Essex, while at Corner Farm, Langley, Kent, the former open hall has been restored to its original condition. A clear indication of the austere living conditions even for the more prosperous farmer can be seen at Bayleaf Farmhouse, which has been reconstructed in the original state with an open hall, central hearth and unglazed mullion windows.

Open-hall timber-framed farmhouses of similar date and size to those in the South-east and in eastern England can be found in other parts of the country. They can, of course, be found in those areas adjacent to eastern England, for instance Manor Farm, Brington, Cambridgeshire (22), Clawdershill Farm, Shillington, Bedfordshire, and Blackwell Farm, Chesham, Buckinghamshire.

There are others to be found in the West Midlands. Many differ from those in eastern England and the South-east in that the medieval concept of a cross-wing was retained (12 B and D) as was the spere-truss supported on two spere-posts which was not a popular feature

21. Pullens Farm, Horsmonden, Kent. A small single bay Wealden hall
house which has had one end bay removed.

22. Manor Farm, Brington, Cambridgeshire, a former open-hall house.

elsewhere. One such example which retains both features is Court Farm, Throckmorton, Hereford and Worcester, a late-medieval hall house of about 1500 with a solar cross-wing. The hall part is of three bays plus the screens-passage with gallery over, and at the lower end there was formerly a service bay, but this has now been destroyed. The hall range, although now floored, still has parts of the spere-truss as

well as much of the central truss. The solar wing is of three bays with
the upper floor comprising a two-bay room complete with a
contemporary fireplace and a small ante-chamber at one end. In the
same county there is Pool Farm, Hereford, a house built in the
fifteenth century with a two-bay open hall and a service bay in one
range and a two-bay solar cross-wing. The porch was added in 1626.
Also in Hereford and Worcester is Manor Farm, Feckenham, built in
about 1500 and a good example of a farmhouse with a single service
cross-wing. The hall range comprises a two-bay hall, a screens-passage
and at the upper end a small parlour with the first-floor room jettied
out at the front. Across the screens-passage at the lower end is the
service wing. Other notable examples of open-hall farmhouses of box-
frame construction in Hereford and Worcester are Chapel Farm,
Wigmore, and Church House Farm, Staunton-on-Wye. Another
example in the West Midlands was Shelfield Lodge Farm, Aldridge,
Staffordshire, which was, however, demolished in 1961.

Even in those areas not renowned today for their half-timbered
buildings, one can still find the occasional box-framed timber hall
house. One such example is Manor Farm, Wimborne St Giles, Dorset,
where the Royal Commission on Historical Monuments has discovered
that the south part of the house was originally a timber-framed
structure built in the sixteenth century with an open hall and solar end.
Others are Manor Farm, Alderton, Gloucestershire, a hall house with a
screens-passage formerly built of timber but with the hall largely
rebuilt early in the seventeenth century in stone, and Parks Farm, near
Chipping Sodbury, Avon, which also contains part of a medieval
timber-framed house.

More common, particularly in the highland zone, are open-hall
farmhouses of both true and jointed cruck construction (23 and 24). In
many cases these farmhouses are comparable in size with those of the
South-east and eastern England, but because of the nature of cruck
construction the houses were generally less spacious with a more
limited range of internal designs. Like those of box-frame
construction, few farmhouses of cruck construction still retain their
open hall. One notable example is Hill, Christow, Devon, a late-
medieval house which, despite being extended and extensively
modernized in the seventeenth century, still retains, together with its
open hall, many important features. Another is Old Manor Farm,
Marple, Cheshire, which has an early fifteenth-century two-bay cruck
hall, which is still open to the roof, flanked at one end with a sixteenth-
century timber-framed solar wing and at the other end by a stone-built
service wing constructed in the seventeenth century.

Open-hall cruck farmhouses are particularly common in the West
Midlands, especially in Hereford and Worcester. In some cases, as at

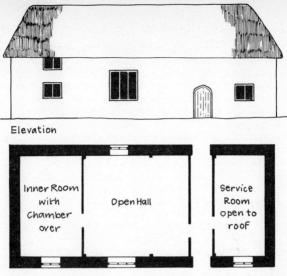

Elevation

Ground Floor Plan

Inner Room with Chamber over

Open Hall

Service Room open to roof

23. Typical cruck house in Devon: farmhouses like this with a chamber at one end reached by a ladder are typical in Devon. Built in the sixteenth century.

24. Typical cruck house in the Fylde, Lancashire; houses similar to this with a chamber over the service rooms reached by a ladder and lit by a window in the gable wall were common in the first part of the seventeenth century.

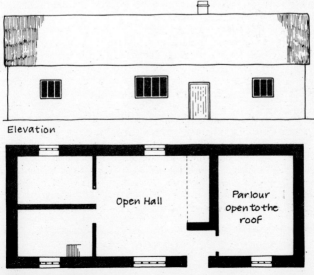

Elevation

Open Hall

Parlour open to the roof

Ground Floor Plan

Upper Poswick, Whitbourne, there was only an open hall and a service bay, while nearby at Lower Poswick and at Eynons Farm, Tyberton, the service bay was replaced by a cross-wing. Similar houses are Upper Limebrook Farm, Wigmore, before the cross-wing was demolished in 1964, and Court Farm, Bishampton, which conceals behind its later brick cladding a former cruck hall with a solar cross-wing. Others, such as Old Hall, Adforton, had the usual arrangement of an open hall with a two-storey bay at each end all arranged in line. These and others such as Dairy Farm, Weobley (25), all appear to be of fifteenth- or early sixteenth-century date.

25. Dairy Farm, Weobley, Hereford and Worcester. A cruck-built open-hall farmhouse of fifteenth- or early sixteenth-century date.

Similar houses appear elsewhere in the highland zone, and many excellent examples can be cited. At Naish Farm, Holwell, Dorset, the Royal Commission on Historical Monuments has recently discovered an almost complete late-medieval eight-cruck open-hall farmhouse with a hall flanked by a two-storey solar bay at the upper end and at the opposite end across the passage a partly replaced single-storey service bay. Bush Farm, Horton, Avon, is another former open cruck hall built in the fifteenth century but which in the sixteenth century had a floor inserted and a chimney stack built at the lower end of the hall to form a cross-passage. Also of fifteenth-century date is Farley's End Farmhouse, Elmore, Gloucestershire, a four-bay house with the two centre bays forming the open hall. A late example is Rodford Hill Farm, Westerleigh, Avon, perhaps built in the second half of the sixteenth century, with a three-bay open hall and a three-bay two-storey cross-wing.

Farmhouses of similar size and date are to be found in Buckinghamshire in an area where both cruck and box-frame construction overlap. The two-bay former open cruck hall at Hill Farm, Chalfont St Peter, was built in the fourteenth century and is all that remains of that period. Whether this stood alone or had a further bay at one end is unknown for the house has been greatly extended over the centuries, and the south-west wing which was built in the fifteenth century may have replaced an earlier bay. Later in date are Grange Farm, Widmer End, and Northend Farm, Long Crendon, both of the fifteenth century and both with a two-bay open hall and a two-storey single-bay service wing at one end. The crucks at Northend Farm, which was demolished in 1965, terminated for some reason just below the collar and may be a late example of a base-cruck.

There are a number of cruck-built farmhouses which were originally of single storey throughout, and from the evidence of the soot-encrusted trusses and rafters some of the houses such as Townsend Farm, Stockland, Devon, Champs Farm, Sixpenny Handley, Dorset, and Old Farm, Standlake, Oxfordshire, were divided up into rooms by low head-height timber partitions, although others, it appears, had full-height partitions. In some houses partial flooring took place, leaving the hall as the last part to be floored. This probably first occurred at the upper end to form a chamber over the parlour and later over the cross-passage and service room. A feature of these inserted floors was the extension of the upper floor beyond the ground floor partition to form an internal jetty. This provided not only a greater floor area on the upper floor but also a decorative feature with the ends of the joists often chamfered and stopped. It generally occurred at the upper end of the hall, as at Sanders, Lettaford, Devon, where it provided a kind of canopy, sometimes at the lower end and occasionally, as at Little Rull, Cullompton, at both ends. These internal jetties indicate that at least part of the house was at one time open to the roof.

Open-hall farmhouses of stone are comparatively rare even in those areas where good building stone was abundant, for in the fifteenth and early sixteenth century, when most of the open-hall houses were being constructed in eastern England, the South-east and parts of the South and West, timber was also the predominate building material at the vernacular level in other parts of the country. However, because timber was scarce in much of the highland zone and the quality less good than elsewhere, these early timber-framed houses were generally replaced by the end of the sixteenth century with ones constructed of stone. There are of course exceptions. Many cruck-built open-hall farmhouses, among them Upper Poswick, Naish, Townsend, Bushes, Rodford Hill and Sanders, had walls constructed of stone. There are others in the highland zone built of stone which still retain the medieval concept of an open hall between solar and service ends, with the roof of the open hall being spanned by an arch-braced collar-beam roof. These are to be found mainly in those counties in the southern half of England and are in many cases clearly farmhouses which were originally of manorial status. Two such examples are to be found in Somerset; one is Blackmoor Farm, Cannington, which is a splendid example of a manor house built about 1500 which retains many of its original features, and another is Lower Marsh Farm, near Dunster, which has its own private chapel. Similar farmhouses are to be found in Wiltshire; for instance there is Bradfield Farm, Hullavington, and Easton Court Farm, Corsham. A fine example of a smaller stone open-hall farmhouse is Higher Abbotts Wootton Farm, Whitechurch Canonicorum, Dorset, with its simple rectangular solar-hall-service arrangement unobscured by later additions. Others in Dorset are Sandpit Old Farm, Drimpton, and Upbury Farm, Yetminster. In Avon one can cite such farms as Green Farm, Olveston, and Rock Farm, Littleton, both former open-hall houses. At Cogges, Oxfordshire, Manor Farm, which forms part of an attractive medieval group around the church, incorporates a substantial part of the hall and kitchen of a house built about 1270. In the same county, at Balscott, there are two houses, Priory Farm and Grange Farm, both probably built by Wroxton Abbey, which are former open-hall houses. Further north in Shropshire there is Manor Farm, Aston Botterell, which incorporates a thirteenth-century hall with its doorway still preserved.

Towards the end of the fifteenth century the open hall began to be replaced in the East and the South-east by houses constructed with two storeys throughout, and from this time onwards the old open halls began to be chambered over and chimney stacks inserted. Elsewhere in the country the abandonment of the open hall occurred somewhat later. In the West Midlands substantial timber-framed houses, comparable with the largest to be found in the South-east and eastern England, such as Court Farm, Throckmorton, Hereford and Worcester, were still being constructed during the early part of the sixteenth century with an open hall. Even here, however, the open hall had generally been divided horizontally to give an upper floor during the sixteenth century, but it is clear from inventories that many still remained in use in the late seventeenth century. The room over the hall became little more than a store in many cases because of the low headroom and was normally referred to as 'the chamber over the hall'. In both the South-east and eastern England by the beginning of the sixteenth century and elsewhere by the reign of Elizabeth, all but those houses built in remote parts of England and for poor farmers and cottagers were being built with two storeys, yet the hall remained as it had always been, the main living-room.

The Cross-passage Farmhouse

The cross-passage was the predominant feature of all late-medieval houses of more than one room. It ran transversely across the building, providing access to the house from both the front and rear and dividing the living quarters from the service rooms or, in the case of the longhouse, the living quarters from the byre. The cross-passage, in the form of the screens-passage, in the open hall has been discussed earlier and developed from a desire to provide greater privacy by the exclusion of the service rooms from the hall and the draughts from the two external doors, thus providing a greater degree of comfort. It had generally been abandoned by the end of the sixteenth century, at about the same time as the open hall, in most of the lowland zone, yet it must be remembered that the open hall was not only an old form but a superior form, the influence of which lasted long after it had disappeared in larger houses, and so a cross-passage, still flanked by the impressive ornamented timber screens, was often retained. This was so in many late-medieval farmhouses which had a floor and chimney inserted into the open hall at the upper end of the hall away from the screens-passage. It remained a popular feature of many farmhouses built in the sixteenth century in Suffolk and Norfolk and to a lesser degree in Cambridgeshire, Essex and Hertfordshire and continued to do so until finally being displaced by the central lobby entry plan. The screens-passage was also a feature of many continuous jettied farmhouses built at the end of the fifteenth century which still retained many of the medieval attitudes, with the hall, with its upper and lower end, and remained so during the following century. This is particularly true of the South-east where it is as equally well defined as the early Wealden house it replaced.

Although the cross-passage in the South-east had generally been superseded by other house plans during the sixteenth century, in the highland zone it persisted, remaining the most characteristic post-medieval feature in many farmhouses throughout the seventeenth and eighteenth centuries. This was especially true of the South-west, West and North-west, parts of the limestone belt (the Cotswolds and North Somerset) and the Pennines. In these areas the cross-passage developed quite independently from that of the lowland zone and the medieval open hall. It seems to have originated from the desire of many

26. 'Old Farmhouse', Higher Stiniel, Devon. An old granite cross-passage farmhouse.

farmers for improved domestic accommodation, which resulted in the ultimate exclusion of animals from the house and the conversion of the byre into a service room. In some areas this change had occurred by the thirteenth century; in the South-west at Hound Tor, Beere and

Hutholes, all in Devon, and at Gomeldon, Wiltshire, excavations have revealed that alterations, which include the blocking-up of one entrance to the cross-passage, the removal of the screen between the house part and the byre, the narrowing of the former passage which had originally been intended for use by cattle, and the filling-in of the drainage channel in the byre, had only one objective and that was to convert the byre into additional accommodation. Clearly, although the cross-passage of the open hall and longhouse developed independently, they are both of medieval origin.

The position of the cross-passage is usually related to the position of the chimney. Although there are exceptions – occasionally one finds a stack built against the cross-passage or more commonly on the rear lateral wall – in most of the lowland zone and in particular the South-east and East Anglia the chimney was nearly always situated away from the cross-passage, the usual position being at the upper end of the hall (27). This arrangement is also to be found in many farmhouses in the highland zone, particularly in the southern half of England, but in nearly all cases they are either of late-medieval origin or large houses built towards the end of the seventeenth century with either three or four large units to each floor (29F).

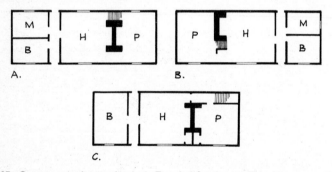

27. Cross-passage house plans – 1. East and South-east: The old concept of the screens-passage lingered on in the South-east and East after the abandonment of the open-hall and in these examples a cross-passage flanked by timber partitions was retained. They first appeared in the middle of the sixteenth century and continued to be built into the seventeenth century. This house type was common in East Anglia as well as in the Weald of Kent and Sussex.

In the South-west too, the chimney was sometimes sited away from the cross-passage on the front wall of the hall adjacent to the main entrance and serving both the hall and the chamber over (29G and H).

Known as a lateral stack, it became a standard feature of many east Devon farmhouses, the earliest dating from the end of the sixteenth century – Poltimore, Farway, dated 1583, and Pinn Farm, Otterton, dated 1587 – and remained popular for over one hundred years and spread, although to a lesser degree, all over Devon and elsewhere in the South-west. One of particularly early date is Methrose, near Luxulyan, Cornwall, a house probably built in the latter part of the fifteenth century or early part of the sixteenth century and similar in plan to Tintagel Post Office, which is of fourteenth-century date. Why it gained popularity is uncertain, for it is less efficient than the axial stack, but it was of high social standing, often being built of contrasting materials, perhaps two types of stone as Barclose Farm, Otterton (28). It had the advantage that the oak plank-and-muntin partition between the cross-passage and hall, which was an important feature in many farmhouses in the South-west, could be retained.

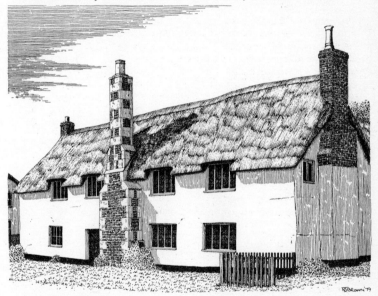

28. Barclose Farm, Otterton, Devon. Built in 1627, this farmhouse has a typical East Devon chimney at the front. Built in two different types of stone, although the house is of cob.

The most common arrangement, however, and the traditional position throughout the highland zone, is where the stack backs onto the cross-passage forming part of the cross-passage wall. At the lower end of the house beyond the cross-passage was the service room. This arrangement can be found in some former stone-built open-hall farmhouses where the stack is placed at the lower end of the hall against the former screens-passage and is to be found in most farmhouses built in the sixteenth and seventeenth centuries in all parts of the highland zone where stone is plentiful and continued to be built into the latter half of the eighteenth century.

Although there are some cross-passage farmhouses which were originally of two units, with only hall and service room (29A and 31A) – one such example is Hill, Christow, Devon – most are of three units, with the hall, an inner room, usually the parlour, and beyond the cross-passage at the lower end the service room. In the highland zone this room was probably agricultural rather than domestic. The parlour was generally the smallest room and in the highland zone was usually divided from the hall by a timber screen and would sometimes contain a fireplace in the gable wall, but this was almost certainly a later addition. The service room too might also have had a fireplace, but once again this was more likely to be an addition when the service room was converted into a kitchen. In the South-east and eastern England the service room was usually divided into two to form a buttery and pantry, each with its own door from the cross-passage and generally with a communicating door between the two. In the South-west the stairs were usually in the hall and often housed in a projection within the rear wall (29C, D and H), although sometimes they are to be found alongside the wall to the cross-passage (29B, E and G).

Many of these houses are to be found in Cumbria (31). R. W. Brunskill, in his survey of the smaller houses of the Eden Valley, indicates that out of a total of 205 houses built by statesmen nearly 50 per cent are of the cross-passage type. They were built for nearly a hundred years, from about 1675 until about 1770, with the greatest number concentrated in the first thirty-five years when they represented some 50 per cent of all dated houses built in the area.

The typical early cross-passage house that the statesmen built consisted of three rooms on the ground floor with a cross-passage dividing the hall and parlour at the upper end from the service room at the lower end, known in Cumbria as the downhouse (32). The upper floor, divided into bedrooms, extended only over the upper end, for in many cases the downhouse was open to the roof or was floored and used as a hay loft with access only from the outside. The bedrooms were reached either by a ladder from the hall or parlour or in the larger houses by means of a newel stair in a projection at the rear of the house. The inconvenience of both the ladder and the newel staircase was soon apparent, and many houses were built and others altered to

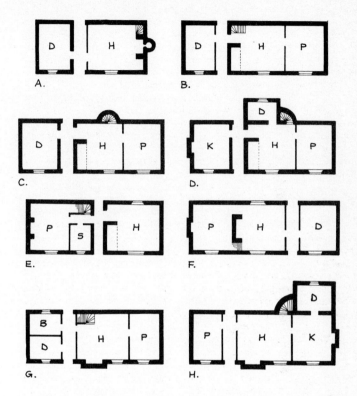

29. Cross-passage house plans – 2. South-west: Type A is a typical small seventeenth-century house with projecting oven. Types B and C show the differing staircase position adopted in the South-west. In Type D the dairy has been converted into a kitchen and the dairy, an important feature in the highland zone, added in an outshut at the rear. Type E shows an example of the service room in the centre giving a more symmetrical appearance which was becoming popular at the end of the seventeenth century. Type F house with stack away from cross-passage. Types G and H are typical house plans with stack on front wall common in East Devon and elsewhere in Devon, Cornwall and Somerset in the late sixteenth and seventeenth centuries. Types B, C, D and F are all typical of houses built at the end of the sixteenth and throughout the seventeenth centuries.

30. Lower Lynch Farm, Bossington, Somerset, stands on the site of an earlier manor house. This cross-passage farmhouse has a chimney at the front, a common feature in the South-west.

incorporate a dog-leg-type staircase, still of stone, in a rectangular outshut at the rear. In many of the larger houses a dairy was incorporated alongside the staircase in this rear extension. The house was heated by a single fire situated in the hall, the rear wall forming one wall of the cross-passage. The hearth was large, occupying from a quarter to a third of the hall, and above this was the typical timber and plaster firehood common in the North. In addition the hearth was invariably lit by a narrow fire-window. In the rear wall of the fireplace between the hearth and fire-window was a spice cupboard, generally carved with initials and date. Positioned opposite the hearth in the timber partition between the hall and parlour was a bread cupboard often carved and usually carrying a date. Most bread cupboards are dated between 1670 and 1700, while the spice cupboards are slightly later, most being dated between 1680 and 1710.

In the seventeenth century there was a desire for some sort of

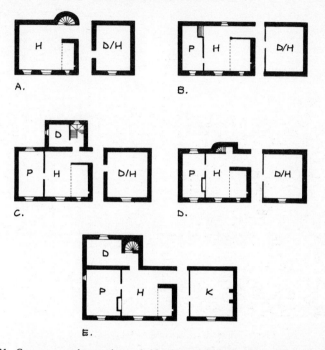

31. Cross-passage house plans – 3. North-west: the cross-passage farmhouse was built in the North-west from about 1625 until 1775 with the highest concentration being between 1670 and 1710. Type A is typical of the earliest surviving example, the spiral staircase indicating its social standing. Type B, although larger, is a humbler dwelling built towards the end of the seventeenth century; the loft above the hall and parlour is reached by a ladder or companion-way. Type C is a more ambitious example of about the same date with the staircase and dairy housed in an outshut at the rear. Type D is probably of an earlier date, perhaps 1650, while Type E is typical of those built around the turn of the century for the more prosperous farmers.

symmetry to the front elevation which was unobtainable with the cross-passage plan so far described. In the South-east and in eastern England this was partly achieved by the introduction of the central lobby-entry house, but in parts of the South-west including Avon and parts of Gloucestershire this was achieved by the re-arrangement of the internal rooms yet still retaining the all-important cross-passage (34). The service room below the cross-passage was replaced by the parlour,

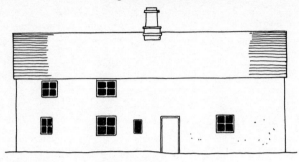

Elevation

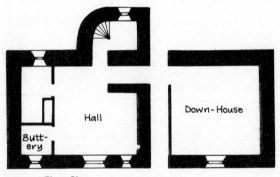

Ground Floor Plan

32. Typical statesman-plan farmhouse of Cumbria.

moving the service room to the centre of the house between the hall and the cross-passage. Both hall and kitchen were heated generally with gable-wall fireplaces, but in some cases the parlour was heated by a fireplace situated on the wall to the cross-passage in the old-fashioned way. The overall appearance was one approaching the then fashionable symmetrical façade, and when the parlour was heated by a fireplace backing onto the cross-passage, it was not uncommon to have a chimney built at the end gable to achieve the overall balance. Although farmhouses of this type can be found, they are not common, for this overall symmetry was usually obtained without retaining the cross-passage.

There has been much speculation as to the reason why the cross-passage remained so popular in the farmhouses of the highland zone

33. Glencoyne Farm, Patterdale, Cumbria. This early example of a statesman's house was built in 1629 for the Howard family. Originally it had only two ground-floor rooms, the hall and downhouse, but in 1700, a two-bay extension was added at the rear and the downhouse converted into a parlour. The stepped gables are rather an unusual feature, but the cylindrical chimneys are to be found on many of the early Cumbrian farmhouses.

long after it had generally been abandoned elsewhere in England. That the cross-passage developed independently in the two areas from differing social needs is quite obvious. In the South-east and East Anglia it developed from the desire for greater comfort and privacy, and as the agriculture in these areas was generally arable or sheep, the service rooms, usually divided into a buttery and pantry, were domestic rather than agricultural. In the highland zone, from Cumbria in the north to Devon in the South-west, agriculture was mainly pastoral, and the service room was nearly always agricultural and from documentary evidence was usually a dairy, which was considered an essential part of the house. This was true in Devon, where one of the rooms in a small two-roomed house – like the house now used as a farm

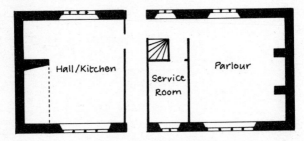

Hall/Kitchen

Service Room

Parlour

34. Late seventeenth-century cross-passage farmhouse with central service room on the limestone belt.

building at Nettacott, Upton Pyne – was often a dairy. In many cross-passage farmhouses where the service rooms were later converted into a kitchen, a dairy was added at the rear of the house, like that at Buskins, Exbourne, Devon, while in many longhouses, such as Nettleslack, Martindale, and Sanders, Lettaford, when the inner room was either built as or later converted into the parlour or kitchen, a dairy was again often provided at the rear. With the service room being agricultural, it was necessary to obtain access to this throughout the day from the yard or farm buildings at the rear without entering the hall, and it was equally desirable for the farmer's wife and domestic

35. A seventeenth-century cross-passage farmhouse at Otretton, Leicestershire.

36. Overfield Farm, Tissington, Derbyshire.

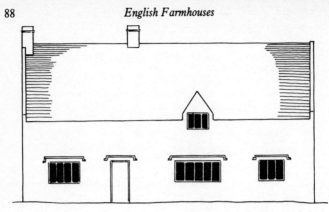

Elevation

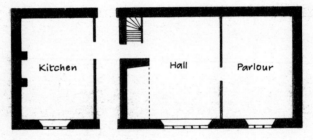

Ground Floor Plan

37. Typical cross-passage house found in parts of Somerset.

staff to obtain access to the dairy without going outside. Also in many areas the medieval concept of the detached kitchen away from the house still prevailed, and this was particularly true of many farmhouses of the South-west. These kitchens were mainly situated at the rear of the house, often facing the rear door of the cross-passage. Once again access was needed from the rear of the house. So we have a house in which access was required at the front to receive visitors and at the rear for farmworkers and domestic servants coming in from the yard. It was an obvious advantage to the smooth running of the house to construct a cross-passage which had access from both ends with a single entry into the hall and which also served the service room as well, rather than constructing two separate lobby entrances into the hall at the front and rear and a separate one into the service room.

38. Warren's Farmhouse, Stanton, Gloucestershire. A typical cross-passage farmhouse found in the Cotswolds.

It seems, therefore, that the continued use of the cross-passage in the highland zone of the country was determined by the daily needs of the cattle and their produce, unlike more seasonal requirements of the arable farmers of the lowland zone. In addition many of these cross-passage farmhouses in nucleated villages, particularly in the Midlands, are associated with dwellings placed with their frontage parallel to the street, the passage providing access from the street to the yard at the back.

The Dual-purpose Farmhouse

The term dual-purpose is one now commonly employed for a dwelling in which the living accommodation and the farm buildings – either the byre or barn – are all housed under the same continuous roof. In England there are three main types, the longhouse with all its derivations, the laithe-house and the bastle-house which has previously been described.

The use of the dual-purpose dwelling in which both men and animals were housed under the same roof was at one time widespread, and the traditional form in England was the longhouse in which the house and byre were separated by the cross-passage or cross-walk which had a door at each end. When this house type first appeared in this country is uncertain, for although longhouses have been traced back to the ninth century in the Orkneys and perhaps also in the Shetlands, no such date has yet been firmly established in England. At Mawgan Porth, near Newquay, Cornwall, excavations have revealed a dry-stone walled building, probably built in the tenth century, which clearly shows the division between house and byre, but the dwelling formed part of a larger complex. It is not until the twelfth and thirteenth centuries that any large number appear. Excavations in Devon, at Beere, near North Tawton, and Hound Tor on Dartmoor, and in Cornwall at Old Lanyon, near West Penwith, Treworld, near Boscastle, and Garrow Tor on Bodmin Moor, and in Wiltshire on Fyfield Down and at Gomeldon all reveal longhouses which have within their sites pottery of late twelfth- and early thirteenth-century date. At Hound Tor and Treworld, excavations have revealed earlier turf and wattle structures built and rebuilt on the same site and in some cases on the same alignment as the later stone structure, clearly indicating occupation at least a century or so before.

In all these dwellings the size and accommodation provided varied greatly; in fact the only common feature was the cross-passage or in some cases a cross-walk dividing house and byre, and they were all built with low dry-stone side walls carrying the roof structure. At Beere the longhouse was divided into three parts; in the middle was the main room with a central hearth and to the left, divided by a wall or screen, an inner room, probably used for sleeping. To the right beyond the cross-passage was the byre. At Garrow Tor the living accommodation was 20 feet by 11 feet separated from the byre by a paved cross-passage, while at Treworld the overall size of the longhouse was 72 feet by 22 feet. All these houses had generally been abandoned by the fourteenth century.

Although the earliest longhouses appear to be in the South-west, there is both archaeological and documentary evidence that during the fourteenth and fifteenth centuries they were built elsewhere in the country. Although most are of fourteenth- and fifteenth-century date, none are earlier than the thirteenth century, and they continued in use throughout the fifteenth and into the sixteenth century. These later examples, for instance at Upton, Gloucestershire, West Hartburn, County Durham, Wharram Percy, North Yorkshire, West Whelpington, Northumberland, and Hangleton, Sussex, were all poorly constructed of dry stone, turf, chalk or timber and, like the earlier ones in the South-west, were of one or two rooms with no structural division between the house and byre.

Longhouses little better than these continued to be used in parts of Cumbria until the middle of the seventeenth century. J. S. Nicholson in his *History of Crosby Garrett, Westmorland* describes houses built with crucks which had the family at one end of the building and cattle at the other, with only "some sort of partition between". In 1853 A. Turner describes these houses and similar ones found in Northumberland and County Durham as comprising only two compartments, one with the only external door, containing the animals, and the other in which the family lived, the two being divided only by a "rude partition" called a "brattish" which extended only up to eaves level.

There were, however, from the fifteenth century similar but more substantial longhouses being built providing accommodation which was in many cases little better. In the Black Mountain area of Hereford and Worcester a number of early longhouses providing limited accommodation are to be found. One good example is Black Daren, Llanveynoe, probably built in the fifteenth century of cruck construction with stone walls. The accommodation provided was a hall and an inner room divided from the hall by a timber partition, with both rooms being open to the roof. There was probably no cross-passage but opposed entrances in the hall, and from the evidence of the mortice holes in the underside of the tie-beam to the cruck-truss, the byre was separated from the hall by a timber partition which was open above the tie-beam. This building, which is no longer occupied, has been greatly altered and was partly rebuilt in the nineteenth century, when the byre was changed to domestic use. Other houses similar to Black Daren which still survive are Great Turnant, also at Llanveynoe, and Cwarelau, Newton, and there are probably others where later

39. Higher Godsworthy, Peter Tavy, Devon. A longhouse showing the
changes that occurred to many over the centuries. The farmhouse originally
had a porch which led directly into the byre with a door immediately into the
house, but this was later blocked up and a new doorway formed and a porch
added adjacent to the old porch and opening.

additions and alterations have obscured the original plan. Similar
houses built in the sixteenth century are to be found in Devon. Higher
Brownston, Modbury, was built with only a hall (open to the roof and
with probably a central hearth) and a byre being divided by nothing
more than a timber screen, and at Higher Dittisham, Walkhampton,
there was only a hall above the cross-passage. It was in Devon, on and
around Dartmoor, however, that most longhouses were built, and
there is perhaps no better place in England to study their development
(40). Most of the existing longhouses in this area were built with the
slope of the land, with the byre at the lower end. Originally above the
passage there was probably only a hall, perhaps divided from the byre
by a timber screen (40B). In many cases the hall was of considerable
size, and it seems likely that later it was sub-divided with a timber

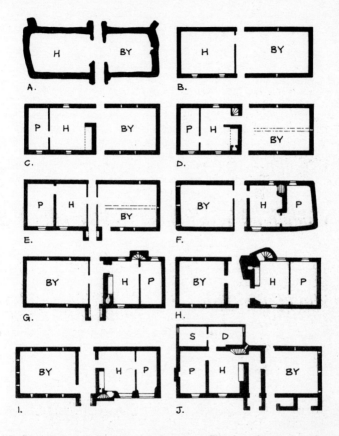

40. Dual-purpose house plans – 1. Dartmoor: The above house plans show
the development of the longhouse on Dartmoor from medieval times
onwards. A. is based on the longhouse found on Hound Tor Down and is of
thirteenth-century date; D. is based on Collihole, Chagford, (after R. H.
Worth); E. on Sanders, Lettaford (after P. Child); F. on Tor Farm,
Widecombe-in-the-Moor (after R. W. McDowall); G. on Warne's kitchen,
Sampford Spiney (after R. H. Worth); H. on Higher Shapley, Chagford (after
R. H. Worth); I. on Shilstone, Throwleigh (after R. H. Worth) and J. on
Lower Tor Farm, Widecombe-in-the-Moor although much altered (after R.
W. McDowall).

partition to provide the fashionable inner room. At this time men and animals still used a common entrance into the byre, the entrance into the house being through the cross-wall containing the hearth. Examples of this type may be seen at Higher Godsworthy in Peter Tavy parish (39) and Collihole, in Chagford (40D). This early type was replaced by the so-called 'classic longhouse' which still had a common entrance for men and animals but in which the cross-passage was divided from the byre with either a timber or stone partition. A massive stone newel staircase in the back wall lead to the upper rooms which had, between 1570 and 1640, generally been formed by inserting a floor. It was not until the latter part of the seventeenth century that a separate entrance was provided to the house, usually adjacent to the original common entrance to the byre. Yet at Shilstone, Throwleigh (40I), dated 1656 and one of the last longhouses to be built in Devon, access was still provided from the cross-passage into the byre. Many other later longhouses were modified to incorporate these improvements. Lake, Poundgate, was probably adapted in 1661 when the porch was added, as was Lower Tor, Widecombe-in-the-Moor (40J and 41), when a porch was added in 1707 and the entrance between byre and house blocked and a separate entrance formed. The old byre end can still be plainly seen though no longer used and is entered through an arched doorway of about 1500. Higher Shapley, in Chagford (40H), was of the classic longhouse design before the porch was added in 1776.

In the hundred or so years in which the Dartmoor longhouse was built, the design was in no way standard, and the four basic plans described above varied greatly. It is impossible to say with any degree of certainty that one type was earlier or later than any other, and it is probable that the various types are coeval, although the last type, with the separate entrance into house and byre, appears to be the latest.

Today no longhouse survives on Dartmoor in which both men and animals are still housed under the same roof, and many byres have been converted to make additional domestic accommodation, but there still survive some byres with the original layout. In most, as at Sanders, Lettaford (42), the drain made of stone slabs ran centrally down the byre to an outlet at the base of the end wall, with two rows of stones sunk in the floor and drilled to accommodate the tethering stakes. Occasionally the drain was set transversely, as at Chapple, Gidleigh, a longhouse which displays many Dartmoor characteristic features such as a pitching-hole in the upper part of the wall, for loading hay, and two small dung-holes to clear out the muck.

Towards the end of the seventeenth century, at a time when the Dartmoor longhouse had ceased to be built and existing ones were being altered and modernized, in other parts of the country they

41. Lower Tor Farm, Widecombe-in-the-Moor, Devon. A remarkable Dartmoor longhouse, much altered over the centuries with the porch added in 1707 and the entrance between byre and house blocked and a separate entrance formed.

42. Sanders, Lettaford, Devon. A Dartmoor longhouse with a cross-passage and the shippon at the lower end in the typical down-slop orientation. The outer walls are of granite in part formed with large dressed coursed blocks with an entrance porch also built of large granite blocks and has a wide-shouldered head doorway.

started to be built. One area was North Yorkshire, where Green Farm, Levisham, is perhaps the most complete example, having a single-storey attached byre which, although dated 1791, is clearly a rebuild of an earlier one. Others include Scar House, Upper Swaledale, where access to the byre could be obtained from the hall-kitchen via the cross-passage, and Kepp House, Burton-in-Lonsdale, and Crow Trees, Cowan Bridge, both of which had at one time doors opening immediately from the hall-kitchen into the fodder gang of the byre. However, it is now impossible to tell in most cases whether there was originally a service room or byre beyond the cross-passage, but it is evident from the width of many of these cross-passages and the description of these houses by many early writers that some at least must have been longhouses. Oak Crag and Duck House, Farndale, Cliff Cottage, Beadlam and Weathercote, Bilsdale, all seem to be former longhouses. Perhaps the best example is Stang End, which formerly stood at Danby and has been re-erected at the Ryedale Folk Museum, Hutton-le-Hole, in its original longhouse form.

It is in Cumbria, however, that most are to be found being built to a more uniform plan than those of Devon (43). Like those in Devon, the farm buildings and dwelling were in a continuous range separated by a cross-passage with doors at each end, but at the far end opposite doors led in one case to the hall and in the other to the byre. The partition between the cross-passage and byre was generally of stone, but in some of the earlier examples this partition appears to be of timber. The house itself resembled in every respect the statesman plan previously described, only the service rooms being replaced by the farm buildings. These longhouses were first built about 1670, probably replacing those earlier examples previously described, and continued to be built for another hundred years, although from the many dated examples most appear to have been built between 1680 and 1710.

Today none survive in their unaltered state, but there are a number of good examples to be found. Bromley Green, Great Ormside, a house surveyed by R.W.Brunskill, was built in 1687 and is one of the few houses in which the farm buildings are still used in conjunction with the house and clearly shows the improvement to both house and farm buildings over the years, reflecting both an increase in prosperity and a change in social needs and values. When originally built, the house comprised a hall and parlour, the hall being heated by the usual hearth with firehood over. Access to the floor above was probably by a ladder; the roof would almost certainly be thatched and the eaves low. The farm buildings, which probably comprised the byre and barn with a loft above, were separated from the house by the cross-passage with doors at both ends and at the far end with doors into the hall and byre. In the middle of the eighteenth century the building was modernized;

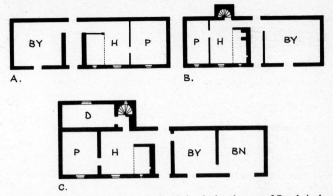

A.

B.

C.

43. Dual-purpose house plans – 2. Cumbria: the longhouses of Cumbria date from the second half of the seventeenth century until the early part of the eighteenth century. Type A access to the bedroom above would have been by ladder, but in some cases a staircase was provided at the rear as with type B. Type C is a large example with a staircase and dairy block in an outshut at the rear.

44. Typical late seventeenth- or early eighteenth-century Cumbrian longhouse.

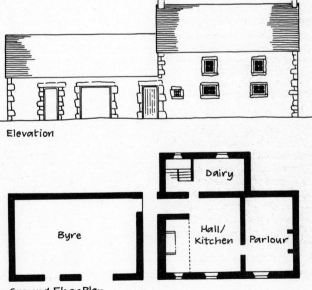

Elevation

Ground Floor Plan

new windows were put in, a rear outshut containing the stone staircase and dairy was built, the external walls to both the house and farm buildings were raised to form one uninterrupted roof, and fireplaces were added to both hall and parlour. The farm buildings were also altered to form a byre, meal-house and loose-box with a hay-loft above. The cross-passage with access to both hall and byre still remained, and it was not until the nineteenth century that the present entrance door was put in and the door between the hall and cross-passage finally blocked in. Ona Ash, Kirkoswald, built in 1693, is another example; originally single-storey, the house has been raised to two full storeys, though the cross-passage and byre remain as first built.

The tradition of the longhouse continued in parts of Hereford and Worcester long after those early examples previously mentioned had been built, and there are a number of timber-framed farmhouses which still retain many of the essential features of the longhouse, of which Lower House Cottage, Staunton-on-Wye (probably the original Lower House Farm before the new farmhouse opposite this cottage was built late in the seventeenth century) is one good example. Built early in the sixteenth century, it originally consisted of an open hall and farm buildings under one roof, and although there is a separate external entrance into the byre, there is direct communication between the byre and hall. There does not appear to have been a cross-passage, but there were opposed entrances in the hall. The house was extended in the seventeenth century to provide two additional ground-floor rooms with bedrooms above, and at the same time a fireplace and chimney stack were built between the new and old building and a floor inserted into the hall. Other houses are to be found in the region which closely resemble in date, size and later extensions that at Staunton-on-Wye, among them Lower House, Burrington, and Olchon Court, Llanveynoe, which was extended in the seventeenth century to form a long range with parlour, service room, kitchen, cross-passage and byre. There are others, such as The Farm, Adforton, which was built at the beginning of the eighteenth century yet still retains direct access between the house and byre.

It seems likely that in other parts of the highland zone longhouses of some form at one time existed. Although the longhouse was the traditional house type on Dartmoor and its hinterland, elsewhere in the region it is virtually unknown. Only two – Higher Brownston, Modbury, and Arnolds, Harberton – have so far been identified with any certainty in Devon, and it is virtually unknown elsewhere in the South-west. In Dorset, in the southern uplands, it seems likely that they once existed, but only Charity Farm, Osmington, now survives. Likewise in Cornwall although none now remain or can be identified with any degree of certainty, there is much evidence of rebuilding

45. Farmhouse at Blencarn, Cumbria. A typical Cumbrian longhouse formerly thatched but raised in the nineteenth century and re-roofed. The painted surrounds to the windows are a feature of the North-west.

below the cross-passage, while at Halton, at St Dominick and Higher Hampt at Stoke Climsland, the lower ends have clearly been reconstructed. There are others that have an end-entry passage where the lower end may have been removed. Clearly some of these farmhouses may originally have been longhouses. If so, why they were abandoned is not clear; it may have been due partly to the decline of dairy farming in the county towards the end of the sixteenth century or perhaps to the adoption of the more practicable courtyard plan which provided greater protection from the high winds and storms so common in the South-west. Some of these courtyard houses are certainly adaptations of former houses.

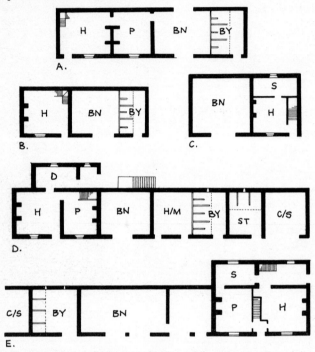

46. Dual-purpose house plans – 3. Laithe and linear houses: Type A is an eighteenth-century laithe-house of West Yorkshire. Type B a nineteenth-century laithe-house. Type C is a typical nineteenth-century house built for smallholders in the North and elsewhere in the highland zone. Type D is a typical linear house of North Yorkshire; Type E a similar house in the North-east.

A derivation of the longhouse, the linear farm, in which house and farm buildings are two or more contiguous buildings each with their own entrance yet sharing the same roof line, can be found in many parts of the highland zone (46). They are broadly classified as longhouses mainly because they form one long, continuous range of buildings. Yet the longhouses' characteristic feature of the cross-passage with entry to both the house and byre is not evident. They are generally of a later date than most longhouses, and consequently the old concept of the cross-passage was abandoned for more symmetrical house types with entry directly into the house. In addition, the farm buildings were located not at the lower end across the cross-passage but at the upper end adjacent to the parlour. Unlike the longhouse, in which the farm buildings comprised only a byre and possibly a barn, with these later houses the extent of the farm buildings varied according to the needs of the farmer, and no regular layout seems to have been adopted. The small farmer still had only a barn or byre, and houses with these attached continued to be built well into the nineteenth century. In many, however, the range of buildings was considerable, containing not merely the barn and byre but a full range of farm buildings, including hay-store, granary, stables, cart sheds and ancillary buildings.

47. West Newhouse Farm, Bishopdale, North Yorkshire. A typical Dales linear farmhouse built in 1635 from stone quarried from the hill behind the house.

These farmhouses were an obvious continuation of the longhouse development, and although they appeared at different times throughout the highland zone, they all date from a time when the traditional longhouse with its internal communication between house and byre began to decline. In Cumbria, where many are to be found, they first appeared towards the end of the seventeenth century when the longhouses in that area had reached their peak and continued to be built well into the nineteenth century. Typical are those at Broom Farm, Gosforth, where the outbuildings comprise two byres, a barn and a calves' pen with a loft over all but the barn, and at Thornbank, also in Gosforth, built in 1795, which has a range of outbuildings 113 feet long. In the Dales of North Yorkshire many are to be found, of which West Newhouse, Bishopdale, dated 1635 (47), is an early but typical example of Pennine construction. Others of a slightly later date but equally typical are Low Oxnop, Swaledale, built in 1685, Lumb Farm, Settle, which is dated 1702, and of the same date Woodhouse Manor, Wharfdale. Similar farmhouses can be found to the southern part of the Pennines in Derbyshire (48), and the adjoining parts of Cheshire (49) and Staffordshire (50) as well as in the South-west and North-east.

In all these houses the front elevation became one approaching symmetry, with the front entrance door placed more or less in the centre of the front wall flanked on either side by windows. This desire for symmetry can be seen at Trenow, Gulval, Cornwall, a farmhouse built of cob in the late eighteenth century with a byre at one end with a loft over. The house has a door placed centrally in the front elevation leading directly into the kitchen with sash window, and at the other end a matching sash window which lights the byre. Entrance into the byre is from the rear.

A local variation to the dual-purpose plan is the laithe-house (52) which is found in West Yorkshire, particularly in the Halifax-Huddersfield-Sheffield area of the Pennines. 'Laithe' is a Yorkshire dialect word for 'barn', and the laithe-house comprises, under one roof, a house, barn and byre, with the barn and byre combined. They are generally later in date than most longhouses. The earliest known example is Bank House, Luddenden, which was built in 1650, but the majority date from the eighteenth century, such as Savile House, Hazelhead, dated 1702, Law Farm, Thornton, dated 1750, Abinger Farm, Holmfirth, Scout Farm, Todmorden, Moorside Farm, Holmfirth, bearing the dates 1777 and 1792, and Unslivenbridge Farm, Stocksbridge. They continued to be built into the nineteenth century, and Catherine Slack Farm, Hebden Bridge, which was built in 1880, is one of the latest.

Unlike the longhouses the laithe-houses are not generally uniform in size or arrangement, the only common feature being that the barns

48. Long Roods Farm, Longstone, Derbyshire.

49. Farmhouse near Fernlea, Cheshire. A typical linear farmhouse found in the southern Pennines.

50. Linear farmhouse at Waterfall, Staffordshire.

51. Typical nineteenth-century farmhouse at Staron, near Gunnerside, North Yorkshire.

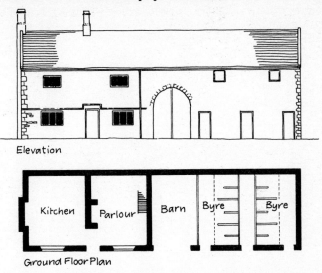

Elevation

Ground Floor Plan

Kitchen   Parlour   Barn   Byre   Byre

52. Typical eighteenth-century laithe-house in West Yorkshire.

were always adjacent to the houses. Generally, however, the later the building the smaller the house part became, while the size of the laithe tended to increase.

None of the later examples, with perhaps the exception of Scout Farm, compares with the accommodation provided at Bank House, and most are only one room deep. Nearly all contain just a hall and parlour on the ground floor, but Bents Farm, Hazelhead, built about 1850, originally had only one room, while Catherine Slack Farm had only an additional small service room. Abinger Farm consists of a very small house in contrast with a very large laithe some hundred feet long. The laithe-house usually comprised a two-storey house, with the laithe the same height as the house and in the same range. Occasionally the laithe was lower or set at right angles to the house, forming an L-shaped group, as at Savile House. Some, like Scout Farm, Woodroyd Farm, Hepworth, Moorside Farm and Savile House, have or at least had access to the laithe from the house, enabling the farmer to enter the laithe without going outside, but the house was never entered through the laithe. The prominent external feature of the laithe is the high, usually curved entry into the barn, tall enough to allow a laden haywagon to pass beneath. Occasionally, as at Scout Farm, Savile House and Moorside Farm, there is another door opposite the main entry to the barn. Access to the byre is usually by a separate smaller door.

The Lobby-entry Farmhouse

Although the divided house in which the service rooms were separated from the living quarters by means of a cross-passage remained the principal house type over much of the highland zone until the end of the eighteenth century, in the lowland zone from the beginning of the sixteenth century the divided house began to be replaced by a superior house type – the lobby-entry house – in which the service rooms were incorporated within the house.

These lobby-entry houses were by far the most popular and earliest type of undivided house and are clearly of a later date than those houses containing a cross-passage. There is evidence that a number of old farmhouses have been converted into a form of lobby-entry house either by the insertion of an axial chimney stack, as at Birds Farm, Barton, Cambridgeshire, or in other cases by the rebuilding of the lower end. Also the majority of dated lobby-entry houses are of a later date than any dated cross-passage houses in the same area. They first appeared at the beginning of the sixteenth century, the earliest example being Old Hall Farm, Kneesall, Nottinghamshire, but it was not until the end of that century that it became accepted for farmhouses. It first gained popularity in South-east England and spread into East Anglia and then into the South and Midlands and finally in the eighteenth century to the remainder of the country. The reason for the abandonment of the divided house in favour of the undivided house was, it seems, the result of the changing social structure in farming. Many of the earlier farms were small, and few men were employed other than relatives, and so those using the hall were all of the same social status. Consequently in the divided house access to the parlour through the hall was of little importance for those using both hall and parlour were of the same social standing. With the increased size of farms and the employment of labour, it became desirable to have a separate entrance to the parlour, thus separating the family from the wage-earning labourers who would in most cases still use the hall for meals.

One form of lobby-entry house was the central lobby house, sometimes known as the central chimney-stack plan (53). It had an entrance towards the centre of the front lateral wall leading into a small lobby formed between two main rooms, the hall and parlour, by the

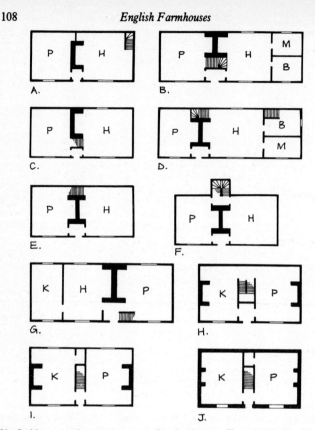

53. Lobby-entry house plans – 1. Lowland zone: Types A–G are of late sixteenth-or seventeenth-century date and types H–J of eighteenth-century date. The main variations in types A–G are in the position of the stack and staircase. Type G is common in Cambridgeshire; having the kitchen unheated and sometimes open to the roof.

introduction of a central axial stack, the lobby being in general the width of the stack. This layout had two main advantages over those houses which contained a cross-passage: the lobby reduced draughts, providing greater comfort to the two principal rooms, while it also provided independent access to both rooms, and unlike the cross-passage of the highland zone in which the parlour was rarely heated, the parlour of the central lobby entrance house was always heated,

54. Shadowbush Farm, Poslingford, Suffolk. A typical Suffolk central lobby-entry house.

either from its own fireplace or when only the hall had a fireplace which radiated heat through the stack from the fire in the hall (53A and C). In addition they provided some degree of symmetry, although there are some, such as Dear's Farm, Elsworth, Cambridgeshire, and Green Tye Farmhouse, Green Tye, Hertfordshire (56), retaining the continuous jettied front elevation.

Most of the early forms of this house type had two ground-floor rooms with only the hall or the hall-kitchen, as it had now generally become, being heated (53A and C). These two-roomed farmhouses continued to be built during the seventeenth century, although by this time both the hall and the parlour had a fireplace (53E and F). From these two-roomed houses evolved what can be termed the classic central lobby entrance house, which in the South-east and eastern England was almost universally adopted for all the larger new

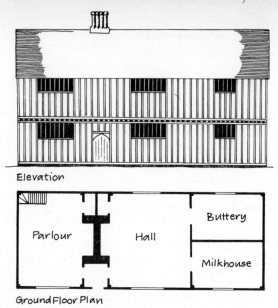

Elevation

Parlour | Hall | Buttery

Milkhouse

Ground Floor Plan

55. Typical sixteenth-century continuously jettied farmhouse in eastern England.

56. Green Tye Farmhouse, Green Tye, Hertfordshire. A late sixteenth–early seventeenth-century jettied central lobby farmhouse.

farmhouses during the seventeenth century. The house comprised simply three ground-floor rooms – a heated parlour, a heated main room (the hall or hall-kitchen) and at the opposite end to the parlour an unheated service room with the entrance lobby situated between the parlour and the main room (53B and D). Entrance to the service room was directly from the main room and was commonly sub-divided into two, often with a communicating door. To this basic two-or three-roomed plan there were several variations, and like other house plans they were generally associated with the position of the chimney stack and its relationship with the stairs. The stack could be placed centrally within the depth of the house so that the return wall of the stack formed one wall of the entrance lobby – the one opposite the entrance door – with the stair, either a newel or straight flight, positioned between the stack and the rear lateral wall (53D and E). Another layout was to place the stack against the rear lateral wall with the stairs placed elsewhere (53C and G). Often it was situated in the entrance lobby, sometimes but not always adjacent to the stack itself, but in the two-roomed unit it was generally placed in the hall, while in those houses with three rooms it was commonly in the service room. In most of these cases the stairs were a straight flight rather than a newel. In some three-unit farmhouses an additional flight of stairs can be found in the service room (53D) to give independent access to the third bedroom without going through one of the other bedrooms.

By the beginning of the seventeenth century the 'classic' three-unit central-lobby house, built of timber, had become universally accepted in the South-east, and even in eastern counties it replaced houses with a cross-passage as the most popular house type being built. As one went further north and west, however, they became progressively rarer and generally of a much later date. Perhaps in these areas, where farms were often small and generally run by the family, the social changes which had occurred in the South-east and East Anglia a century before accelerated during the eighteenth century, and so the transition from the cross-passage house where access to the parlour was still obtained through the hall to ones with an entrance lobby were overtaken by later and improved house types.

In some houses this old-fashioned concept of gaining access to the parlour directly from the hall remained popular, and a lobby-entrance house was developed to retain this requirement. Known as an end lobby-entry house, they were of only two units – the hall-kitchen and parlour, of which only the hall-kitchen was heated by a chimney or firehood situated on the gable wall, with the entrance lobby formed between the side wall of the stack or heck of the firehood and the front lateral wall, with a door from this lobby leading into the hall-kitchen (61E, F and G). In some instances the entrance door was placed on the

57. Low Farm, Elsworth, Cambridgeshire. A timber-framed and plastered central lobby farmhouse, dated 1595.

gable wall instead of the front lateral wall (61H). In many cases what now appears to be an end entry-lobby house was originally built as a baffle-entry house (described later) and has had a partition and door added between the stack and front lateral wall. Often the stairs were situated in the hall, sometimes adjacent to the stack but commonly elsewhere. Occasionally the end unit would be sub-divided into a parlour and service room (62). Although this house type can be found in parts of the lowland zone, it is in the highland zone and in particular along the Pennines that many can be found. Most were built at the end of the seventeenth and during the eighteenth century and continued to be built throughout the following century by many small farmers.

Although houses with a central lobby against the stack produced an elevation with a degree of symmetry, there was a desire for complete symmetry. This was achieved by another type of central-lobby house, one in which there was no axial stack, the entrance door placed in the centre of the elevation opening directly either into a small entrance hall, extending the full depth of the house, or into a small lobby (53H,

58. Popefield Farm, Smallford, Colney Heath, Hertfordshire. An early
seventeenth-century timber-framed farmhouse.

59. Willow Farm, Assington, Suffolk. A central lobby entry farmhouse with earlier jettied cross-wing.

60. Church Farm, Church Minshull, Cheshire. A central lobby entrance farmhouse.

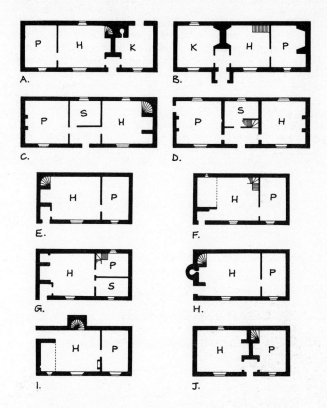

61. Lobby-entry house plans — 2. Highland zone: Types A, B and J are of the central lobby type similar in layout to those in the lowland zone, but are generally later in date, dating mainly from the second half of the seventeenth century and continuing to be built for most of the eighteenth century. Types A and J are to be found in the southern part of the limestone belt while B is typical of those built further north. Types C and D are examples of houses with a central service room found in the South-west and are of late seventeenth–early eighteenth-century date. Types E, F and G are to be found mainly in the moorland areas of the North and Cornwall. Type H with a gable entrance and a projecting oven, both features common in the Cotswolds and Somerset until about 1700. Type I is common in Cumbria and is of the statesman plan built between 1670–1720.

I and J). The entrance hall or lobby, in which was situated a straight flight of stairs, divided the house, there being two rooms – one on each side, both reached independently from the entrance hall or lobby and each being heated by a fireplace in the gable wall. In some of the larger and later examples the entrance hall or lobby was increased in width and the simple straight flight of stairs replaced with an impressive open-well or dog-leg staircase with turned or twisted balusters so positioned that it could be seen by any visitor. In these larger farmhouses the service rooms were often located in a wing at the rear. Houses of this type built in brick or stone are to be found in most parts of the country with the possible exception of northern England and the South-west. They first appeared at the end of the seventeenth century and, because of the ease with which the fashionable symmetrical façade could be achieved, remained popular throughout the Georgian period.

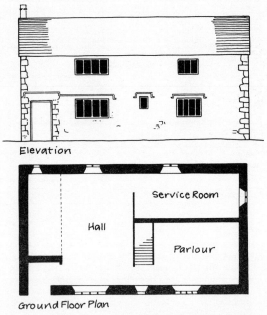

Elevation

Ground Floor Plan

62. Typical end lobby-entry house in the highland zone.

This desire for symmetry was the principal reason for another type of farmhouse which appeared in the seventeenth century. The entrance door was placed towards the centre of the front wall and opened out into a wide entrance lobby with the two principal rooms placed either side. Each room, the hall and parlour, was reached independently from the lobby, and both were heated by gable stacks. Between these two rooms and occupying the remains of the central core was an unheated service room with access either from the lobby or from the hall (61C and D). These houses are not especially numerous but can be found in many parts of the country, for example Brockley Farm, Elsworth, Cambridgeshire, although most are located in the South-west and parts of Avon and Gloucestershire.

Perhaps more readily than any other house type the lobby-entry houses could be extended by means of an outshut at the rear or side. In the two-unit house this was often the buttery, but in the three-unit house it frequently housed the kitchen, known in East Anglia as the back kitchen. In some houses the service room was converted into a kitchen, and a chimney stack was inserted into the gable end, with the service room added at the rear either as an outshut or sometimes by building a two-storey extension to provide both an extra ground-floor room and an additional bedroom over. Similarly, a cross-wing could be provided at either the parlour or the service end to provide additional accommodation, depending on the needs of the household. In most cases these additions to the basic two-or three-unit house would all be later extensions rather than part of the original plan.

The Direct-entry Farmhouse

Not all farmhouses were entered via a cross-passage or entrance lobby; in many cases access was directly into the house. Known as the direct-entry plan, it can be found in most parts of the highland and lowland zones, but those in the highland are generally of later date than those in the lowland zone. In the South-east and East Anglia they are generally of fifteenth- and sixteenth-century date while in the North, West Midlands and South-west they are mainly of seventeenth- and eighteenth-century date and in fact continued to be built by small farmers well into the nineteenth century. In many cases in the highland zone farm buildings, usually a byre or barn, were attached to the house. In nearly all cases the houses were of two or three units, and although there are of course exceptions, entry was directly into the hall, and from this access to both the parlour and service rooms was gained.

In many cases in the South-east and the eastern counties this access was at the lower end of the hall in the position formerly occupied by the door to the screens-passage (63A, E and F). There is evidence that in some cases, when the medieval open hall was chambered over and a chimney inserted at its upper end, the screens-passage was removed, although both external doors were retained to form a way through. Some new houses built in the sixteenth and seventeenth centuries retained these opposed entrances, and this was especially true in East Anglia.

However, in most cases a single entrance was provided into the hall. With the small two-unit farmhouse it was situated towards the centre of the house close to the parlour, achieving a certain degree of external symmetry (63A and B), while in the larger three-unit farmhouse the entrance was at the lower end adjacent to the service rooms (63C, E and F). Wydard's Farm, Cratfield, Suffolk, is an example of this. Built in the fifteenth century, it was enlarged at the beginning of the seventeenth century, by the insertion of an axial stack and a new parlour at one end yet still retains its medieval position for the main entrance. Unlike Wydard's Farm, most halls were heated by a chimney stack in the gable wall or in the rear lateral wall. It was probably the only heated room, although in the three-unit house the parlour was occasionally heated by a gable-wall stack. Even when a

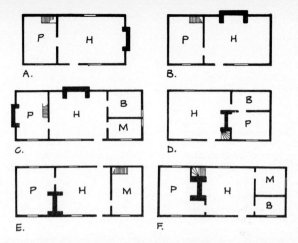

63. Direct-entry house plans – 1. Lowland zone: Types A, B and C are of sixteenth-century date and Types D, E and F of late sixteenth- or seventeenth-century date. Type E shows the old concept of opposed entrances. In some examples of Type F the staircase was located in the buttery or milkhouse and there was often an intercommunicating door between the two.

64. Place Farm, Ashdon, Essex. A sixteenth-century farmhouse with continuous jetty to the front and direct entry into the hall.

house was built with an axial stack between the hall and parlour, direct entry into the hall was sometimes retained. This was particularly true where the axial stack was built against the front lateral wall.

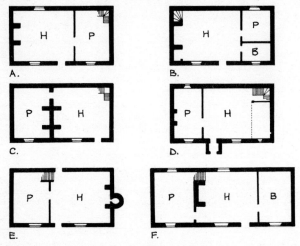

65. Direct-entry house plans – 2. Highland zone: Types A, B and C are common in the North and are generally of eighteenth-century date. Type D is found in the North-west and dated from 1690 to 1750. Type E is common in the southern part of the limestone belt and of seventeenth- or eighteenth-century date. Type F is of similar date and is to be found at the northern end of the limestone belt.

Although it can be found in most parts of the lowland zone, the direct-entry farmhouse was more common in the highland zone (65). Some direct-entry farmhouses consist of only a single unit, and although on occasions an early example is to be found, such as the former farmhouse situated at the rear of Yeo, Chagford, Devon, most are of eighteenth- or nineteenth-century date. Yew Tree Cottage, recorded by J.W. Tonkin, is one such example at Burrington, Hereford and Worcester, a former stone and timber farmhouse built in the eighteenth century with one large ground-floor room with a fireplace and oven at one end and at the other end a flight of stairs leading to the loft above. The house, which is now derelict, is typical of many farmhouses which once existed in the same area. These single-roomed farmhouses continued to be built in many parts of the highland zone, often with a barn attached, well into the nineteenth century, as for instance Bents Farm, Hazelhead, West Yorkshire, which before it was extended had only one small room downstairs with a gable fireplace and a newel staircase in one corner leading to two rooms above.

The majority of these direct-entry farmhouses consisted of only two rooms – the hall and parlour – with the parlour sometimes sub-divided to provide in addition a small service room (65B). When they first appeared, they began to replace for the first time the farmhouses constructed with a cross-passage, which had been the predominate feature of most farmhouses in the highland zone for so many years, yet in many instances they retained the old concept of obtaining access to the parlour directly from the hall.

In Cumbria there is a small number of two-roomed farmhouses built in the latter part of the eighteenth century in the declining years of the statesman class which retained this old concept (65D). These generally were smaller, often providing less accommodation than earlier ones, yet often retained many of the characteristics, such as spice cupboards, generally associated with earlier and larger examples. In nearly all cases these houses consisted of a hall and parlour with entry into the hall from the gable wall alongside the only fireplace in the house. This fireplace was screened from the entrance by the back of the firehood, which was still of considerable size and still lit by a small fire-window. Access to the bedroom above was generally obtained by an internal ladder or staircase. The general arrangement of these houses was the same as in earlier statesman houses but without a cross-passage, downhouse or byre. Farmhouses of similar arrangement can be found elsewhere in the highland zone, especially along the Pennines, in Hereford and Worcester, the Cotswolds, Derbyshire and many of the moorland districts.

In all these houses the accommodation and general arrangement of the rooms resembled closely the upper ends of those farmhouses with cross-passages and are generally in areas where such houses had been widely used. Some are of similar age to those with cross-passages built in the area, but many are of a later date, built by small farmers in areas in which the old traditions still lingered. In many of the later examples the gable-end entry was replaced by one placed in the front wall opposite the return to the stack or heck of the firehood. An entrance so placed is called a baffle entry.

Not all these farmhouses had a gable-end fireplace; some had axial fireplaces heating both hall and parlour. Entry to the house was still into the hall, usually at the lower end away from the fireplace and alongside the gable wall (65C). Occasionally, although the fireplace was placed along the wall dividing the hall and kitchen, only the hall was heated. Access to the parlour and to the rooms on the first floor was still obtained directly from the hall. Houses of this type can be found in many parts of the highland zone and were particularly common in Yorkshire, where they first appeared at the end of the seventeenth century and continued to be built for over a hundred years.

66. Low Bridgend Farm, St-John-in-the-Vale, Cumbria. A typical Lakeland farmhouse with direct entry into the hall.

In many instances, however, these direct entries made the first dramatic change on the overall appearance of the farmhouses throughout the highland zone. With the omission of the cross-passage the entrance could be moved towards the centre of the front elevation, and so for the first time the house became one at least approaching symmetry. The house again had only two rooms, the hall and parlour, with the entry directly into the kitchen, generally alongside the partition to the parlour. Alongside the entrance door were two windows, one in the hall and the other in the parlour, and in addition often a small fire-window lighting the hearth to the only fireplace in the house, which was situated on the gable wall away from the entrance. In later examples there was often a fireplace in the gable wall of the parlour. The upper floor, reached by an internal ladder or staircase from the hall, had one or two bedrooms. Houses of this type began to be built in the latter half of the seventeenth century and continued to be built into the nineteenth century. They were probably the first genuine replacement for the cross-passage farmhouse. This is certainly true in Cumbria where, in the survey carried out by R.W. Brunskill, most houses of this type were built between 1695 and 1745, coinciding with the last fifteen years of the peak period of the statesman plan but extending for a further thirty-five years.

The inconvenience of the direct-entry house is evident. In nearly all cases there was only one external door, and this was into the hall from where access was gained to all the other living-rooms and to the floor above. The hall remained the main living-room in which the family lived, cooked and ate and, with the continuing comings and goings of visitors, farmworkers and the family, must have been a cold and draughty place. To overcome this some form of protection was sometimes provided. In some areas, particularly in Cumbria and the West Country, single-storey gabled porches with stone seats were provided to protect the entrance and for the farmer and farmworkers to remove their muddy boots. Far less common was the provision of an internal lobby or baffle screen.

The Cross-wing Farmhouse

Farmhouses with cross-wings at either one or both ends are to be seen in many parts of the country, but in many cases these are not contemporary with the main range and are either later additions or possibly the enlarging or rebuilding of a former service or solar bay. There are some, however, in which the medieval concept of a hall range with a cross-wing or wings are retained. They are to be found generally in the southern half of the country, from Derbyshire southwards, with the highest concentration to be found in the western counties. In nearly all cases they were adaptations of existing house plans, generally the lobby-entry or direct-entry type, but there was a greater variation in the arrangement of the rooms. Unlike their medieval predecessors, these houses were two-storey throughout and often had in addition an attic.

In the eastern counties the traditional rectangular ground-floor plan of a hall with solar and service end bays, jettied on the upper floors and each under a separate roof to form cross-wings, continued to be built in the sixteenth and early seventeenth centuries. They retained the standard medieval ground-floor layout of parlour, hall and service room or rooms with entry either into a cross-passage or directly into the hall with a fireplace either on the rear lateral wall or on the wall between the hall and parlour. Of course, with the hall being of two storeys throughout and the first floors of the end bays therefore being connected, only one staircase was usually provided. Externally these later houses are often indistinguishable from those built in the fifteenth century which have had the roof to the hall raised when the upper floor was inserted, but generally these earlier former open-hall farmhouses have a steeper-pitched roof than later ones.

Farmhouses built in an 'L' or 'T' plan are fairly common in many parts of the country. In the lowland zone the main block was generally rectangular in plan and comprised the general arrangement of parlour, hall and service room built in line with the wing placed, normally at the rear (67A, B and C), at either the solar end to provide more living accommodation or more commonly at the service end. When placed at the service end, the end bay was often the kitchen, with the rear extension becoming the service room. Often, however, and this is true in Essex and parts of Hertfordshire and Suffolk, the rear extension

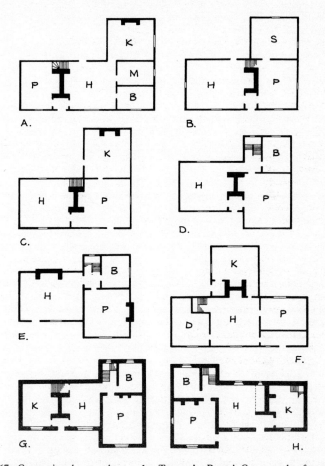

67. Cross-wing house plans – 1.: Types A, B and C are to be found throughout the East and South-east and are generally of late sixteenth- or seventeenth-century date. Types D and E are of seventeenth-century date and are a feature of Hereford and Worcester, as is Type F which is a typical solar house. Type G is also found in the West Midlands and further north into Derbyshire as well as in Lancashire. In some cases these houses incorporated a separate entrance into the parlour as Type H.

became the kitchen with an end-gable chimney stack (67A and C). In some cases a wing was built at both ends to provide both additional living and service accommodation and to form a 'U' plan, also known as the half-'H' plan (69A and B).

In the highland zone the cross-wing was almost universally located at the upper end to become a solar or parlour wing (67D, E and G). This wing was generally of two bays, the parlour to the front projecting beyond the main range, with a service room, usually a buttery, at the rear. In nearly all cases the staircase was also placed in the solar wing alongside the buttery. Very occasionally in a few larger farmhouses there were two parlours – the inner and outer – both heated by a back-to-back fireplace in the wall dividing the two. In the hall range the main variation was its length; occasionally it contained only a two-bay hall, but more often there were three bays with the bay at the lower end being the kitchen (67G). The entrance was either in the old medieval position at the lower end of the hall (67E) or more commonly into an entrance lobby against the axial stack (67D and G). In many of the timber-framed farmhouses of Hereford and Worcester this axial stack occupied the upper bay of the hall, serving both the hall and the parlour as well as the two upper rooms (67D). They are particularly popular in this area, where the cluster of four chimneys at the junction of the hall and cross-wing is a common feature of many farmhouses. They first appeared in about 1600 (Tardebigge Farm, Stoke Prior, and Keys Farm, Bentley Pauncefoot, are two excellent unaltered examples) and continued to be built in Hereford and Worcester and other parts of the West Midlands until the eighteenth century. Elsewhere the axial stack was placed between the hall and kitchen in the hall range, serving both, with the main entrance into a lobby between the stack and external wall (67G). In this case the parlour in the cross-wing was heated by a separate stack.

A variation to the cross-wing farmhouses of the highland zone were those in which there was a secondary entrance, generally located on the return wall of the cross-wing and the hall range, which opened directly into the parlour (67H). The general arrangement was similar to other cross-wing houses found in the stone-bearing areas of the highland zone, but these were undoubtedly houses of higher social standing, for they gave direct access for the family to the parlour and other private rooms without entering the hall, which was in many parts, particularly the North, still used by the farmworkers. These houses can be found as widespread as Gloucestershire – Potters Farm, Buckland; Derbyshire – Old Hall Farm, Youlgreave; and Lancashire – Hodgkinson House, Great Eccleston, and Kennedy Ridge, Pilling. Although Old Hall Farm is dated 1630, most of these houses are of late seventeenth- and early eighteenth-century date.

68. Manor Farm, Tredington, Gloucestershire, a typical cross-wing timber-framed farmhouse.

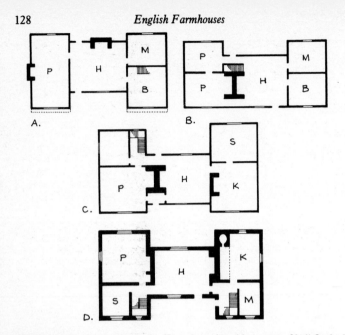

69. Cross-wing house plans – 2.: Type A retains old concept of hall flanked by cross-wings often jettied and is of sixteenth-century date. Type B still retains the hall but now has an axial stack and is of late sixteenth/seventeenth-century date. Type C is a typical cross-wing timber-framed farmhouse built in the second half of the seventeenth century in East Anglia. Type D is a typical large stone farmhouse of mid-seventeenth-century date on the limestone belt; there is a separate entrance to the service wing to keep the servants away from the rest of the house with a staircase to serve the chambers above used by the servants.

A variation of the 'U' plan was the 'E' plan, in which the wings were placed to the front, with a projecting porch placed centrally between the two. These houses were generally impressive, providing far superior accommodation than most other farmhouses. Generally the entrance door led into a central lobby staircase area, with doors leading to the living accommodation one side and the service rooms the other side. The living accommodation often comprised a hall and in the end wing one or two parlours. The service rooms generally comprised a kitchen and in the wing probably a buttery, with one or two other service rooms depending on the nature of the farm. Both the hall and the kitchen would be heated by a stack between the central range and the cross-wings, and in addition the parlour would be heated. These houses, although resembling the Elizabethan 'E' plan, are generally of seventeenth-century date, built of brick or stone, with those of brick often with shaped or Dutch gables to the cross-wings and porch, as at Bridge Farmhouse, Lower Kinnerton, Cheshire, a house built in 1685, and Redhouse Farmhouse, Knodishall, Suffolk, dated 1678.

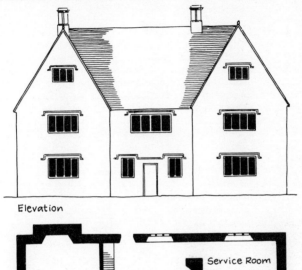

Elevation

Kitchen   Hall   Service Room

Parlour

Ground Floor Plan

70. Typical seventeenth-century cross-wing house found along the limestone belt.

The largest of these cross-wing farmhouses is the 'H' plan in which there is a cross-wing at both ends. Many closely resembled the layout of the 'T' plan, with the entrance into a lobby against the axial stack which served the hall and parlour in the cross-wing and at the rear a store and staircase. However, the kitchen at the lower end of the hall was replaced by a cross-wing containing a kitchen at the front and a service room at the rear, with the kitchen usually heated by a stack backing onto the hall (69C). Houses of this type are to be seen in many parts of the country, for their distribution is widespread although they are not common. It is along the limestone belt that most are probably to be found (69D and 70). In nearly all cases they are of mid or late seventeenth-century date and continued to be built into the eighteenth century.

In Hereford and Worcester another house type, less common than those previously described but still a direct development of the medieval hall plan, was the so-called 'solar' farmhouse in which the solar wing was enlarged – usually three bays and two storeys plus an attic range – while the hall became no more than a rear wing (67F). Moat Farm, Dormston (71), dated 1663 above the beam to the end gable, is one good example. The solar wing is of three bays and two full storeys high with the third storey within an elaborate gabled roof – three to the side and one at each end. The hall, now relegated to the kitchen, is a single-storey projection at the rear. Close by, Lane Farmhouse, Feckenham, is of the same type; built about 1600, it too has a solar wing of three bays of two storeys and an attic lit by an original dormer window. A later and very much larger example is Lower Tundridge Farmhouse, Suckley. Unlike the previous two, which have the rear wing so placed as to form the standard 'T' shape, at Lower Tundridge it is so placed as to form an 'L' with the three-bay solar wing, and in addition to the usual two storeys and an attic it has a cellar. The plan also differs slightly, for in the two later farmhouses, Lower Tundridge and Moat Farm, the middle bay of the solar wing is the smallest and used as the staircase bay, while at Lane Farm it is the largest. At Lower Tundridge this staircase bay is flanked by two symmetrical windows of the two main rooms.

All these cross-wing farmhouses provided greater accommodation than most farmhouses built in the same period. Although the 'L'- and 'T'-shaped farmhouses provided only one or perhaps two additional ground-floor rooms, in many cases the 'U'- and 'H'-shaped plans doubled the accommodation that was provided in average farmhouses. Yet even in the seventeenth century when many of these farmhouses were built, because of the continuing difficulty in spanning much over eighteen feet, the main block and the cross-wings were still only one room deep, producing large, rambling houses in which access to one room could only be obtained from another. It was not until the following century that a more compact farmhouse became possible.

71. Moat Farm, Dormston, Hereford and Worcester. A timber-framed house dated 1663 with tiled weatherings above ground- and first-floor windows.

72. Church Farm House, Boningale, Shropshire. A handsome timber-framed cross-winged farmhouse.

The Double-pile Farmhouse

In all the house types so far described the common feature has been that the principal rooms were only the complete depth of the house, although some, such as the service rooms, may have been divided. In addition the service rooms were in nearly all cases situated at one end – the lower end. Towards the end of the seventeenth century a change began to develop to this medieval design which had lasted for over five hundred years. Houses began to be built more than one room deep, and for the first time the service rooms were relegated to the rear of the house behind the principal rooms. Houses of this type first appeared in England towards the end of the sixteenth century, but it was not until the second quarter of the seventeenth century that it began to descend the social scale, with the earliest dated example being perhaps Little Park Farm, Ampthill, Bedfordshire, built in 1629. Although there are others of similar date or slightly later, such as Manor Farm, Dewlish, Dorset, and Old Hall Farm, Thoralby, Yorkshire, it was not until the first part of the eighteenth century that these 'double-pile' houses with their symmetrical façade had become the standard design for all larger farmhouses; by the second half of that century the plan had become universally accepted for all new ones. Unlike most earlier house types which gained greater popularity in one region than another or else spread slowly from one region to another, the double-pile house gained popularity throughout the country at more or less the same time, due no doubt in part to the increasing number of pattern books available to the country builders. In fact the North adopted this house type for small farmhouses more readily than parts of the Midlands and South-east.

Even by the first half of the seventeenth century this desire for the service rooms to be located at the rear began to develop in the South-east, and houses with a continuous outshut at the rear under a catslide roof began to be built. By the end of the seventeenth century they had gained popularity throughout southern and eastern England. Generally they were adaptations of earlier house plans, either with a central lobby entrance opposite the stack, or into a central lobby with the staircase with an outshut at the rear containing perhaps a back-kitchen and buttery. Similar houses began to appear in the North at the end of the seventeenth century and continued to be built for over one hundred years. Again they were adaptations of earlier house plans, with the direct entry being the most commonly used. The main entrance door, which was placed more or less centrally with windows symmetrically about it, led directly into the hall as before, but in most cases both the hall and the parlour were heated by gable fireplaces. In the outshut at the rear was generally the staircase and two other small rooms, one invariably a dairy and the other a kitchen or scullery. In nearly all cases access to the rear of the building could be obtained from the outshut. These houses could be said to be the forerunners of the double-pile house. In the South the steep pitch required for thatch or plain tiles made it impossible to have an outshut more than a single storey, but in the North, where the pitch of the stone slate roofs was much shallower, the main roof could be extended over an outshut of at least 1½ storeys. Many farmhouses originally built with an outshut of 1½ storeys were later raised to provide two full storeys.

Although builders had for many centuries both built and extended farmhouses by the means of a service wing at the rear of and set at right angles to the main block to form an 'L' or 'T'-shaped plan, it was not until the seventeenth century that an attempt was made to build a house of two sections, one containing the living quarters and the other the service rooms, side by side. Each section still spanned the customary eighteen feet, and each had its own pitched roof forming an 'M'-shaped roof with a gutter in the valley formed between the two. Although this roof type is more common in the South-east and East Anglia, where the use of plain tiles made it the only practicable roof for a double-pile house, it can also be found on some of the farmhouses in the North where stone slates were common. However, the inherent weakness of the valley gutter, combined with the increasing availability of the thinner and lighter Welsh slates which could be laid at a low pitch, soon encouraged the adoption of the single-roof double-pile plan.

The basic layout of a double-pile house is four rooms, the two principal living-rooms – dining-room and parlour – at the front and at the rear the kitchen and another service room which was usually the buttery or in northern England a dairy (73). In nearly all cases the living-rooms were deeper than those of the service rooms, but in some the partition wall divided the living- and service rooms equally. In the North the staircase was generally situated at the rear between the two service rooms (73B, C, D and F) and in most of the South in the entrance lobby between the two living-rooms (73A and E). The front entrance was placed more or less centrally along the front elevation and opened either directly into the dining-room (73C, D and F), in which case access to the parlour was gained from the hall, or when there was a central staircase into an entrance lobby with direct access to both the

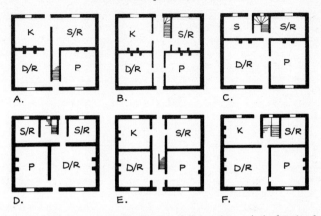

73. Double-pile house plans: The feature of all these houses is the fact that for the first time houses are two-room deep with the living-rooms at the front and the service rooms at the rear.

hall and the parlour (73A, B and E). This entrance lobby on occasions ran the full depth of the house, providing access as well to the two service rooms. Both the living-rooms and in most cases the kitchen as well were usually heated by a fireplace situated on the gable walls, although it was not uncommon, especially in eastern England, to find the fireplaces back-to-back on the partition walls between the living- and service rooms. Occasionally, as at New House Farm, Wormingford, Essex, one finds the stacks rising up from the valley of an M-shaped roof. If extra accommodation was required, in addition to the four rooms provided under the basic plan, further rooms were added at one end.

The double-pile farmhouse was the ultimate development in house design at the vernacular level, providing a degree of comfort not found in earlier houses. In most and especially the later ones, access to each room was gained from the central hall, and there was no need to pass through one room in order to gain access to another. The old hall-cum-kitchen became the new dining- or living-room, the parlour became the sitting-room, and a kitchen became for the first time an essential part of the house. Unlike older houses, in which only the hall or at the most the hall and parlour were heated, in the double-pile house the ground-floor rooms, with the possible exception of the service room as well as the upstairs bedrooms, were all heated. The old steep newel

74. Foscote House Farm, near Abthorpe, Northamptonshire. A double-pile
house, one of three, built by the Grafton Estate in about 1840.

stairs or straight-flight stairs were replaced with the fashionable
framed stairs. The general result of all these improvements was to
provide a house which for the first time was designed for the needs and
comfort of the family rather than for those of the farm.

PART TWO

Materials, Construction and Characteristics

Introduction

The differing building materials employed in the construction of farmhouses, as with all vernacular buildings, affected their appearance, for the distinctive regional characteristics are invariably not a result of the plan and general arrangement of accommodation but from the local materials used. Up until the nineteenth century all building materials were usually obtained from as near as possible to the site, and it seems that the maximum distance for haulage of materials for small buildings was about five miles. This gives a building a particularly local personality, and in spite of the close similarities in both design and plan in various regions there is a marked visual contrast between buildings in different geological areas. Above all it is the geology of each area that is the principal factor determining regional building styles. Yet because geological classifications are based on the age of the formation and not the quality of the stone or soils it yields, there are often considerable differences in the physical properties contained in any one geological system.

Of all the materials used, those for the walls had the greatest effect. This is particularly true of the stone-producing regions where the character of the buildings differs greatly with the type of stone available; the mellow farmhouses of the limestone belt, for instance, contrast greatly with the rugged, simply fashioned ones constructed of the less tractable slates and igneous rocks of the harsher parts of the country. These walling materials can be divided into two groups: mass construction, in which the walls are solid and form both a load-bearing and a weatherproof wall, and framed construction in which only the frame is load-bearing with either the panels filled in or the frame clad to weatherproof the building. The materials for mass construction were stone, brick and unbaked earth, and of these only unbaked earth in the form of cob did not require to be bonded and jointed. Where the stone was of good quality which could be dressed, there was little problem, but where the stone was of poor quality, such as chalk, flint, cobble, slate, granite and many of the limestones and sandstones, the stability and the final weather-resistant properties of the wall relied on the skill and in many cases the ingenuity of the local craftsmen. Often dressings and lacing courses of better-quality material, either brick or a good-quality stone, were introduced, and as the strength of the wall was reduced with each opening, the number and size were restricted. So where walls were constructed of poor-quality stone, the window openings were fewer in number and narrower, contrasting with the long, tall ranges of the mullioned and transomed windows in those areas with good-quality stone. The irregular shape of many of the poorer stones required thick joints, and until the supply of lime became plentiful, clay was the principal jointing material used on humbler buildings, further reducing the capabilities of the building stone. Bricks, being of uniform size, did not present to the vernacular builder the same problems as did many of the poorer stones.

With framed construction timber was of course the material used and was either of box-frame or cruck construction. With both forms of construction, differing techniques produced a variety of styles throughout the country, and this applied not only to the frame but also in the method of weatherproofing the building. The panels were filled in either with wattle and daub or with brick nogging, exposing the structural and non-structural timbers, or the frame was entirely clad with plaster and lath, plain tiles, mathematical tiles or weatherboarding.

Timber was of course used in roof construction, and the vernacular builder was often restricted, because of the length of available timber, to the construction of a long, narrow, rectangular building rarely more than eighteen feet from front to back, and the many irregular-shaped houses that survive today are generally the result of additions to the original plan. One common form of this is an outshut at the back or end with the main roof extending as a catslide. The choice of roof covering affected not only the shape of the roof – hipped or gabled – but also the construction, for each material had its appropriate pitch, and so the builder had to choose a form of roof construction suitable for the chosen or available roof covering.

Yet it was not building materials alone which dictated the style. The craftsmen in each locality had to learn how to handle and work their particular building material in the most satisfactory way to produce a sound, stable building. Local traditions also had an influence and so account, for instance, for the difference between the 'black-and-white' timber-framed house of the Welsh border counties and its mellower counterpart in the South-east. Climatic and environmental conditions also had a hand in the evolution of the farmhouse. The bleak, exposed nature of some parts of the North and the South-west, the harsh climate and the isolation all helped to contribute to the rugged low-pitched roofed farmhouses of these areas which blend so happily with their respective surroundings yet which would undoubtedly look out of place elsewhere in the country. Sometimes a regional style became established by a foreign influence. In those areas along the East and

South-east coast which traded with the Continent, Dutch fashions in both brickwork and roofing are to be encountered.

It is the vivid diversity of both style and texture and the understanding of our ancestors to exploit the full potential of the materials available that makes the study of vernacular buildings in general and the farmhouse in particular so absorbing. It is not necessary to travel any great distance to observe this diversity. In one county, Wiltshire, one can find unbaked earth, timber, flint, chalk and various kinds of limestones and sandstones as well as brick, often with two or more of these materials incorporated within one building.

Timber

The use of timber as a building material has been known from medieval times. Up to some four hundred years ago timber was plentiful in all but a few areas and had the advantage of being readily available, easy to handle and perhaps the most flexible of all materials. Timber framing was more widely used than is evident today, many houses being clad at a later date in brick or stone. Even in the major stone-producing areas there is evidence of the former use of timber in the construction of walls which were originally built of timber and have been largely rebuilt or clad in stone.

Oak was the timber predominantly used in construction, for its strength and durability was unrivalled, but elm and to a lesser extent sweet chestnut and later, in the eighteenth century when the country's forests were depleted, imported softwood were all used. The use of softwood for flooring was, of course, widespread but in some areas such as Cambridgeshire from the eighteenth century onwards it replaced the traditional oak as wall framing. It can be found in many cottages in the county and also in a number of small farmhouses such as Long Lane Farm, Hatley, Fen Farm, Lode, Childs Farm, Elsworth, and Old Woodbury Farm, Gamlingay. The oak was not seasoned for any length of time, for its peculiar nature and the large scantlings required made it impracticable, and so after felling the timber was stood up so that any movements could be examined and then left to season in position. The timber was generally used within a year or so of felling.

The oaks were felled with a narrow axe, although a large tree was often cut around with a broad axe before the narrow axe was used on the heartwood. The larger trees were split into baulks by means of an axe and iron wedges, but for the smaller ones the baulks were often formed by roughly squaring the tree by means of an axe or adze. The baulks were then cut to length by means of a two-handled cross-cut saw, known as a 'twart-saw'. The length of these timbers was usually between ten and twenty feet, but lengths up to thirty feet were not uncommon, and very occasionally timbers up to fifty feet were used. For the principal timbers (posts, wall-plates and main beams) the timbers were simply shaped by means of an axe before finally being trimmed with an adze. For smaller timbers (the studs, braces, rafters

142

and joists) the baulks were generally cut along their length to the required scantling. This was done either over a pit or on trestles, with a pit-saw operated by two men, one above and one below.

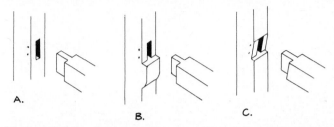

75. Typical joints between horizontal members and vertical posts: A. unrefined mortice and tenon; B. mortice and tenon with hewn-bracket; C. mortice and tenon with housed soffit-shoulder or ledge.

With the timbers so prepared, it was necessary to cut the joints. These joints were either mortice and tenon, half-lap or scarf. The mortice and tenon was the most important and was the basis of all traditional framing. The tenons were cut with a hand-saw – a one-handled tool with a scimitar-like cutting edge – while the mortices were formed either with a chisel and mallet or with a series of holes bored by an auger, with the remaining wood being chopped away with a twibill. Scarf joints were used to join two beams together to form one continuous member – mainly purlins, wall-plates and sill-beams. These often occurred near a main post, and unlike the mortice and tenon joints there were many different forms. Lap joints, although an important element in early medieval forms of construction, were later used in relatively few positions in timber-framed buildings, being almost entirely restricted to the joint between the collars and rafters in roof construction and in cruck construction to the joints between the blades and the tie-beam and collar.

Extensive research undertaken by C.A.Hewett during the last fifteen years or so has established that joints used in the construction of timber-framed buildings are an important criteria in dating a building. Lap joints, as previously mentioned, were important in medieval times, for relatively few mortice and tenon joints were used at this time, with many of the subsidiary members such as scissor bracers being inserted after the main frame had been assembled, and so a lapped joint was essential. These joints were either notched or dovetailed, open or secret, and were generally superseded by the beginning of the fourteenth century when the use of long braces declined. More important as an aid to dating are the scarfed joints of

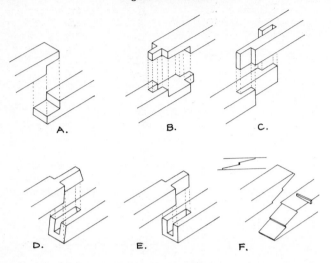

76. Scarfed joints: A. lapped; B. edge-halved; C. faced-halved; D. and E. bridle; F. splayed.

which there are many varieties and which varied considerably over the centuries. The earliest are of the splayed variety (76F) and are almost certainly of thirteenth- and fourteenth-century date. These were followed by various types of edge-halved scarf joints (76B) used from the fifteenth to early seventeenth century and finally followed by face-halved scarf joints (76C). There are other types of scarf joints, such as the bridle (76D and E), but these are less common than the other three major types.

Another important joint is the complexed joint between the post, wall-plate and tie-beam known as the tie-beam lap-dovetailed joint (77). The tie-beam is secured to the wall-plate by a dovetail joint, generally of a lap-dovetail type, although sometimes they are of the bare-faced variety, that is with a shoulder to one side only. In some instances the lap-dovetail joint would open up due to the strain showing a gap, and to overcome this the shoulder of the joint was sometimes entrant or housed. The post is secured to both the tie-beam and the wall-plate with a mortice and tenon joint. To enable the joint to be undertaken satisfactorily, the maximum amount of timber was required and thereby the maximum rigidity in the joint could be achieved. This thickening out of the post is known as the 'jowl', and though associated with the reversal of the trunk, that is root uppermost

77. Tie-beam lap-dovetail joint: an important lap joint used from the thirteenth until the nineteenth century.

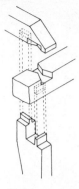

and so using the expanded growth of the tree's root, it has like many other techniques undergone many changes (78). First used in the thirteenth century, the jowl finally declined in the sixteenth and seventeenth centuries, when it became highly decorative but structurally poor. Also in the seventeenth century long swelling jowls were used before in the eighteenth century generally being dispensed with altogether. The tie-beam lap-dovetail joint was a very satisfactory joint and was used from the thirteenth until the nineteenth century with little variation.

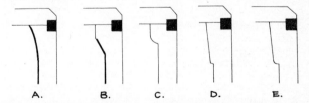

A. B. C. D. E.

78. Jowls: A. flared; B. splayed; C. round; D. tapered with square cut return; E. tapered with curved return.

In addition most of these joints were secured with pointed heart-of-oak pegs, often referred to in medieval times as 'trashnails', driven into holes pre-drilled through the joints with the head of the peg left projecting. Iron bolts and nails were rarely used, for iron was too precious a commodity to be employed, and moreover if they had been, the acid in the unseasoned oak would soon have corroded them. In any case heart-of-oak pegs were equally effective as untreated bolts and more so than nails.

79. Medieval carpenters' numerals.

All this work was undertaken in the carpenters' yard – the 'framynplace' – the timbers being framed on the ground with the components incised at the joints for identification and assembling on site. A system based on Roman numerals (79) was used, the carpenters' numerals being cut adjacent to the joints with a scribe, gouge or chisel. The system was based on various combinations of I, V and X with often, but not always, the V being inverted. Also one cross-cut was often made to do when X and V were used together or when two or more Xs were used. To assist in erecting the building on site, carpenters' marks were added to the Roman numerals, each mark denoting a particular section of the dwelling, so enabling the timbers to be easily sorted prior to erection. Once framed at the yard, the timbers were dismantled and transported to site for re-erection.

TIMBER WALL FRAMING

Most medieval timber-framed buildings have walls with very large open rectangular panels formed by the main posts, wall-plates, bressummer and sill-beam. Their most characteristic feature is the use of large curved or elbowed wall-braces. These are of two basic types, the arch-brace rising from the post to the wall-plate or bressummer, and the tension-brace running down from the post to the sill-beam or bressummer. Occasionally both types of bracing are to be found within one panel to form a St Andrew's Cross or in each corner of the panel to form a circular pattern. Sometimes a number of diagonal braces were provided within one panel to form a herring-bone pattern, as at Wymondley Bury, Little Wymondley, Hertfordshire. At Raven's Farmhouse, Woodham Walter, Essex, serpentine bracing can be seen in one of the gables. All these variations are rare, and the two basic types were most commonly employed. The arch-brace is to be found mainly in the Midlands and West and the tension-brace in the East and South-east, although of course there are exceptions. Winkhurst Farmhouse, a fourteenth-century farmhouse which formerly stood at Bough Beech, Kent, and which has now been re-erected at the Weald and Downland Open Air Museum, is one example of the use of arch-braces in the South-east; another is Aldhurst Farm, Capel, Surrey (80).

80. Aldhurst Farm, Capel, Surrey. An old timber-framed farmhouse with large open panels and arch-braces.

Large, open panels were a feature of most houses in the first half of the fifteenth century and remained popular until the beginning of the sixteenth century. Examples are fairly common, especially in the South-east, and one can cite Selby's Farm, Hildenborough, Kent, Crookhorn Farm, Southwater, and Bell's Farm, Slaugham, both in Sussex, and in Surrey there is Hookstone Farm, Chobham, and Aldhurst Farm, Capel (80). Farmhouses constructed of these large panels continued to be built until the seventeenth century. Home

Farm, Chalfont St Giles, Buckinghamshire, is one example built in about 1600 with large rectangular panels and no braces. Another is Pound Farm, Fetcham, Surrey, built at the beginning of the seventeenth century.

Later timber wall framing can be classified into three schools: the eastern school with close studding forming tall narrow panels, the western school where the panels are square, and the northern school where the studs instead of rising from a sill-beam rise from a sill framed between the main posts. Although there are without doubt these differing techniques, they are not, except for the northern school, in any way restricted to these regions. Close studding is concentrated in East Anglia and may, although there is no real evidence, have originated there, but it is also common in the South-east; by the middle of the fifteenth century it had spread into most towns, and in the following two centuries it was used in many buildings of high social status throughout the country. The use of square panels first appeared in the West, particularly in Hereford and Worcester, Shropshire and Gloucestershire, during the fifteenth century, and it spread throughout the following two centuries northwards into Cheshire and eastwards towards Kent but never into East Anglia where close studding persisted unchallenged until well into the seventeenth century, when, with the need to economize, the studs were set wider and wider apart. The northern school of carpentry differs greatly from the other two, having a distinctive style of its own which did not spread outside the North.

In close studding the studs were storey height, framed into the sill-beam at ground level, the bressummer at the upper-floor levels and the wall-plates at roof level. Up until the middle of the sixteenth century these studs were placed at intervals approximately equal to their own width, but later the spacing became wider – as much as two feet or more – although this was probably due more to the lack of timber than to any desire to change the overall visual effect. In order not to affect the overall close-studded appearance, internal tension-braces were introduced of smaller depth than the studs and halved over the inside face of the intervening studs and concealed externally with plaster. Later tension-braces of the same scantling as the studs were used, with the studs being cut and framed into the braces. With the eastern school of English carpentry, unlike the other two schools, much of the roof load is taken on external framed side walls instead of being transmitted to the ground by means of transverse frames. Also there is no obvious division into bays as with the other forms of construction. This is not to say, however, that all buildings with closely spaced studs do not have transverse frames, for even with a crown-post truss, the roof truss most commonly employed in the area up to the end of the fifteenth century, the size of the timbers supporting the crown-post was generally increased. Unlike elsewhere in the country, however, the framed truss supporting side purlins was not employed until about 1600.

This form of construction was used extensively in eastern England in the late fifteenth and sixteenth centuries, but due to the popularity of cladding buildings with plaster in the sixteenth and seventeenth centuries, much is no longer visible. Such is the abundance of timber-framed buildings, particularly in Essex and Suffolk, that there are still plenty to be seen, especially in the villages where there has been a tendency in recent years to remove the plaster. Farmhouses too with exposed close studding are not by any means rare, and in many cases these have never been plastered. In Cambridgeshire studs were almost always of smaller section and spaced wider apart than those in the neighbouring counties of Suffolk and Essex.

Similarly in the South-east, although much is hidden behind plaster, tiles, weatherboarding and Georgian brickwork, there are many farmhouses with close studding still to be seen. It is a feature of many of the Wealden houses in the area; Old Bell Farm, Harrietsham (17), Eldridge Farm House, Littlebourne, Claxfield Farm, Lynsted, Brewerstreet Farmhouse, Bletchingley (18), Corner Farm, Langley, and Sands Farm, Warnham, all have closely spaced studs, as have such houses as Hagbrook Farm, Alkham, Manor Farm, Cliffe, Pond's Farm, Frittenden, Pounds Farm, Fletching, Old Maypole Farm, High Hurstwood, and Gatehouse Farm, Kilndown.

The characteristic feature of the western school is the use of full height posts, spaced at determined intervals – bays – on both sides of the building, which are framed into the sill-beam at the bottom and the wall-plate at the top and tied together across the width of the building by a tie-beam, which also acted as the tie-beam of the roof truss. This form of construction was formerly known as post-and-truss, for the weight of the roof is conveyed by means of the purlins and wall-plates to the trusses and finally by way of the posts to the ground. To increase stability diagonal arch-bracings were introduced between the posts and wall-plate, but from the middle of the sixteenth century these became straight. Consequently the wall between the vertical posts had no structural importance and was generally of lighter construction, to form plain rectangular panels more or less equal in size. The storey-height was usually divided horizontally into two, but in the West Midlands, especially in Shropshire, there were sometimes three horizontal divisions. This form of construction can be found throughout the West Midlands and also, although to a much lesser degree, in the South-east and East Midlands.

Close studding was also employed, but unlike the eastern school in

81. Timber-framed farmhouse near Sledge Green, Hereford and Worcester.

which the timbers ran the full storey height, the western school has an uninterrupted middle rail. Also, because these studs had no structural importance, it was not unusual for boards rather than studs to be used to give the desired effect. Farmhouses where close studding is employed throughout can be found (one example is Lane Farmhouse, Feckenham, Hereford and Worcester), but more common is the combination of close timbering and square panels. Often this comprised close studding to the ground floor with the upper floor formed of square panels, as at Cross Lanes Farmhouse, Feckenham, and Lower Tundridge Farm, Suckley, both in Hereford and Worcester, and Top Farm, Knockin, Shropshire. At Keys Farmhouse, Bentley Pauncefoot, Hereford and Worcester, the front of the hall range is close-timbered throughout, while the cross-wing has close-studding below and square panels above. Sometimes this combination of both close studding and square panelling denotes a house of two builds. At Burton's Farm, Wellington Heath, Hereford and Worcester, a farmhouse originally built at the beginning of the sixteenth century and extended in the seventeenth century, the earlier part has close studding while the later has square framing.

82. Hall Farm, Deuxhill, Shropshire. A timber-framed farmhouse dated 1602, the right-hand gable and cross-wing is of later date.

A feature of many of the timber-framed buildings of the West Midlands is the use of decorative framing within the panels formed by the studs and cross-members. In the sixteenth and seventeenth centuries and when the panels were fairly large, diagonal strutting often in the form of a herring-bone pattern was popular. This form of decoration can be found on a number of farmhouses, and one can cite such examples as Cross Lanes Farmhouse, Feckenham, Combe Farm, Byton, and Moat Farm, Longdon, all in Hereford and Worcester, and Bearstone Farm, Bearstone, Shropshire. During the second half of the sixteenth century the panels became smaller and squarer and were filled in with a variety of ornamental motifs. Concaved lozenges, cusped concave-sided lozenges, stars, crosses, quatrefoils and many other highly decorative shapes were all found. These are to be found mainly in the West Midlands, in Cheshire and in some of the larger houses in southern Lancashire, with the highest concentration being in

Shropshire and Hereford and Worcester: Hillhouse Farm, Bosbury, built about 1600; Wilton Farm, Breden Bury, which has a cross gable with lozenges within lozenges and also cusped concave-sided lozenges; Court Farm, Sollers Hope, also with lozenges within lozenges; Middle Beanhall Farm, Bradley (3), Aston Hall, Aston (84), and Top Farm, Knockin, which has lozenges so heavily cusped that the plastered area inside appears to be elongated pointed quatrefoils.

Like the western school, the northern school of carpentry is of post-and-truss construction, but whereas in the western school the main posts are framed into the sill-beam, in the northern school they rest on large stone foundations, known as 'stylobates', with sill-beams framed into them at ground-floor level – a feature known as the 'interrupted sill'. The walls are framed with closely spaced studs arranged in two rows of unequal height framed into a horizontal rail spanning between the main posts. Curved arch-braces are provided between the main posts and the wall-plate. A large number of timber-framed buildings in the North were cased in stone in the seventeenth and eighteenth centuries and later in brick, and few can be recognized from the exterior.

Today all the above types of timber-framed walling are collectively known as box-frame construction to distinguish it from cruck-construction, and the old distinction between box-frame (where the walls provided a continuous load-bearing wall) and post-and-truss (where a framed cross wall and roof truss carries the roof) has largely been abandoned, although these terms are perhaps more appropriate in describing the characteristics of these two differing techniques.

In all these forms of construction the sill-beams rested on a plinth of local material – stone, flint, brick or occasionally baulks of timber – laid in a shallow trench directly on the sub-soil with no foundation and no damp-proof course, the sill-beam itself, as long as it remained sound, acting as a damp-proof course to prevent rising damp. Later these plinths were often tarred to help prevent the sill-beams from rotting.

INFILLING

The oldest method and by far the most common form of infill panel was what is known as 'wattle and daub' (86C). Where the panels were square, it was usual to have vertical staves, usually hazel, cleft chestnut or oak, which were pointed at one end and a chisel shape at the other, which were either fitted into holes in the upper horizontal member and slid and wedged into a groove in the lower one or sometimes slid and wedged into grooves top and bottom. These uprights were generally fixed about twelve inches apart, although they could be as much as

83. Old Farmhouse, Houghton, West Sussex. An old farmhouse with jettied
cross-wing and large open square panel with tension-braces.

84. Aston Hall, Aston, Shropshire. A picturesque timber-framed farmhouse with concave-sided lozenges.

85 Old Hall Farm, Woodford, Greater Manchester. Built about 1540, this old farmhouse now surrounded by new houses is an excellent example of the complicated decorations evolved by the carpenters of Cheshire and Lancashire.

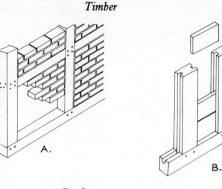

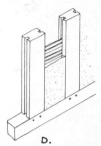

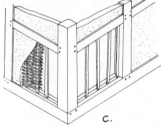

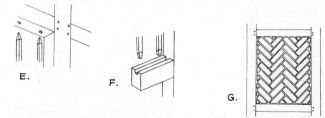

86. Infilling to timber-framing: A. isometric view of brick-nogging; B. isometric view of infilling using stone slabs; C. isometric view of wattle and daub infilling; D. isometric view of lath and daub infilling to close spaced studs; E. and F. detail of fixing for staves; G. herring-bone brick nogging.

eighteen inches apart, between which the wattle – pliable wands – usually unbarked hazel or ash sticks, were interwoven to form hurdle-like panels. In better-class work riven oak or beech laths were used in place of the hazel or ash sticks. When the panel was tall, a short cross-piece was sometimes wedged between the studs to which the uprights were tied. Where the studs were closely placed, often only uprights were used, sometimes merely wedged between the horizontal members, but more commonly they were fixed in a similar way as staves. In East Anglia stout cross-pieces were fixed horizontally between the studs in V-grooves cut into their sides, to which upright ash or hazel sticks were tied or less often woven. Another method when the panels were narrow was to omit the uprights completely, and instead of a woven panel, ash or hazel sticks or more commonly oak laths were wedged horizontally into grooves cut in the side of the studs (86D). All these various methods of framing the wattle were constructed without the aid of nails.

To this panel was applied the daub, a mixture of clay, chopped straw or cowhair, cow dung and where available lime. The daub was then thrown onto both sides of the wattle at the same time so as to fill in the interstices between the sticks. It was then left to dry before successive layers were applied until the required thickness was obtained. Although the daub set hard, it was liable to shrink or swell in dry or wet weather, and to overcome this either the surface was limewashed or where possible a coat of plaster was applied prior to the application of limewash to give the panel greater protection.

From the seventeenth century onwards brick began to replace wattle and daub as an infilling, often replacing old wattle and daub which had become defective. Why this transition took place is difficult to say, for most old bricks were more porous than good plastered daub, so dampness was encouraged, while the extra weight of the bricks caused many structural problems. Brick-nogging, as this infilling is known, was generally laid in stretcher bond (86A), or, on larger buildings, in herring-bone pattern (86G), but sometimes it was laid in a haphazard manner with no form of pattern. Often a combination of stretcher bond and herring-bone pattern was incorporated in the same building. In Essex and Suffolk brick-nogging was often recessed and plastered, but in the West Midlands the brickwork was usually left and lime-washed.

Although wattle and daub and brick-nogging were by far the two commonest forms of infilling, many other local materials were used. Flint, chalk and stone were all used, and where the stone could be cut into slabs, these were fitted horizontally one above the other into grooves in the side of the studs. Slate was used in a similar manner, and so too were oak boards. In these forms of infilling, where slabs fitted into grooves (86B), it would have been necessary for them to be inserted at the same time as the frame was erected and not, like wattle and daub and brick-nogging, afterwards.

If the framing between the panels was left untreated, it weathered to a silvery hue, and this was the common treatment in East Anglia and the South-east. In East Anglia, Essex, Cambridgeshire and the adjoining part of Hertfordshire, however, where much of the timber work was subsequently clad in plaster, exposed timbers are somewhat rare, especially for farmhouses. In Cambridgeshire for instance nearly all timber-framed houses are clad in plaster. In recent years as well there has been an increasing tendency to blacken these timbers, giving a more striking effect than that obtained from untreated timber. There are, of course, many examples still to be found in the eastern counties in which the timbers are exposed and left in their natural state. Some of the most attractive are at Parsonage Farm, Stebbing, Lower Dairy Farm, Little Horkesley, and Martins Farm, Newport, all in Essex, Nether Hall Farmhouse, Cavendish, Suffolk (87), and Castell Farm, Raveningham, Norfolk.

This blackening of timber is particularly common in the Welsh border counties as well as in Lancashire, Staffordshire and Warwickshire, and all but a few farmhouses, among them Lane Farmhouse, Feckenham, and The Leys, Weobley, both in Hereford and Worcester, have been so treated. Whether this practice was common is unknown, but it is unlikely to be of any great age, for it was not until Victorian times that a permanent black was manufactured. Such buildings as Little Moreton Hall, Cheshire, one of the finest black-and-white buildings in England, did not have their timbers blackened until Victorian times, and it has been decided by the National Trust to return Little Moreton Hall's timbers to their former condition. This desire to return the timbers to their natural state can be seen elsewhere in the West, the most notable example being Moat Farm, Dormston, Hereford and Worcester, which has in recent years been stripped to reveal the timber beneath. Despite this there are many hundreds of farmhouses which still retain their blackened timbers and which are visually most striking.

CLADDING

From the end of the sixteenth century onward many old timber-framed buildings as well as many new ones were clad to provide more comfortable weather- and draught-proof dwellings. This was achieved by plastering the face of the building, cladding it with tiles, slates or bricks or covering the face with timber boards.

The oldest of these methods was plastering, which started in the sixteenth century and gained popularity in the seventeenth and eighteenth centuries with the availability of wood laths and an improvement in the quality of plaster (89). On old buildings the old

87. Nether Hall Farmhouse, Cavendish, Suffolk. A sixteenth-century house with a two-storeyed porch with close-spaced studs left untreated, typical of the Eastern school.

88. Farmhouse at Wick, Hereford and Worcester. A typical western timber-framed house with an attached barn.

wattle and daub often remained, the external face only being covered with closely spaced riven laths nailed to the face of the studs and subsequently plastered over leaving the timbers exposed on the inner face. Where the wattle and daub was removed or on new timber-framed buildings, both the external and internal faces were covered with laths and subsequently plastered.

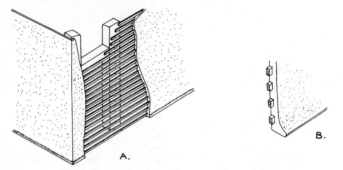

89. Plaster cladding: A. isometric view showing plaster and riven timber laths; B. detail of plaster and lath showing bellmouth.

The plastering of timber-framed houses is a feature in eastern England, where it became the most popular treatment of external walls. In the sixteenth and seventeenth centuries many houses originally constructed with exposed studs were subsequently clad, while others often built with inferior timber were clad from the outset. Sadly today much of this old plasterwork has been stripped off to expose the timbers, in many cases timbers that were never intended to be exposed, leaving timber badly marked and stained from the old nails used to fix the laths. In spite of this there are many hundreds to be found with parts at least of the original plasterwork remaining. The plastering of timber-framed houses is also to be found in the South-east, but it is far less common than in Essex, Suffolk and Cambridgeshire.

All the plaster cladding and wattle and daub infilling needed some form of protection against the elements. Limewash was the traditional material to be used, but it was porous and gave the plasterwork or daub little protection, and other means were often employed to throw the water away from the walls. It has been suggested that this was one of the reasons why jettying was employed, and certainly this attractive form of construction had this effect. However, when no jetty was provided, other means were devised. In eastern England a prentice

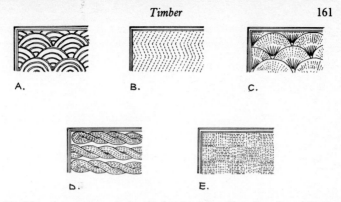

90. Pargetting patterns: A. fan; B. herring-bone; C. scallop; D. cable; E. basket weave.

91. Oxenbridge, Iden, East Sussex. A fifteenth-century plastered Wealden hall house extended in the eighteenth century.

board was employed. This was a timber board fixed to the face of the wall with timber brackets and so built as to throw the water away from the wall. It was generally fixed on the gable end. In the West Midlands, particularly in Hereford and Worcester, tiled weatherings were a feature. These comprised a narrow bracketed pentroof built out from the face of the building some eighteen inches or so at each storey height. It was not only an extremely practical but also an ornamental method of protecting the wattle and daub panels. Sadly few remain today, for over the past century throughout the area the wattle and daub panels have been replaced with brick and at that time the weatherings were also removed. Thankfully there are some that still survive: Lane Farmhouse, Feckenham, Moat Farm, Dormston, and Upper Beanhall, Bradley, have all retained this attractive feature.

There were several local variations using both wattle and daub and plaster. One was mud-and-stud, a form of construction used in the Lincolnshire Wold where the houses were built with a slender timber frame with the posts merely having intermediate rails, and where the only cross rail was one to support the floor joists. Consequently the panels were of considerable size and were covered with thin staves fixed to the outside of the frame with the daub applied to both sides of the wall and extended across the outer face of the timbers. A few houses of this construction built in the sixteenth and seventeenth centuries still survive, amongst them Clapgate Farm, Somersby, a house built in the sixteenth century and later clad with brickwork. In Lancashire another form of construction known locally as 'clam-staff and daub' was used. Unlike mud-and-stud construction there was no frame, the houses generally being of cruck construction with the walls being of clay stiffened with studs morticed to the wall-plate and sill-beam. For added protection the whole face of both these forms of construction was subsequently covered with a thin coat of plaster.

Ideally the composition of plaster was a mixture of compounded lime and coarse sand – three to six times the volume of sand as lime – mixed for additional strength with chopped straw, cowhair, horsehair, road-scrapings or cow dung. Water was added, the ingredients beaten and mixed to produce a plaster which when set was as 'tough as leather'. The toughness of this plaster made it possible to form ornamental enrichments to the face of the plaster, known as pargetting (90). Two forms were employed: incised or inscribed work, also known as 'stick-work' or 'combed work', and the other, more ornate but less common, raised or relief work. With incised work the process was simple, and the implements used were largely home-made; the idea was to impress a pattern into the surface of the wet plaster with the use of a pointed stick, a group of sticks tied together to form a fan, a wooden comb or simply a large nail. Sometimes the whole face of the

92. Farmhouse at Shillington, Bedfordshire.

93. Lordship Farm, Shillington, Bedfordshire. An old timber-framed farmhouse clad with pebble-dash, a common feature in Bedfordshire on the old timber-framed houses.

building would be covered with one design, but more frequently the walls would be divided into rectangular panels, each panel with a slight border and filled in with one of a variety of patterns. Raised pargetting was more difficult and required great skill, and it reached its zenith in the late seventeenth century.

The best pargetting is to be found in eastern England, although today it is far less common. Incised work can still be found occasionally on such farmhouses as Dales Farm, Barton, and Low Farm, Elsworth, both in Cambridgeshire, Willow Farm, Assington, and Giffords Farm, Shimpling, both in Suffolk, and Dairy Farm, Tacolneston, Norfolk. Perhaps the best surviving pargetting can be seen at Walnut Tree Farm, Walpole, Suffolk. The work there, which dates from 1708, is both relief and incised, there being a broad decorative frieze across the whole of the upper part of the front of the house with rolled plaster-moulded string course between the ground and first-floor windows and a vine trail running the full length of the house. The spaces between the windows are divided into panels, with two picked out in relief, one with the date 1708 in the spandrels. At Yew Tree Farm, Finningham, there is also a pair of oval panels in relief placed each side of the porch. Pargetting can also be found on occasions elsewhere in England; at Hunt Street Farm, Crundale, Kent, a later large-gabled bay, placed in the centre between the two jettied wings of a former Wealden house, has the infilling between the timbering decorated with geometrical pargetting. In Hereford and Worcester it can also be found, the notable example being on that remarkable farmhouse The Leys, Weobley, which has a sun head and a spray of thistles and oak leaves on one of the gables.

Tile-hanging (94), as a method of weatherproofing timber-framed buildings, first appeared in the latter part of the seventeenth century. Plain tiles (94B) were the first to be used, being the same as for roofs though sometimes a little thinner, and were hung on horizontal battens fixed to the face of the studs. They were hung to give a triple lap – each tile lapping two others – with the upper ends often bedded in lime and hair mortar to make a permanently waterproof wall and might in addition be secured with wooden pegs or nails. For corners and jambs special tiles were generally manufactured.

Although plain tiles were more commonly used, pattern tiles (94C, D and E) of considerable variation of design have been employed to give decorative effects, sometimes used in conjunction with plain tiles but often by themselves to give an all-over pattern (94 F, G, H, I, J and K). Most patterned tile-hanging belongs, however, to the Victorian period.

Tile-hanging is to be found almost exclusively in the South-east in the counties of Kent, Sussex and Surrey. Of these three counties Kent

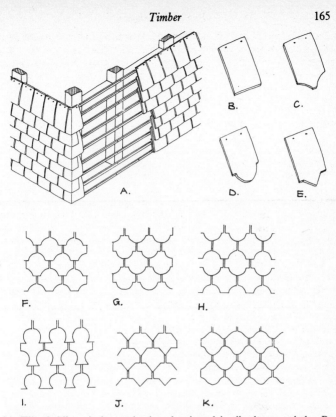

94. Tile cladding: A. isometric view showing plain tiles hung on laths; B. plain tile; C. hammer-head tile; D. fish-scale tile; E. arrow-head tile; F., G., H., I., J. and K. various tile patterns.

has the best and most, in particular in the villages and towns of the Weald, where the clays produced the beautiful terracotta tiles seen today, which over the period of time have toned down yet have still retained their glowing red. In Kent most of the tiles are plain, but the slightly cambered face and the irregular shape add a great deal to their overall appearance. Plain tiles are also to be found in Sussex and Surrey, particularly in the Weald and the surrounding area, but in these counties there is an increasing use of pattern tiles, and in Surrey there is more patterned tile-hanging than plain. Most belong to the Victorian period, and although the earlier hand-made tiles can look

attractive, the later machine-made ones are less so, often producing a
rather monotonous and somewhat distracting effect.

95. Great Job's Cross Farm, Rolvenden, Kent. A timber-framed farmhouse
built in the seventeenth century clad with plain tiles.

Generally tile-hanging is restricted to the upper floors and gable
ends, these being more exposed than other parts of the house, but
there are examples of farmhouses in which the tiles cover one or more
walls completely. One example is Great Job's Cross Farm, Rolvenden,
Kent (95), a seventeenth-century timber-framed house where the
entire front and the upper storey and gable of the end walls are all clad
with tiles. Another is Pix's Farm, Rolvenden, a farmhouse clad in tiles
with the exception of its three gables.

Another cladding material was the brick-tile or mathematical tile
(96). They were hung or more commonly nailed to either horizontal
battens or boarding and were designed to give the illusion of
brickwork, and to this end the joints were bedded and pointed in
mortar. Special return bricks were manufactured for corners to
maintain the bond and the illusion, but in many cases the ordinary tiles
were returned, leaving the thin edge of the tile exposed. These tiles are
usually to be found in many of the villages and towns of Kent and
Sussex but only occasionally in rural areas, as at Manor Farm, South

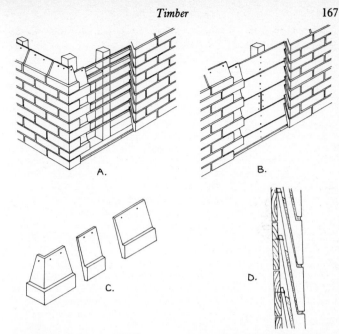

96. Mathematical tile cladding: A. isometric view showing tiles fixed to battens; B. isometric view showing tiles fixed to boarding; C. typical mathematical tiles; D. section through tiles showing method of bedding.

Heighton, Sussex.

During the seventeenth and eighteenth centuries, with the increasing production of bricks, it became popular to modernize old timber-framed houses by providing a new false brick front. It is a common feature in the South-east, among the finest being Netherhale Farm, St Nicholas-at-Wade, Kent, Mansion House Farm, Crowhurst, Sussex, Hill Farm, Thursley, Surrey, and Hussey's Farm, Lower Froyle, Hampshire. Others, such as Chillenden Court Farm, Goodnestone, Kent, Winchcombe Farm, Crundale, Kent, and Chennell's Brook Farm, Horsham, Sussex, have been encased or largely encased in brick. Similar farmhouses can also be found in eastern England, but they are less common than in the South-east. In other parts of the country too a false brick front or the cladding of a timber-framed house can be found. For Hereford and Worcester one can cite Warndon Farmhouse, Warndon, which was encased in brick in the seventeenth century and is perhaps the earliest example of a brick-built farmhouse in the county. Others in the county include Court Farm, Bishampton, which is entirely encased, and Astwood Farm, Dodderhill, which though of early seventeenth-century date has been refronted in brick.

In addition from the late sixteenth century onwards it became a common practice to underbuild the jetties, and many farmhouses which today appear on first evidence to be plain brick or tile-hung houses are on closer examination former jettied houses. The advantage of this undertaking was two-fold, for it provided extra space to the ground-floor rooms – usually some eighteen inches – and at the same time the front of the house could be modernized. Generally a brick wall was built up under the projecting jetty, and in the case of the Wealden house this brickwork was carried up to eaves level between the projecting end bays, to support the floors or wall-plates. When all the timbers were securely fixed, the front wall beneath the jetties or wall-plate could be subsequently removed without fear of structural damage. The whole of the upper storey would then be clad with tiles or sometimes weatherboarded, and with the insertion of contemporary windows and doorways the modernization would be complete. There are numerous examples of this type of construction to be found in the South-east, particularly in the Weald. Three examples in which the original character of the building has been completely lost are Gatehouse Farm, Blindley Heath, Surrey, Cleavewater Farm, Haywards Heath, Sussex, and Jarves, Whitewood, near Horne, Kent.

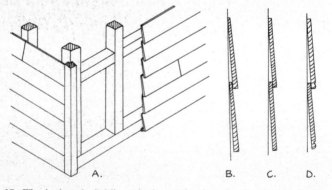

97. Weatherboard cladding: A. isometric view showing boards fixed to studwork; B. feather edge boarding; C. square-edged boarding; D. beaded-edged boarding.

The last cladding material used on dwellings was horizontal boards

98. Maytham Farm, Rolvenden, Kent. A typical weatherboarded and brick farmhouse to be found in the Weald.

99. Paul's Farm, Leigh, Kent. A sixteenth-century timber-framed farmhouse with continuous jetty and two-storeyed porch later clad with weatherboarding.

known as weatherboarding or clapboarding (97). Its use in preference to other cladding materials was probably the need to economize, and it is therefore found principally on small houses, cottages and farm buildings. There is evidence that it was first used on barns and other farm buildings as early as 1600, but it was not until the eighteenth century that it began to be used on domestic buildings. Early weatherboarding was oak or elm, pegged to the frame and left untreated, but later softwood was generally used, nailed directly to the studs. The boards were fixed horizontally, each board lapping the board below; at the corners vertical battens were provided, and at the window reveals a rectangular batten was fitted to provide a stop for the boarding.

100. Creeds Farm, Epping, Essex. A weatherboarded eighteenth-century central-lobby farmhouse.

101. Collops Farm, Stebbing, Essex

Weatherboarding is indigenous to the South-east and occurs more often in the Weald of Kent than anywhere else in the country, but it is also to be found in the adjoining part of Sussex and to a much lesser extent in Surrey. Like tile-hanging, the weatherboarding was generally restricted in these counties to the upper floors and gables (98). Occasionally, however, the whole house was clad, and Paul's Farm, Leigh, Kent (99), a sixteenth-century timber-framed house with a continuous overhang and a two-storeyed porch, is one of the finest. Unlike tile-hanging, weatherboarding is to be found elsewhere in the country. In most of the eastern counties it was used extensively for the cladding of barns and other farm buildings as well as for wind- and watermills, but apart from Essex (100) and the adjoining part of Hertfordshire it was rarely used in the cladding of domestic buildings other than cottages and an occasional farmhouse such as Goodwin Manor Farm, Swaffham Prior, Cambridgeshire. Even in Essex, although weatherboarding was once more popular than it now appears, for much has been replaced with plaster in recent years, it is nowhere as common as it is in the South-east. A feature to be found in the eastern part of Hertfordshire close to the Essex border is the combined use of plaster and weatherboarding. There are a number of cottages, farm buildings and the occasional farmhouse – Bury Green Farm, Bury Green, Green Tye Farm, Green Tye (56), and Walnut Tree Farm, Luffenhall (14) – in which the lower part of the wall, generally up to ground-floor windowsill level, is weatherboarded and tarred with plaster above. This treatment can also be found on an occasional farmhouse in Essex such as Collops Farm, Stebbing (101). Occasionally, as at Cutting Hill Farm, Bennington, Hertfordshire, the weatherboarding is carried up to the top of the ground-floor windows.

CRUCK AND OTHER ROOF TYPES

The characteristic feature of cruck construction (103) is the use of two inclined timbers which rise from the ground and meet at the apex, which are tied together by a collar or tie-beam to form an A-frame serving as a roof truss to support the purlins. In this respect it is similar to post-and-truss construction in that the weight of the roof is transferred to the ground by means of transverse frames. Consequently the vertical walls had no structural importance and when constructed of timber depended greatly on the crucks for both support and stability. The inclined timbers of the cruck frame, known as 'blades', were cut from trees which had, whenever possible, a natural curve, or from the trunk of one tree split in two along its length to ensure a symmetrical arch. The blades varied in shape according to the curvature of the tree and could be nearly straight, smoothly curved or elbowed. The ends of the blades were either supported on a stylobat or framed into a sill-beam and at the apex either simply butted, crossed or halved or terminated below the apex and joined with either a saddle, a link or a yoke. Between each cruck frame ran the ridge-beams and purlins which supported the common rafters. When the external walls were of timber, the tie-beams were extended until their ends were directly above the base of the blades, and vertical posts were introduced pegged to the base of the blades and to the end of the tie-beams. Wall-plates running between each cruck frame were fixed to the end of the tie-beams, and the panel between each post was filled in with studs and horizontal members. Often, however, in order to obtain more headroom the tie-beam was omitted, and in these cases the wall-plate and vertical post were tied back to the cruck by means of a cruck-spur.

102. A cruck and timber-framed farmhouse at Styal, Cheshire.

The above briefly describes the 'true' or 'full' cruck, but there are several other forms of cruck construction which, although not full crucks, are obviously related, some more than others, to the cruck family. First there is the 'raised' cruck which is similar to the full cruck in all respects other than that instead of starting at ground level it starts instead some way up a solid wall. In fact, full crucks are often referred to as raised crucks because the starting-point of the cruck, being concealed within the wall, is uncertain. With the 'base' cruck the blades, although rising from the ground, are truncated well below the apex and are tied together at the head with a tie-beam or collar which supports the roof structure. Most surviving examples of base-cruck construction are from the fourteenth century. In the raised base or truncated raised cruck only the middle – the curved part of the cruck – is used, while in the 'upper' cruck the blades rise to the apex from a tie-beam at or near eaves level. Another form of cruck construction is the 'jointed' or 'scarfed' cruck where a vertical post is jointed to an inclined blade to obtain a cruck-like form.

Today most crucks are to be found in cottages or barns, and so it is a popular view that cruck construction was developed for humbler dwellings. This is not so, for the surviving examples erected in the fourteenth and fifteenth centuries are in houses of considerable standing and are of heavy scantlings with well-finished timbers, very different from those built in the sixteenth and seventeenth centuries.

With other forms of construction – both timber wall framing and mass wall construction – the width of the building was governed by the limitations imposed on it by the roof construction, for it was difficult to achieve roof spans greater than the length of timber available. Roofs can be divided into two groups: single-framed, consisting of rafters with no longitudinal members but often with various bracing members, and double-framed, consisting of rafters and purlins which either span from wall to wall without intermediate supports or are supported along their length by trusses.

The earliest roof at the vernacular level is the crown-post (104 B and 105), which appears to have developed from an earlier, simpler form of single-framed roof using only rafters with each pair pegged at their apex and tied together with a collar (104A). There was no longitudinal member to stiffen the roof, its stability relying on the roof battens and coverings. Obviously such roofs were liable to collapse, and it is thought that to overcome this problem a longitudinal member was inserted, running for the whole length of the roof placed immediately below the collars but not fixed to them. This longitudinal plate, known as the 'collar purlin', restrained by friction any tendency for the rafters to collapse and transferred much of the weight of the roof by means of crown-posts to the centre of the tie-beams. These crown-posts were set at regular intervals along the length of the roof framed into the tie-beam at the bottom and to the collar purlin at the top. The crown-posts themselves required braces between post and collar to prevent lateral movement, and usually in addition longitudinal braces were provided between the crown-posts and collar purlin. In fact the variations in crown-post roof construction are mainly in the arrangement of these diagonal braces and the height of the crown-post. When exposed in the open hall or solar, the crown-posts were often decorated, with the cap

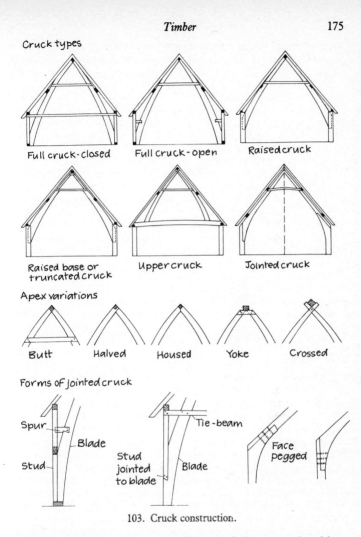

Cruck types

Full cruck-closed   Full cruck-open   Raised cruck

Raised base or truncated cruck   Upper cruck   Jointed cruck

Apex variations

Butt   Halved   Housed   Yoke   Crossed

Forms of jointed cruck

Spur
Blade
Stud

Tie-beam
Stud jointed to blade
Blade

Face pegged

103. Cruck construction.

and base moulded and the post itself shaped. In less exposed positions and later on humbler buildings, these crown-posts were square without decoration.

The crown-post roof truss belonged predominantly to the South-east and East Anglia, and in other parts of the country other types were

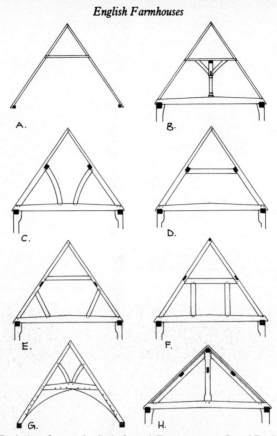

104. Typical roof types: A. single-framed; B. crown-post; C. and D. clasped-purlin; E. butt-purlin; F. through or trenched purlin; G. arch-braced collar-beam; H. king-post.

used. In the North it was the king-post truss (104H and 106), in which a stout post, the king-post, rises from the tie-beam to support the ridge-piece, with the principal rafters rising from tie-beam to ridge being framed to the tie-beam and the side of the king-post. Between each principal rafter run the purlins trenched into them to support the common rafter. In addition the principal rafters were sometimes supported by struts off the tie-beam. Although there are a few early king-post trusses in other areas, they are extremely common in the

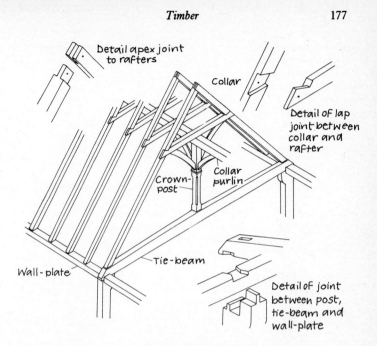

105. Details of crown-post truss.

North in medieval and post-medieval buildings and, unlike the crown-post trusses of the South, were widely adopted in the rest of the country in the eighteenth and nineteenth centuries.

Another, and perhaps the most ornamental type of truss used in medieval secular buildings, was the arch-braced collar-beam (104G), being the standard truss in western England. In this roof truss the tie-beam was eliminated and a collar-beam provided at high level supported with arch-braces framed either into the underside of the principal rafter and down onto the main post or directly to the main post at the bottom and at the top into the underside of the collar. The area above the collar-beam was often highly decorative. Usually this took the form of bold trefoils or quatrefoils frequently formed by two raking struts between the collar and principal rafters, foiled or finely cusped, and forming, with equally foiled or cusped principals and collar, a decorative panel. In addition the wind-braces, of which there may be one or more tiers, were similarly foiled or cusped.

With the abandonment of the open hall, the roofs were no longer

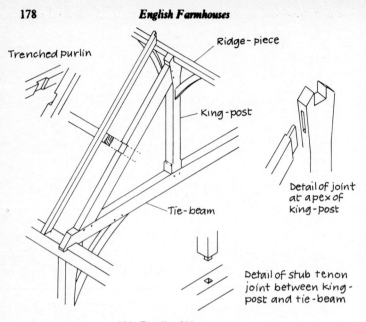

Trenched purlin

Ridge-piece

King-post

Tie-beam

Detail of joint at apex of king-post

Detail of stub tenon joint between king-post and tie-beam

106. Details of king-post truss.

intended to be visible, and so with their decorative function removed there became a desire to utilize the roof space by forming an attic. For this both the crown-post and the collar purlin were a hindrance, and so the side purlin roof, which left the whole of the attic space free from obstructions, came into its own on smaller houses. In the South-east and the East the crown-post roofs were replaced by two types of side purlin roofs, the clasp-purlin (104C and D) and butt-purlin roofs (104E). The features of these roofs are that the principal rafters are in the same plane as the common rafters and are, in most cases, only slightly larger in section, with the purlins being either clasped at the back of the principal rafters by a collar or strut (107) or alternatively butted between the principal rafters and tenoned to them. When the purlins are clasped at the back of the principal rafter, that section of the rafter from this point to the ridge is often reduced in size to that of a common rafter.

In many ways cruck roofs and king-post roofs were similar in that they both employed ridge-pieces and side purlins laid on or trenched into the crucks or principal rafters. In the West and Midlands during the sixteenth century, when cruck construction began to dwindle, and

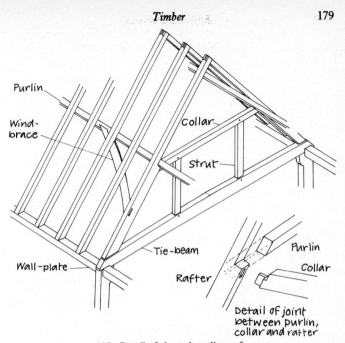

107. Detail of clasped-purlin roof.

in the North, when the use of the medieval king-post declined, the trusses that succeeded them continued to adopt this same trenched or through purlin technique (104F). With this type of roof the principal rafters are of a much larger scantling and in a lower plane than the common rafters, with the purlins trenched into their upper face onto which the common rafters sit (108). Also, more often than not, the roof incorporated a ridge-piece, a feature not normally employed in the clasp and butt-purlin roofs of the South-east and East.

In all these forms of roof construction, with the exception of cruck and arch-braced, the trusses are built off a tie-beam preventing any outward movement of the principal rafters. However, there were buildings in which the tie-beam was often in an inconvenient position. To overcome this problem several methods were adopted. One method was to eliminate the central part of the tie-beam, the end being framed into a post which rose from the main cross-beam at floor level to the underside of the principal rafter or collar-beam. This system was generally adopted in trenched-purlin roofs. In clasped- or butt-purlin

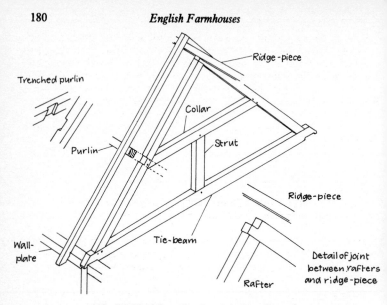

Ridge-piece

Trenched purlin

Collar

Strut

Purlin

Ridge-piece

Wall-plate

Tie-beam

Detail of joint between rafters and ridge-piece

Rafter

108. Detail of through- or trenched-purlin roof.

roofs a similar method was used, but the post was replaced by a diagonal member, introduced from the main post to the principal rafter, into which the remaining length of the tie-beam was framed. Finally there was the use of upper crucks which rose from first-floor cross-beam level but which did not always continue to the ridge being held together by a collar.

From the seventeenth century onwards the development of the double-pile house provided the carpenter with another problem to overcome. When the chosen roof covering required a steep pitch, the resultant roof over the house would have been of excessive height. To overcome this, two identical roofs were placed side by side to form an 'M' roof with a valley gutter between. The disadvantage of this roof type was that it divided the roof space into two, needing two separate accesses and both being small with little headroom. A roof was, however, devised in which the valley wall was raised and the purlin forming the valley was supported on a tie-beam strutted off ceiling beams. The result was to provide a single attic with reasonable headroom over much of its area. When the roof coverings were slate or stone-slates requiring a lower pitch, the double-pile house proved less of a problem, the roof being supported by purlins bearing on the external walls and internal partitions.

From the eighteenth century imported softwood replaced oak as the predominate timber used in roof construction. Carpentry techniques became progressively simpler, with nails, bolts and metal straps often replacing the elaborate joints formerly employed. The trusses used were often adaptations of old ones; the king-post truss found almost exclusively in northern England up to the seventeenth century was adopted in many parts of the country, while the more elaborate queen-post truss, which was used in many houses, some of only moderate size, in the lowland zone during the sixteenth and seventeenth centuries, was another commonly used.

AISLED AND QUASI-AISLED CONSTRUCTION

A roof could only span a limited width, usually about eighteen feet and rarely more than twenty feet, without increasing the size of the timbers so much that it would become both impracticable and uneconomical. In order to increase the roof span and also the floor area, it was necessary to support the roof structure across its span (109). This was achieved by the introduction of timber posts, known as 'arcade posts', which supported the 'arcade plate', a longitudinal plate running between each post for the full length of the building. The arcade plate supported the common rafters which ran from the ridge of the main roof over the aisle to the wall-plate at the external wall. To increase rigidity a tie-beam was introduced, spanning the building and sitting on top of the arcade beam above the post into which the principal rafters were framed. These rafters were further strengthened by a collar at high level. Stability was further increased by the introduction of straight braces between the arcade post and the beam, as at Purton Green Farmhouse, Stansfield, Suffolk (7), or later in such farmhouses as Stanton's Farm, Black Notley, Manor Farm, Little Chesterford (2), and Lampett's Farm, Fyfield, all in Essex, with curved braces between the arcade post and beam and arcade post and tie-beam.

In early aisled buildings, transverse rigidity was obtained by the introduction of 'scissor bracing' (109B and C), comprising ties fixed to the face of the main structure extending from either the external wall posts or the arcade posts to a point high on the principal rafter on the opposite side. These timbers are often referred to as under or secondary rafters. In addition duplicate passing braces extending from either the external wall post or the arcade post to the tie-beam or to the under rafters were on occasions provided, as at Purton Green Farmhouse. At Edgar's Farm, formerly at Stowmarket, Suffolk, built in about 1300, longitudinal stability was obtained by the introduction of a collar purlin and crown-posts (109A). This became the standard form of construction in later aisled farmhouses such as Lampett's

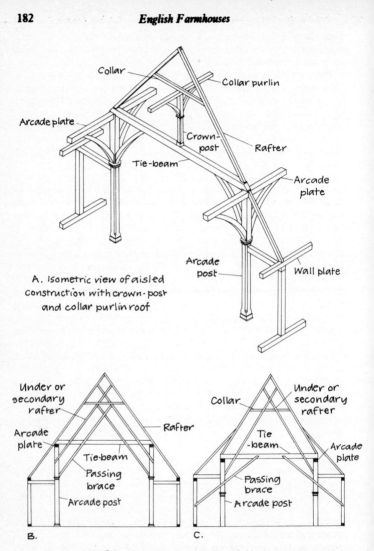

A. Isometric view of aisled construction with crown-post and collar purlin roof

B.

C.

Examples of aisled construction with scissor bracing

109. Aisled construction.

Farm and Manor Farm, Little Chesterford. One feature of all these aisled houses was the free use of lapped joints instead of or in addition to mortice and tenon joints.

Most aisled houses were built before 1400, but so suitable and economical was aisling that, long after it was abandoned for domestic work, it continued to be used in the construction of barns. Throughout the lowland zone in the counties of Kent, Essex, Sussex, Surrey, Hampshire, Berkshire, Buckinghamshire, Suffolk, Norfolk and Cambridgeshire, barns of aisled construction can be found, and in Kent and East Anglia they continued to be built well into the eighteenth century.

Although aisling provided a greater floor area, the arcade posts caused an obstruction, and the problem was to overcome this yet still maintain the overall span and support the arcade beams. One solution was the use of the base-cruck (110A), which enabled the arcade plate to be supported from the external wall. The base-cruck, an adaptation of the true cruck, was truncated and did not extend above the arcade plate. The two blades were tied together at their top by a collar-beam supported on arch-braces springing from the crucks. The arcade plate was supported at the top of the base-cruck and was secured by various methods (110 B, C, D and E). The most common device was the introduction of a second collar-beam, with the arcade plate being clamped between the two. Another was to introduce subsidiary framing in the spandrel between the base-cruck and the arch-brace to cradle the plate. A third and simpler method sometimes used was for the arcade plate to be notched or tenoned into the top of the base-cruck. Few base-crucks in houses survive intact without considerable alteration and mutilation. One of the finest examples still to be found is at Hyde Farm, Stoke Bliss, Hereford and Worcester. The timbers are extremely large and very heavily moulded, with the arch-braces each having a moulded capital at its lower end with the moulding continuing down onto the cruck itself, this concealing the joint between the two. The timbers in the spandrel above the collar-beam are all cusped. Another and very similar base-cruck can be seen at Amberley Court, Marden, Hereford and Worcester, although it is considerably later than Hyde Farm.

The base-cruck was never adopted in eastern England, and here raised aisles were used to provide the required unobstructed floor space. It was a comparatively simple method in which the arcade posts supported off the ground floor were omitted and replaced with shorter arcade posts supported on an extremely large cambered tie-beam spanning the full width of the building. (110F). The tie-beam was usually low, as at Gatehouse Farm, Felsted, Essex, only some six feet above floor level, and at this old farm it was supported at its end by

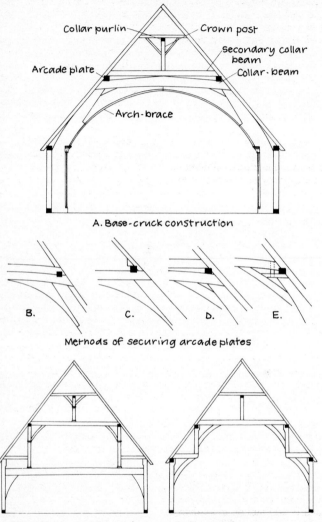

Collar purlin — Crown post

Secondary collar beam

Arcade plate — Collar-beam

Arch-brace

A. Base-cruck construction

B. C. D. E.

Methods of securing arcade plates

F. Raised aisled construction G. Hammer beam construction

110. Quasi-aisled construction.

curved braces springing from floor level and having the moulding of the tie-beam mitred and continuing down the braces. Above the tie-beam are the two posts complete with braces and with moulded base and capitals supporting the arcade plate or purlin and an upper tie-beam in the usual way. Above this tie-beam was usually a collar-purlin and crown-post as at Wymondley Bury, Little Wymondley, Hertfordshire. A variation to this design is to be seen at the disused hall at Church Farm, Fressington, Suffolk, in which instead of two posts on top of the lower tie-beam there are three, two at each end supporting the arcade plates and one in the centre beneath the crown-post.

The use of the hammer beam provided another solution(110G). However, because of the excessive thrust on the external walls it was not commonly used on domestic buildings, especially timber-framed ones, although it was widely used in churches and other large buildings with stone walls which could be supported with buttresses.

UPPER FLOOR CONSTRUCTION

Whether in a timber-framed building or one with solid walls, the construction of the upper floors was basically the same. The floor joists spanned either across the building or along the building from bay to bay. When the span was too great, a large beam, the bridging-beam, was introduced to reduce the span, with the joists jointed into it (111). Generally these beams spanned between bays with the joists spanning between them and the front or rear wall. In solid wall construction the ends of the joists and bridging-beam were built into the wall, but with timber-framed buildings a different technique was necessary. The ends of the joists either sat on or more commonly were framed into the bressummer or on poorer-quality buildings sat on a ledge pegged to the inside of the frame. The bridging-beams, however, were almost always tenoned into the bressummer or the girth of the cross-frame.

The bridging-beams were the largest timbers in any building and always acquired some form of decoration (112). The plain chamfer was the basis of many of these mouldings, but during the seventeenth century the ovolo moulding with many varieties of stopped ends became popular.

One of the outstanding features of some timber-framed buildings is jettying – the projection of an upper storey beyond the one below. It can occur on one or more sides and even on occasions on all four sides and in addition on more than one storey projecting in some cases as much as four feet. When jettying was to one side only, the construction was simple, for all that was required was for the floor joist to cantilever over the wall below and rest on the 'summer', the beam situated at the

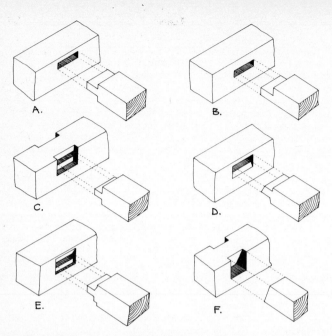

111. Typical joints between bridging-joists and floor joists: A. thirteenth–fourteenth century; B. fourteenth century; C. and D. fifteenth century; E sixteenth century; F. seventeenth–eighteenth century.

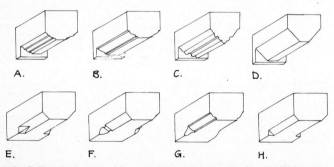

112. Ceiling beams – arris mouldings: A., B. and C. moulded beams fifteenth- and sixteenth-century date; D. late sixteenth–early seventeenth century; E. mid-seventeenth century; F. early seventeenth century; G. late sixteenth–early seventeenth century; H. seventeenth–early eighteenth century.

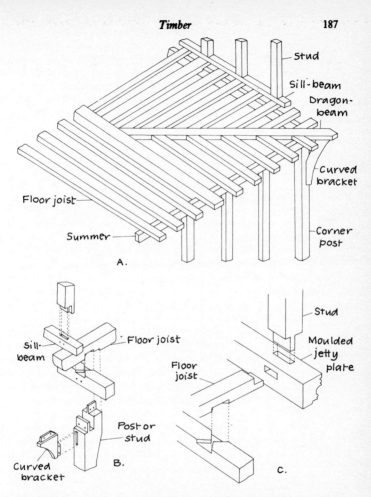

113. Jetty construction: A. general layout showing arrangement at corner with jetty to two sides; B. detail of joint between stud, summer, floor joist, sill-beam and stud; C. detail of joint between floor joist and jetty plate.

back of the overhang. When the overhang was on two adjacent sides, the process was a little more complex (113A). It was necessary to change the direction of the floor joists, and to enable this to be undertaken one of the floor joists was replaced by a larger one to which

114. Houchin's Farm, Feering, Essex. A farmhouse built in the sixteenth
century with a continuous jetty on first and second floor.

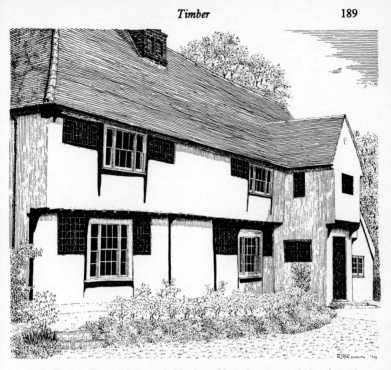

115. Tewes, Essex. A remarkable late fifteenth-century timber-framed former manor house with original oak-mullioned windows constructed before glass was used and still retaining an old reed window. The porch and bay are twentieth-century additions.

was framed another horizontal beam, called the 'dragon-beam', which ran diagonally to the corner of the floor. Into this beam the ends of the floor joists were framed, each pair set at right angles, although sometimes the last few were framed at an angle. Towards its end the dragon-beam was supported by and framed into a massive corner post, usually finely carved, which often had in addition a curved bracket to support the outer end of the dragon-beam. To support the jetty along its length additional curved brackets, occasionally carved, were sometimes provided framed to the studs and floor joists. Once the floor joists were in position, the framing of the next storey could continue with a sill-beam laid along their ends. The ends of these joists were generally shaped into a quarter-round and left exposed, but in early jettying the ends were often concealed behind a fascia. These are today rare, for later their use was discontinued, and once they decayed they were not replaced. Jettying was first introduced in the thirteenth century and remained popular until the latter part of the sixteenth century, when its use began to decline.

One of the earliest examples is the thirteenth-century Tiptofts Manor House, Wimbish, Essex, but jettying became a common feature of many medieval farmhouses. In most of the houses built in the fourteenth and fifteenth centuries the end bays or cross-wings flanking the open hall were jettied. Generally it was confined to the front, as at Abbotts Hall Farm, Stanway, Essex (15), and Cromer Farm, Cromer, Hertfordshire, but sometimes, and this is particularly true of the Wealden houses such as Old Bell Farm, Harrietsham, Kent (17), the jettying returns along the ends and even on occasions at the rear as well. Towards the end of the fifteenth century, when the open hall had generally been abandoned in the South-east and eastern England and farmhouses began to be constructed with two storeys throughout, it became possible to extend this overhanging upper floor the full length of the building. These continuous jettied houses are perhaps more numerous in towns and villages than in the countryside, but there are a good number of farmhouses with this form of construction to be found. This is especially true in the South-east and in particular in Kent.

Jettying was not only restricted to the first floor for where there was a second storey this was often jettied as well, like the floor below. This was fairly common in many of the gable cross-wing houses built not only in eastern England but also in the West Midlands. Less common is the use of the continuous jetty at both first and second floors. An excellent example of this is Houchin's Farm, Feering, Essex, (114), built in the sixteenth century, which has a continuous jetty not only at the front at both first and second floors but also returning along one end. So popular was the continuous jetty in the South-east that it is not uncommon for the central recess between the jettied end bays of a Wealden house to be filled in, when the open hall was divided horizontally, to form a continuous jettied front, as at Baxon Farm, Bredgar, Kent.

Unbaked Earth

The use of unbaked earth as a building material is as old as if not older than that of timber. The widespread use of turf in medieval times is well known, but the use of other forms of unbaked earth in the construction of walls continued until this century. Today three methods are to be encountered: 'cob', a mixture of clay, stones, straw and water used without the aid of shutters, '*pisé*', similar to cob but used dry and rammed between shutters, and 'clay lump', again a similar consistency as cob but shaped into rectangular blocks with the aid of moulds and laid and jointed with puddle-clay mortar.

Of these three methods the oldest and most extensively used was cob. It was the traditional walling material of most of eastern, central and northern Devon but was also commonly found in northern Somerset, in Cornwall, in parts of central Dorset along the chalk uplands and in the extreme west of Hampshire. Most cob can be found in cottages and farm buildings, of which a surprisingly high number still survive although hidden beneath a coat of rendering or numerous coats of limewash. Although it is thought that some of the cob at Pilliven, Witheridge, Devon, must date from around 1300 and that at Bury Barton, Lapford, also in Devon, from a little later, most cob farmhouses are of sixteenth- and seventeenth-century date. In Devon there are many examples: Buskins, Exbourne, Barclose Farm, Otterton, dated 1627, Poltimore, Farway, dated 1583, Cordwents Farm, Harberton, Fishleigh Barton, Tavistock, and Brown's Farm, Woodbury (116) are all typical. In Somerset one can cite such farmhouses as Hagley Bridge Farm, Ashbrittle, Henley Farm, High Ham, Little England Farmhouse, Othery, Court Farm, Stawley, and Old Farm House, Isle Abbotts. They are less common in Cornwall, Dorset and Hampshire. Unbaked earth was also used extensively in the construction of all types of buildings in Cumbria until about 1700, after which its use was generally restricted to cottages and farm buildings. A few farmhouses stand, such as Lamonby Farm, Burgh-by-Sands, built in the latter part of the seventeenth century in the longhouse tradition with hall and parlour separated from the byre by a cross-passage. As well as the building there is a small cottage in the range.

Cob's consistency varied from area to area according to the materials

191

116. Brown's Farmhouse, Woodbury, Devon. A cob house built about 1700.

117. Sheldon, Doddiscombsleigh, Devon. The two-storeyed porch was added in the seventeenth century to an existing cob building of an earlier date.

available locally. In Devon the material consisted of loamy earth, containing sufficient lime to enable it to set, mixed with water and chopped straw with, on occasions, small stones and cow dung to increase its strength. Further west, in Cornwall, the consistency was two parts of clay to one part of shilf – small pieces of broken slate. In the sandy and heathy districts of Dorset loam, gravel and sand were used, and heather was used in place of straw as a binding material. Chalk was considered an invaluable ingredient and where available, in Wiltshire, Dorset and the adjoining parts of Hampshire and Berkshire, was widely used. The chalk was crushed and mixed with water, mud and straw, usually in the proportion of three parts of chalk to one part of clay, though the higher the proportion of chalk the greater the strength. Road scrapings were another ingredient, and there is much evidence of their use in the nineteenth century in Dorset, Leicestershire and Oxfordshire, where they produced walls of such durability that it was almost impossible to demolish them with a pick. In Buckinghamshire, in an area south-west of Aylesbury and extending towards Long Crendon, a mixture of chalk and clay known as wychert, found some two feet below the surface of the ground, was used. When mixed with straw and water, it had much the same consistency as cob.

The methods of constructing cob walls were as varied as the consistency of cob itself, varying in differing locations. The materials were mixed, water was added and the whole was trodden into a malleable mixture by horses or oxen or, more often, by human feet. In the South-west the cob mixture was thrown onto the walls by one man and trodden down by another, known as the 'cob mason', who stood on the wall. The first layer was some 2½ feet high, and subsequent layers were about a foot high. Each layer, known as a 'raise', was left to dry for a week or so, depending on the weather, before another layer was placed in position. The excess cob, projecting beyond the face of the wall, was pared off when dry. In the North another method was used. There the wall was built in layers which varied from five to seven inches in thickness, with each layer separated by a thin layer of straw, laid across the wall with the ends of the straw pointing outwards. Each layer of cob was left to dry before any subsequent layer was placed in position. Once the building had been roofed, the projecting ends of the straw were trimmed flush with the wall. The construction of cob walls was undertaken without the aid of shuttering, and the work was based on the craftsman's eye and innate skill. Consequently these walls undulated due to the uneven paring of the surplus cob which gives many cob walls their attractive appearance. These cob walls were seldom less than two feet thick and sometimes exceeded four feet thick.

118. Trenow, Gulval, Cornwall. An eighteenth-century farmhouse built of cob. Its symmetrical façade conceals at one end what was at one time a cowshed with barn over reached from the back by stone steps.

By the very nature of the material the construction of cob walls was a laborious process, and from about 1820 in Devon, as elsewhere, shuttering began to be used. The cob was packed down between boards or hurdles which were later removed when the clay had dried. This method of construction produced a thinner wall – between about twelve and eighteen inches – which could be built faster and more accurately.

The subsequent use of shutters in the construction of cob walls in the early part of the nineteenth century may have been derived from a similar form of construction known as '*pisé*', introduced into this country from the Continent by the architect Henry Holland at the end of the eighteenth century. In this form of construction the mixture comprised gravelly or sandy earth mixed with a little clay but no water, for it was essential that the material remain dry. The mixture was placed between shutters and rammed down with a hardwood or iron heart-shaped rammer. As the wall was kept dry, the process was faster than other forms of cob construction, and a height of nine feet was sometimes reached in a single day. Despite the fact that much of the soil in England is ideally suited to this form of construction, the method never gained popularity.

The other – and technically the most advanced – method using unbaked earth was clay lump. Introduced into this country in the early part of the seventeenth century, it remained in use into the nineteenth century and was also used on occasions in this century. The method of construction was, compared with cob, a simple one. The earth was dug out, generally near the site of the building, and spread out into layers about a foot thick. The large stones, in excess of an inch diameter, were removed and the clay was watered, before short straw or grass was spread over it and trodden in to assist in binding the material together. The mixture was then pressed into wooden moulds and left to harden for a few days before being taken out and turned up on end. The 'bats', as they were known, were then placed on a platform to dry out completely, generally for a month or two. The bats were normally 18 by 9 by 6 inches, but the size varied greatly, depending on local traditions. The bats were bonded in a similar manner to brickwork, being jointed in puddle-clay mortar. The method was considerably faster than other forms of unbaked earth construction, and once the bats had been made, walls were relatively easy to construct.

Clay lump was widely used in eastern England in the construction of cottages and farm buildings, but only in Norfolk, particularly in central-southern Norfolk, was it also used in the construction of farmhouses. There are a few of seventeenth-century date, like Mary's Farm, Tacolneston, dated 1628, Church Farm, Blo' Norton, which is partly timber-framed, and Valley Farm, Bressingham. Many more, however, are from the eighteenth century, but many have been encased in brickwork, and sadly some have been demolished.

To survive it was essential that all these materials were kept dry, for once subjected to the damp they soon disintegrated. To this end all unbaked earth walls were built on a plinth foundation, usually between one and two feet high, of either local stone or later brick, and to give the wall added protection from rising damp it was also frequently tarred. The external face of the wall also required some protection from water penetration. Before any covering could be applied, it was necessary for the wall to be completely dry, and with a cob wall, over two feet thick, this would take a considerable time, possibly over a year. With clay lump, which was at least partially dried before erection, the period was greatly reduced, and with a *pisé* wall, which was used without water, the wall could be covered almost immediately. The traditional covering for these walls was limewash. The material was cheap and easy to apply with the added advantage of being porous, so enabling any rising damp in the wall to dry out. Before the widespread use of lime plaster, which today is the most common form of protection to be found on these walls, other forms of rendering using local materials – clay and where available chalk together with other admixes such as cow dung and straw – were all used.

Stone

The use of stone jointed in mortar in the construction of walls was well established in England in the Middle Ages in the construction of castles, churches and houses for the nobility. By the twelfth and thirteenth centuries it had begun to be employed in the construction of houses for lesser gentry, the earliest of these being some of the first-floor hall houses such as those at Boothby Pagnell and Little Chesterford.

These, like other surviving houses of the period, were generally of manorial status while others were of ecclesiastical origin. Despite these rather rare examples in stone, timber remained the predominate building material throughout the thirteenth and fourteenth centuries, and one rarely finds one of comparable size like Grange Farm, Haversham, Buckinghamshire, built of stone. Again they are, like those built of timber, generally of manorial status. Even in the fifteenth century, at a time when many well-constructed timber-framed houses were being erected in much of eastern England, the South-east and parts of the West Midlands, houses of stone were rare. Some, such as the one at Neadon, Manaton, Devon, still retains its first-floor hall, while others compare with the best of those in the South-east and East. Most are former manor houses, for instance Slough Farm, Stoke St Gregory, Somerset, a remarkable former small manor house of late fifteenth-century date which still retains part of its original two bay-windows. Others now farmhouses, such as Priory Farm House, Stoke-sub-Hamdon, and Rectory Farm, Stanton Drew, both in Somerset, Bury Court Farm, Donhead, Wiltshire, and Manor Farm, Ashbury, Oxfordshire, are former ecclesiastical buildings of some sort.

By the fifteenth and sixteenth centuries a number of stone-built houses began to appear, all comparable in size, if not in architectural detail, with many of the timber-framed houses being built elsewhere. Many appear to be of cruck construction, such as Lower Farm, Beer Hackett, Dorset, Bush Farm, Horton, Avon, Farley's End Farmhouse, Elmore, Gloucestershire, Rodford Hill Farm, Westerleigh, Avon, and Old Farm, Standlake, Oxfordshire, and in the main were of three or four bays with an open hall. As one can see, their distribution is widespread although restricted to southern England,

and the majority were undoubtedly former manor houses. In only one part of the country, in Devon on and around Dartmoor, are there small houses of any number. Built for the more prosperous farmers, they were generally small – the former house at Yeo, Chagford, having only one room on each floor – usually comprising a hall and inner room perhaps separated only by a timber screen. Many, such as Clannaborough, Throwleigh, Lower Tor Farm and Tor Farm, both at Widecombe-in-the-Moor, Sanders, Lettaford, and Luggs Farm, Membury, are longhouses with the byre at the lower end.

Not until the beginning of the seventeenth century did small stone houses, although generally larger than those in Devon, appear in any number in other parts of the country. Examples, although not common, can be seen throughout the limestone belt from Dorset into Lincolnshire. Isolated examples can be seen elsewhere; in Derbyshire there is Old Hall Farm, Youlgreave, dated 1630, and Vicarage Farm, Wheston, dated 1637; in West Yorkshire, Cat Hill Farm, Penistone, of 1634 date; in North Yorkshire there is Leighton Farmhouse, Healey, of 1608, West Newhouse Farm (47) of 1635 and dale Foot of 1640, both in Bishopdale, and Old Hall Farm, Thoralby, dated 1641; in Cumbria there is Townend, Troutbeck (119), built about 1626, Glencoyne, Patterdale (33), dated 1629, and Derwent Farm, Grange-in-Borrowdale (although the house is undated, the adjoining barn was built in 1677, with the house itself almost certainly pre-dating this building), all three in Cumbria, built for a new class of independent dalesmen, the statesmen. In some areas houses formerly of timber began to have their outer walls rebuilt or clad in stone. One such area was in West Yorkshire around Halifax, where the prosperous farmers-cum-clothiers began at the beginning of the seventeenth century to give their fifteenth- and sixteenth-century houses, built of timber, a cladding of stone. One of the earliest is Home Farm, Scriven, originally a timber-framed hall house with one aisle at the rear, which had its outer walls rebuilt in stone in about 1600.

From the evidence of the numerous dated examples of late sixteenth- and early seventeenth-century date, substantial houses in considerable numbers began to appear along the entire length of the limestone belt. Elsewhere, too, stone-built farmhouses began to appear in a greater number. This was true of the Yorkshire Dales, where substantial houses began to replace those earlier constructed of cruck. In Cumbria too there are many dated examples, and there are few other parts of the country with such a concentration of dated farmhouses dated between 1670 and 1710. Often in a single parish half a dozen houses with dates of this period survive. In the village of Shap, for instance, there are eight examples dated between the years 1671 and 1704. In the Fylde, Lancashire, this general rebuilding occurred

119. Townend, Troutbeck, Cumbria. This statesman house was built about 1626 by a prosperous farmer in the traditional style with a further wing and a dairy added. The house is now owned by the National Trust and is open to the public.

120. Manor Farm, Alderton, Gloucestershire. A much altered medieval timber-framed farmhouse with open hall. Largely rebuilt in stone in the seventeenth century although retaining the timber-framed cross-wing.

between 1650 and 1725.

In Durham and Northumberland, stone farmhouses of the seventeenth century are not unheard of – Newhouses, Hunderthwaite, Durham, dated 1668, and Dykehead, Corsenside, Northumberland, dated 1680 – but in general, apart from the bastle-houses, small stone houses before the eighteenth century are rare, with the majority of dated examples being from the second half of the century.

In all those areas where there was an adequate supply of local stone, this was used, and it was not until the nineteenth century, with the revolution in transport and the mass production of bricks, that the reliance on local stone declined. Brick slowly replaced it as the principal building material in all but a few isolated places which either had a plentiful supply of workable stone or were too remote.

Clearly then early small stone farmhouses occurred only where there was a plentiful supply of local stone. In general these houses did not begin to appear until the sixteenth century, and it was not until the following century that any quantity appeared in a number of areas. They probably replaced the less substantial earlier timber-framed or cruck house, and this can clearly be seen in those marginal areas which lie between the predominately stone regions and the timber ones. In Cambridgeshire, in the strip which separates the stone area around Peterborough from the timber areas further south, the early farmhouses such as Manor Farm, Brington, of mid sixteenth-century date, are of timber while Carr's Farm, Elton, Marholm Farm, Marholm, and Eye Bury Farm, Eye, are of stone and are of seventeenth-century date. Similarly on the western edge of the Cotswolds the stone ones are always of later date than those of timber. In some parts one finds farmhouses built of timber and stone; Manor Farmhouse, Frampton-on-Severn, has a ground floor of stone with the upper floor with close-set studs, and Breadstone Manor Farm, Hamfallow, is also partly stone and partly timber-framed. Sometimes an earlier timber-framed house has been rebuilt in stone, as at Manor Farm, Alderton (120), a medieval timber-framed house largely rebuilt in stone early in the seventeenth century yet still retaining the gable end of the cross-wing in timber.

BUILDING STONES

Stones used in building in England can be divided into three major groups, igneous, metamorphic and sedimentary, and within each group many geological formations are classified on their age rather than the physical properties of the rocks they yield. So within each geological classification one often has a number of rocks each differing in texture, colour, durability and workability, and it is this great variety of differing building stones that has such a profound influence on the appearance and architectural character of so many of our vernacular houses.

IGNEOUS ROCKS

Igneous rocks are formed by the solidification of molten rock called 'magma', which originated in temperatures well in excess of 600 degrees centigrade at considerable depths beneath the surface of the earth. It either reached the surface by means of volcanoes and lava flows or was emplaced within other rocks within the earth's crust and reached the surface by the subsequent erosion of the softer strata above. Of the igneous rocks only one is employed to any great extent in building in England, and that is granite, a stone of immense strength and durability. Because of its intractable nature it was difficult to cut and dress, and most vernacular buildings built of this stone are built from 'moorstone' – surface stones lying around the hills and moors of Devon, Cornwall and Cumbria. Even before the end of the Middle Ages the mason had learned how to chisel granite roughly, but it was not until the seventeenth century that the method of dressing improved and dressed quoins and jambs, sometimes formed of very large blocks, began to be incorporated, although the remainder of the building was more often than not still of moorstone. It was not until the nineteenth century that granite was quarried to any great extent, and then it was principally to supply the demands of the engineers for the construction of bridges and lighthouses rather than for the domestic house builder.

Granite is to be found in Cornwall and Devon, in Leicestershire and in Cumbria and in these areas was extensively used. Of all the counties, however, the number of granite buildings found in Cornwall far outnumber the combined total of the other three. The main areas in Cornwall are Bodmin Moor, the region around St Austell, the area encompassed by Falmouth, Helston and Camborne, and most of the Land's End peninsula to the south-west of St Ives, and in Devon it is of course on and around Dartmoor. In all these areas granite was the traditional building material for farmhouses, cottages and farm buildings, usually constructed of moorstone often incorporating large, roughly dressed stones to openings and quoins. The granite farmhouses of Dartmoor are generally older than their counterparts in Cornwall although there are a few such as Methrose, near Luxulyan, probably one of the best farmhouses in Cornwall which is undoubtedly comparable in age with any in Devon.

Because of the indestructible nature of granite several early farmsteads survive, and these older buildings are to be seen behind the present farmhouses at Clannaborough, in Throwleigh, Neadon,

121. Old whitewashed granite farmhouse at Throwleigh, Devon.

in Manaton, Yeo, in Chagford, and Cudlipptown, near Tavistock. In all these instances a more modern house, perhaps built in the seventeenth or eighteenth century, has been built nearby and the old ancestral home abandoned and put to some other use. There are others that retain much of their medieval appearance (Sanders, in Lettaford, Uppacott, in Widecombe, and Old Farmhouse, Stiniel, near Chagford) but many original farmhouses were rebuilt during the seventeenth and eighteenth centuries and represent what is often thought of as a typical moorland farmhouse, examples of which are to be found in most moorland parishes.

These later Dartmoor farmhouses of the eighteenth century are similar to the many plain gabled granite farmhouses to be found in Cornwall. These granite farmhouses rarely demonstrate the richness and elaboration shown in some of the other parts of England. In general they are well built but usually plain and unassuming, and the one outstanding local feature is the use of slate cladding to the walls. Usually this was restricted to the upper storey, but sometimes an entire face, usually the windward one, was similarly clad. This type of construction gained popularity from the late seventeenth century onwards. In Cornwall and in particular around Bodmin Moor there are a number of small two-roomed farmhouses to be found; Leaze, in St Breward, is one, built in the middle of the seventeenth century of moorstone (some of considerable size), and another is Smith's Farm, Altarnun, built about 1800. Both these and others which surround the moor clearly indicate the continuing encroachment of the moor by the peasant farmers. There are also many old, mellow granite manor houses in Cornwall which are now farmhouses, and this is especially true around Blisland, where there are such farmhouses as Helligan and Tredethy (both partly built in the seventeenth century) and to the south of the village Trewardale, a house built in 1773 and later enlarged.

Granite also occurs in Cumbria in the Lake District, mainly in and around Eskdale and from there towards Bootle. In this area granite buildings are not rare, formed of an attractive pale pink colour, while the field walls are usually grey. This stone is one of the most attractive granites, as can be seen in the farmhouses around Ennerdale Water. Like the granite houses around Dartmoor, those in the Lake District are often whitewashed. Granite is also to be found in Leicestershire, being quarried at Mountsorrel together with the closely related syenite and porphyry, both of which are to be found in the Charnwood Forest. Buildings of this stone, built of rubble with brick dressing to jambs and quoins, can be seen. A particularly good example is Home Farm, Mountsorrel, a dwelling probably built about 1700 in the middle of the village and of special interest as being a now rare example of the use of two local materials – granite and Swithland slate.

There are a number of other igneous rocks which are to be found in England which were used locally. Syenite and porphyry have already been mentioned and are to be found in Leicestershire, where with granite and slate they are collectively known as 'forest stones'. In Cornwall too there are a number, elvan, polyphant, serpentine and cataclouse occurring locally in the north and east and porphyry in the south. Of these, serpentine, a dark green and red-veined stone found on the Lizard, helps to give the area its own distinct appearance.

METAMORPHIC ROCKS

Metamorphic rocks, of which slate is the principal one used in English building, the other being marble, are rocks which have changed from their original form by the effect of either immense heat or extreme pressure over a long period, or often a combination of the two. They may have been of either igneous or sedimentary origin, but their transformation often makes it impossible to say which. It is this transformation that is such an important feature of slate, for with the layers of rock being forced together under pressure, it is of close texture, usually extremely hard, extremely durable and non-porous, and above all it can easily be split into thin slabs along its natural cleavage lines. The ease with which slate can be split and fractured is one of the disadvantages when using it in walling for it is almost impossible to square, and most pieces tend to be of irregular shape and size, usually long and thin and often wedge-shaped, requiring a considerable amount of mortar to make a satisfactory wall. Yet it is this ability to be split into relatively thin layers that has long been its greatest asset not only in roofing but in the slate areas in its use as paving, steps, window sills, copings, shelves, fencing and gravestones.

Although slate walling can be found occasionally in Leicestershire, it is in the North-west and South-west that this stone had a predominant effect. In the North-west most of the slate came from the Ordovician and was frequently a by-product in the production of roofing slabs, being the pieces cut off in the trimming. Slate-stone was the principal building stone of the Lake District and can be seen on many of the farmhouses, farm buildings and field walls in the area. In many cases, as at Fell Foot Farm, Little Langdale, slate-stone is found in combination with random lumps of volcanic rocks or cobbles. The pieces of slate were, by the very nature of the material, rather long and thin, and because of the exposed nature of many of the farmhouses a method of laying them, unique in England, was devised in order to keep out the driving rain (see page 228). In addition it became the tradition for the houses to be roughcast or rendered and then whitewashed to assist in making them weatherproof. Outbuildings, which in the Lake District, as elsewhere in Cumbria, were frequently attached to the farmhouse under one continuous roof, were left untreated. Above the windows, in place of the moulded hood-mould to be found elsewhere in the country, a continuous row of slates embedded in the wall was often employed to throw the rainwater clear of the walls. Another feature to be found on many of the early farmhouses is the tall cylindrical stone chimney stack so built because of difficulty in building square quoins with such an intractable material. Another feature, although today somewhat rare, is the use of stepped gables formed with large slate slabs, as at Glencoyne, Patterdale.

In Devon and Cornwall the slate belongs to the Devonian rock formation. In Cornwall it has made a significant contribution to the county's vernacular architecture for it covers a larger area of the county

122. Old farmhouse at Crackington Haven, near Boscastle, Cornwall. This old whitewashed slat-stone farmhouse with its large stepped chimneys is typical of those found in parts of Cornwall.

than granite. This is particularly true around Delabole where the largest slate quarry in England, some four hundred feet deep and about a third of a mile across, still produces slate. In the area there are many slate-stone farmhouses, most around Tintagel, of which Trewitton, which is reputed to be of thirteenth-century origin, Trebarwith, of Elizabethan date, and Trewinnick are the most noteworthy. The stones in Cornwall are very roughly dressed on the face but are rarely square, and all are rather long and thin, needing a good deal of mortar, with on occasions a few lumps of granite forming a patchwork of greys, fawns and brown tints. In many cases, and in particular along the coast, the old stone-slate farmhouses have been covered with successive coats of whitewash. In Devon too slate-stone was used although not so extensively as in Cornwall, where in the sixteenth and seventeenth centuries there was a preference for cob for many of the farmhouses although in the South Hams district from the eighteenth century onwards the slates, and schists, were generally used. However, the numerous quarries in the north of the county and those to the south of Dartmoor have left their mark on the landscape, producing not only many farmhouses of slate-stone but numerous miles of dry-stone field walls.

SEDIMENTARY ROCKS

By far the most important group, however, to which most of the building stones of England belong are the sedimentary rocks. It is to this group that limestone and sandstone belong, of which, it has been estimated, some 90 per cent of the stone buildings of England are built, and if flint is not included, the proportion would be even higher. Limestone consists essentially of calcium carbonate formed by chemical precipitation from sea or lake water or by the accumulation of the remains of living organisms such as shells, fossilized animal life and other forms of marine life like algae and seaweed. These deposits are further cemented together by calcium carbonate in solution. Although the majority of limestones consist basically of calcium carbonate, some contain various quantities of magnesium carbonate and are known as magnesian limestones. Sandstones are composed essentially of the durable particles of igneous rocks, quartz, felspar and mica cemented together with silica, calcium and magnesium carbonates, iron compounds or even clay. It is these materials, the matrix, which determine the stones' durability.

Both 'limestone' and 'sandstone' are very general terms, and within each group are rocks of many geological ages which differ greatly. The principal limestones used in building in this country are to be found in four geological systems: Cretaceous, of which chalk and some ragstone are the principal stones; Jurassic, to which oolitic and liassic limestones belong; Permian which comprise the magnesian limestones, and Carboniferous of which the main stones are carboniferous limestone. In addition to the four systems there is the pre-Carboniferous system to which the Devonian limestones of the South-west belong. Yet within each series the characteristics and texture of the stone vary considerably.

Chalk, the youngest of the limestones used for building, was at one time extensively used at the vernacular level. Described as the whitest of our building stones, it often contains tinges of colour, such as cream, yellowish and greeny grey and sometimes even pink, caused by either muddy impurities or other minerals. Compared with other building stones chalk is soft, and this is one of its attractions, being easy to quarry and cut into blocks; its only disadvantage is that some weathered badly and needed some form of protection. This softness makes it generally unsuitable for quoins, jambs and plinths, and here a more durable stone or even brick was introduced. Although the ease with which chalk could be cut into blocks made it possible to be coursed and even given an ashlar appearance with fine joints, as at Grange Farm, Uffington, Oxfordshire, (123), often walls of farmhouses and humbler buildings were built of chalk rubble.

123. Grange Farm, Uffington, Oxfordshire. A chalkstone eighteenth-century farmhouse with brick dressings.

Chalk is to be found mainly to the east of the limestone belt, the only area to the west of the belt being around Beer, Devon, where a shelly chalkstone was quarried and used extensively. The use of chalk in the construction of farmhouses is not extensive, its use in most areas where chalk is to be found being generally restricted to cottages and farm buildings. In Norfolk it can be found on a number of farmhouses in the north-west of that county often in conjunction with brown carstone and flint. Around Hunstanton this chalk is often red in colour.

In Cambridgeshire chalk was far more extensively used, and quarries at Eversden, Harlton, Haslingfield, Barrington, Orwell, Reach, Burwell and as far north as Isleham, on the edge of the Fens, have for centuries all yielded a good hard chalk, known as 'clunch'. Within this area it was widely used, but although it was used in Roman times and from the twelfth century in Ely Cathedral and prior to 1500 in many colleges in Cambridge, in domestic architecture it is rarely earlier than the seventeenth century – Parsonage Farm, Burwell, built about 1600, and Tunbridge Farm, Burwell – and continued in use until the nineteenth century when such farms as Hall Farm, Burwell, and Church Farm, Barrington (124), were rebuilt and extended. Chalk was once again used further south in Oxfordshire, Berkshire, Buckinghamshire, Wiltshire, Dorset, Hampshire, Sussex and Surrey, but once again its use was generally restricted to cottages and farm buildings and only occasionally for instance along the foot of the Berkshire Downs, notably around Uffington, Oxfordshire, which like Burwell, Cambridgeshire, has houses constructed of chalk dating from the seventeenth century.

Another product of the same geological system as chalk is Kentish ragstone, a very different stone, for unlike chalk, which is soft and easy to cut, Kentish rag is hard, brittle and difficult to work. The term rag or ragstone applies to any stone with a hard, coarse texture that is not in fact a freestone. Because of the scarcity of good stone in the South-east, Kentish rag was at one time widely used although not to any great extent at the vernacular level, though it was popular with Victorian architects.

Of all the sedimentary rocks, limestone from the Jurassic series is the most important and most widely used for building purposes. The main area is the limestone belt which spreads from Dorset in the south to North Yorkshire in the north, comprising oolitic limestone to the east and liassic limestone to the west. Of the two the former is of more use to the builder, yielding such stones as Portland and Bath and producing the stone from which the Cotswolds were built. Along the entire length of the limestone belt were famous quarries, Portland, Purbeck, Chilmark, Painswick, Guiting, Campden, Taynton, Weldon, Kellar, Barnack, Clipsham, Ancaster and Collyweston, and all yielding a fine-grained stone which was comparatively easy to work when first quarried, rendering it possible to be dressed and carved.

It was this capacity to be carved that rendered it possible for the refinements seen on many of the farmhouses of the Cotswolds to be undertaken. The well-moulded mullioned windows with an elaborate hood-mould above, the four-centred arches over doors, the gable coping stones, the ashlared chimney stacks crowned with generous cornices, the date stones and the abundance of ornamental finials are all characteristics of the Cotswolds. Even where the house is built of rubble, ashlared quoins, window dressings and chimneys are still universal. Similar farmhouses are to be found in the extreme north of Northamptonshire and the surrounding parts of Leicestershire and Lincolnshire. The stone here was a pale grey and possibly slightly less attractive than the honey-yellow of the Cotswolds but could be worked equally as well, and the farmhouses of this area have many of the

124. Church Farm,
Barrington,
Cambridgeshire. A
timber-framed
farmhouse of late
medieval origin
extended at one end
and rebuilt the other
end in clunch in the
nineteenth century.

125. Farmhouse at
Collyweston,
Northamptonshire.
Built of limestone and
rendered.

refinements associated with those of the Cotswolds.

Liassic limestone is a less reliable stone, often weathering badly, although it was widely used in the Midlands, Dorset and Somerset. The best of the stone is obtained at Hamdon Hill which produces the famous Ham Hill stone, which is not only one of our most durable limestones but also one of the most attractive, with the surface of this rich, golden-brown stone often covered with lichens. The stone could be readily squared and dressed and was widely used in the Montacute area of Somerset and in north-west Dorset (Strap Farm, Chiselborough, and Priory Farm House, Stoke-sub-Hamdon). Another attractive feature sometimes met with is the banding of this stone with pale grey stone from the blue lias. One excellent example is Slough Farm, Stoke St Gregory, Somerset.

Apart from Ham Hill the most attractive liassic building stone comes from the Middle Lias formation. Marlstone, as this rock is often called, is of various shades of brown induced by the presence of iron within the stone. It was used extensively in north Oxfordshire and the Northamptonshire hills, where the yellow, brown and orange stones produce a marked architectural change from the oolite areas to the south. The stones are larger and squarer than those of the oolite, and the paler colour of the mortar emphasizes the individual blocks. In those areas where the oolite and ironstone meet, the yellowy-brown ironstone is sometimes banded with the grey limestone, as at Manor Farm, Gretton, dated 1675.

A totally different stone to ironstone is blue lias, a whitish-grey stone obtainable only in relatively small pieces which are difficult to dress. It is for this reason that this stone is one of our less attractive limestones for it is seldom obtained other than in small pieces and tends therefore to be 'over-coursed'. Consequently the farmhouses built of this limestone have a rather undignified appearance with their even courses of horizontal stones with little or no decorative features and a profusion of mortar joints. However, it was widely used and can be found in Dorset, between Bridport and Lyme Regis, and further inland in Somerset around Somerton and in other isolated areas in the Somerset marshes as well as in Avon and the south-west corner of Warwickshire.

Two other limestones from the Jurassic series, coral rag and cornbrash, were also used. Coral rag is difficult to saw and was normally used as rubble lumps but it is very durable and virtually unaffected by the climate. Because of the nature of this stone the rubble was laid with plenty of mortar, giving the appearance of great strength. It can be found to the south-west of Oxford and into the adjoining part of Wiltshire as well as in Dorset to the south-west of Shaftesbury. Cornbrash on the other hand is an inferior coarse stone liable to spall and crumble, yet despite these disadvantages it was at one time extensively used in central Oxfordshire, north Buckinghamshire and along the Bedfordshire, Northamptonshire and Cambridgeshire borders. Because of the soft nature of this stone it was often rendered or roughcast.

Magnesian limestone is a fine-grained stone which, like other limestones, is comparatively soft when quarried, hardening on exposure and capable of being dressed and carved. It stretches in a narrow strip from Nottingham northwards, along the Nottinghamshire and Derbyshire border into Yorkshire, where it outcrops in a narrow band to the west of the Vale of York and as far as Ripon before widening in a triangle across County Durham to the coast between the Tees and Tyne. Although an attractive creamy white when quarried, it tended to change to a drab grey and produced white patches when exposed to the weather and could not withstand the chemicals in coal smoke which attacked the stone below its surface.

The other limestone of the North belongs to the Carboniferous series of rocks, sometimes known as 'mountain limestone', for it is generally found in the sparsely populated mountainous regions of England. One such area is the Peak District, where it is the principal building stone of the central and southern part, and it is found in most parts of the limestone plateau where this greyish-white stone lightens the whole landscape. Outside the Peak District, carboniferous limestone is to be found in Cumbria, on the west side of the Pennines across the border into North Yorkshire where it forms much of the Yorkshire Dales, as well as further north in and around Richmond and into County Durham. In Northumberland too its use was widespread, and like the stone of Cumbria, North Yorkshire and County Durham, it is a somewhat darker grey than those of the Peak District. In all these areas it is not unusual for the walls to be whitewashed.

Grey in colour, this limestone is hard, rough-textured and intractable, being completely resilient to the mason's chisel. Consequently in Derbyshire and the Yorkshire Dales much of the stone is roughly coursed rubble with quoins and surround to windows and doors often of gritstone. A walling technique frequently seen in the Dales is the use of projecting 'throughs' – long bonding stone built through the wall tying the inner and outer skins together and projecting beyond the face of the wall enabling rainwater to be thrown clear. Its use is almost universal on the farm buildings and field barns of the Dales, and it is sometimes also used on the gable walls of farmhouses.

Older than the Carboniferous are the Devonian limestones which, like the 'mountain limestone', are hard and intractable. The stone is also grey, of various shades from almost black to nearly white although

126. Rectory Farm, Castle Bytham, Lincolnshire. An attractive limestone farmhouse roofed with stone-slates.

127. Deverell's Farm, Swanbourne, Buckinghamshire, dated 1632.

sometimes they are pink. They are to be found in the South-west and in particular in South Devon in isolated pockets in the Devonian slate.

Like limestones, sandstones are classified according to their geological age. However, of the nine systems that yield sandstone for building the vast majority come from only three: Cretaceous, which yields the Upper and Lower Greensand stones and Wealden Sandstone; Triassic, from which New Red Sandstones are obtained, and Carboniferous, which supplies the Coal Measure Sandstones, the Millstone Grits, the Culm Measures and the Lower Carboniferous Sandstones.

The Greensands from the Cretaceous system vary considerably in colour, and although some in fact are greenish-yellow or grey, the majority are stained by iron oxide to produce stones of every shade from the palest yellow to the darkest brown. These stones are often referred to loosely as 'ironstones'. Many of the stones, although freestones, such as Reigate stone which could be carved and moulded, are not very durable.

Most are to be found in the South-east, a region not renowned for its building stone, and where they do occur there is strong local variation. In parts of Surrey and Kent there occurs a dark brown 'ironstone', known as carstone. Its use is generally restricted to cottages, their joints galletted with either small pieces of similar stone or else ragstone. A similar stone is to be found in Hampshire and used occasionally for farmhouses, for instance, at Goleigh Farm, Greatham, an old farmhouse probably of Elizabethan or Jacobean origin. Another of these Greensand stones is Bargate (sometimes referred to as Burgate), a greenish sandstone found in parts of Sussex – Dawes Farm, Fenhurst – and also in Surrey around Guildford – Peper Harow Farm, Peper Harow. To the Cretaceous sandstone of the South-east can be added the so-called Wealden stone, which as the name implies is to be found in and around the Weald of Sussex and Kent. This grey-fawn stone is possibly the best of the Cretaceous sandstones, being a freestone of fine grain which weathers extremely well. Consequently the stone could be dressed and ashlared as at Moat Farm, Crowhurst, and Court Farmhouse, Penhurst, both in Sussex.

Greensand can also be found in a continuous narrow band to the western side of the chalk escarpments from Hunstanton in the north to Abbotsbury in the south. In Dorset, Somerset and Wiltshire this soft grey and brown stone, rarely is it green, could be easily squared and coursed and even on occasions ashlared. In Wiltshire it was often used, together with limestone, to form the chequered pattern with flint so popular in parts of that county.

The narrow belt of this stone which crosses Oxfordshire, Bedfordshire and Cambridgeshire plays no significant part in the domestic architecture of these counties, and it is not until Norfolk, from Downham Market northwards to the coast, that the Greensand stone, known here as carstone appears again. The principal quarry was at Snettisham where a very dark brown coarse, gritty stone, which could only be obtained in relatively small pieces, was quarried. Generally its use was restricted to humbler buildings, but farmhouses constructed entirely of carstone, like Manor Farm, Snettisham, can sometimes be seen, though more often it is to be found in conjunction with brick and chalk or occasionally flint.

Greensand appears not only to the west of the chalk escarpment in Somerset but also over a large area of south Somerset and west Dorset from Chard to Lyme Regis and extending into the adjoining parts of east Devon. In these areas it was commonly employed in combination with chert and flint often as quoins and dressings. Greensand is again to be found to the western side of the Lincolnshire Wold, and this attractive buff-coloured stone can be seen to good effect on a number of farmhouses in the Teably–Spilsby area.

The New Red Sandstone comes mainly from the Triassic and to a lesser extent from the slightly older Permian systems. The stone, which was the principal one of the western side of England from Devon to Cumbria, varied greatly not only in colour, for although known as red sandstone this was not always the colour, but also in its durability. Although many quarries produced sandstone of excellent quality, there were regrettably more that produced stone that once exposed to the English weather blistered, spalled and crumbled.

Despite this disadvantage it was widely used; in eastern Devon extending northwards through Somerset the stones were of an attractive dark pinky-red which were often used but which do not weather well; it is again found in the West Midlands although rarely used for housing, and in Cheshire where it can be found in the construction of cottages, farm buildings and walls but rarely farmhouses. It was in Cumbria that it was most widely used, in the Vale of Eden, in the coastal plain around St Bees and the Solway Plain. Occasionally the larger farmhouses are rendered and whitewashed leaving the dark red quoins and window dressings unpainted. More often, however, the entire house is rendered and whitewashed, with the window and door surrounds picked out in black, browns or dark grey.

The Jurassic series is composed mostly of limestone, but there are two places in England where the characteristic features of limestone and sandstones are almost equal. One such area is in Northamptonshire around Northampton where from the base of the oolite beds a stone varying in colour from buff to a deep reddish-brown was produced. It was widely used in the villages around Northampton,

128. Hall Fam, Micklefield, West Yorkshire.

129. Swinithwaite Farm, Swinithwaite, North Yorkshire.

130. Manor Farm, Downham, Lancashire.

the best-known quarry being at Duston. It was used extensively in the area, Manor Farm, Naseby, and Park Farm House, Harlestone, being notable examples. A stone of a similar nature is to be found in North Yorkshire; here, however, it yields a yellow-grey sandstone, from which most of the farmhouses of the Yorkshire Moors and surrounding districts are built. These farmhouses are often isolated, spaced out along the length of the valley, and are almost universally of eighteenth-century date and two-storey, with a simple pantiled roof, often with a single-storey byre attached at one end. The windows of these eighteenth- and nineteenth-century farmhouses are sashes either of the vertical double-hung variety or often of the horizontal sliding sort – the so-called Yorkshire sash.

For strength and durability no sandstone can compare with those belonging to the Carboniferous system. Although found in the south-western counties, it is in the North that they are of paramount importance. The rocks from the Coal Measures, the Millstone Grit and the sandstone from the Carboniferous Limestones, known as the

Lower Carboniferous Sandstones, all have much in common. The quartz, the principal material from which all stone is formed, together with some felspar, are all cemented together with silica, a substance extremely hard and virtually indestructible, producing a stone which is hard, intractable and difficult to work but which adds much to the rugged simplicity associated with the vernacular buildings of the North. As if to match the architecture the colours also are sombre, usually brown, buff or various shades of grey, and only the Lower Carboniferous Sandstones of Northumberland produce the more pleasing yellows.

Of the three, Millstone Grit, known as gritstone, is the most important, for the sandstones from the Coal Measures are usually associated with the industrial regions of the North, whereas gritstone is more characteristic of rural areas. Millstone Grit is the principal stone of the southern Pennines and extending to the east and west of the limestone plateau in Derbyshire, northwards into Staffordshire and Cheshire, South and West Yorkshire, Lancashire and into North Yorkshire as far north as Richmond, and appears again to the west of the carboniferous limestone in North Lancashire.

This hard, coarse, uncompromising rock varies when quarried from a pale buff to a dark grey colour and only in areas of atmospheric pollution does it assume its almost black appearance. The stone when quarried was easy to cut and dress, and although the farmhouses of the North are plain in comparison with those further south, moulded mullioned windows with a hood-mould or continuous string course over, were a popular feature during the seventeenth century. These can be seen on the long row of mullioned windows, sometimes as many as nine lights long subdivided by king mullions, introduced into some of the farmhouses of West Yorkshire to light the specially constructed workrooms for the weavers. These long weavers' windows are most common in the Pennine areas south of Huddersfield but two- and three-light mullioned windows were also universal in small houses elsewhere until around 1800. Another and later feature is for the jambs to doors and window openings to be constructed of one or two relatively thin pieces of stone, which because of the nature of the stone could be readily obtained, set vertically but not bonded to the remainder of the wall. Stones of similar size formed the sill and lintel so forming a complete surround. Often, and this is true of Lancashire, this surround projected from the face of the wall. Where mullions were retained, these were of a simple square section. Another and particularly prominent feature of farmhouses of West and North Yorkshire and to a lesser extent Lancashire is the stone kneeler which serves as a visual termination of the sloping gable. They are often large, highly carved stones projecting some way beyond the face of the wall.

131. Seventeenth-century farmhouse at Gargrave, North Yorkshire.

Another feature of many of the seventeenth-century farmhouses of West Yorkshire is the elaborate carved, dated and often initialled door lintels, such as those at Lainger House, Bordley, and Springs Farm, Ingleton, dated 1717.

The Culm Measures are also of the Carboniferous period and cover much of central Devon and extending over north Cornwall to the coast. The hard, dark brownish-red shales, grits and rubble sandstones which the Culm yields were occasionally used for houses, but generally cob was preferred or sometimes a combination of the two with stone on the ground floor and cob above. In most instances these farmhouses were whitewashed.

Apart from the Cretaceous, Triassic and Carboniferous systems, several of the other systems produce sandstones which were used in buildings. From the Tertiary system comes sarsen – the youngest of all our sandstones. Found just below the surface of the ground, they are boulders of indeterminate size being firmly cemented remains of what was once a more continuous layer which has subsequently been largely eroded away. They could, like the moorstones of Devon, Cornwall and Cumbria, be picked from the surface of the ground although some were of an enormous size – the stone circle at Avebury and the larger stones at Stonehenge are all sarsens. The stone has a cold grey appearance and because of its hard nature is almost impossible to work, imparting a rather grim aspect to the buildings. This can clearly be seen at Middle Farm, Winterbourne Monkton (132), an eighteenth-century house which, like its barns and farm buildings, is built of this uncompromising stone. The sombre appearance that this stone gives was relieved at Kingstone Farmhouse, Ashbury, Oxfordshire, a house dated 1730, where the front wall is of chalk while the sides are of Sarsen.

It is at the other end of the time scale that one finds the other systems which produce some stone for building. The Old Red Sandstone rocks formed some 345 to 395 million years ago and, like the New Red Sandstone, yield rocks of many colours – pinks, purples, browns, greys of various shade as well as darker reds – often changing from block to block or even within the same block. Also like the New Red it is only moderately satisfactory for buildings, being liable to spall and crumble when exposed to the weather. Here and there, however, the stone is of excellent quality although it seldom yields a freestone and generally is quarried in rather small pieces. An important rock in parts of Wales and Scotland, in England it is to be found only in Hereford and Worcester, in south Shropshire and in Gloucestershire, west of the Severn.

The Devonian rocks, formed during the same geological period as the Old Red Sandstone, differ considerably. Most of these rocks are of slate with some limestone and also here and there some sandstone. These Devonian rocks cover much of north Devon and west Somerset including the whole of Exmoor as well as most of Devon to the south of Dartmoor and spreading over a large area of Cornwall. Where found, the sandstone from this series was an important building material to the local builder.

Even older sandstones belong to the Silurian and Ordovician series which are perhaps up to 575 million years old. Silurian stones are hard stones normally used as rubble containing particles of grey shale and are of rather sombre greys, browns and black tones. They are found only in the Lake District and were used extensively around Ulverston, Windermere and Hawkshead and spreading down to the coast to Grange-over-Sands and Ireleth. Because of the nature of this stone it is common practice to roughcast and whitewash the walls, as can be seen around Hawkshead.

132. Middle Farm,
Winterbourne
Monkton, Wiltshire.
A double-pile
eighteenth-century
house built of coursed
sarsens.

133. Hall Farm,
Hunworth, Norfolk.
A flint farmhouse
formerly dated 1699
with shaped gable.

134. Nineteenth-century flint farmhouse near Aylmerton, Norfolk.

The Ordovician series, which produces the slates of the Lake District, also produces an uncompromising building stone, often extremely dark and sombre in colour. This is in contrast to the stone from the same series to be found in Shropshire below the Wenlock Edge around Church Stretton. Here the stone is an attractive variety of buffs and browns.

FLINT, CHERT AND COBBLES

One material not previously mentioned is flint, which was, when found, used extensively. As a building material it has been known since the Early Iron Age; the Romans made extensive use of it and during the Saxon and Norman periods it was a building material of paramount importance. It was not, however, until the seventeenth century that it was generally used at the vernacular level. Flints are irregular-shaped nodules of silica and, although extremely hard and virtually indestructible, are brittle and can be easily fractured. Found in the upper layers of the chalk formation, they are when first dug practically black, often with a white 'rind' over the surface. They vary considerably in size, anything from a few inches to over twelve inches across.

Flint was the principal building stone of East Anglia and was used extensively in Norfolk in the south-west of the county around Feltwell, Methwold and Northwold and northwards towards Old Hunstanton and then eastwards along the north Norfolk coast to Happisburgh and spreading inland some ten miles or so. There is a distinct difference between the flint found in the two areas; in the west the flints were generally mined and are larger and more irregular in shape than those found in the north of the county which were generally either picked from the fields or sea-washed cobbles and pebbles from the beach. Apart from the occasional brick-built farmhouse, most farmhouses are of flint dating from the late seventeenth and eighteenth centuries although there are a few of Elizabethan date such as Green Farm, Thorpe Market, and Manor Farm, Metton, dated 1608, both with brick-stepped gables and pedimented brick windows. In the eastern counties the use of flint was not only restricted to Norfolk and can be found elsewhere along the chalk ridge in Suffolk, Cambridgeshire, Hertfordshire and Essex but to nothing like the extent that it does in Norfolk, and apart from the occasional farmhouse like Manor Farm, Horseheath, Cambridgeshire, it is almost entirely restricted to cottages and farm buildings.

In the South-east too flint was employed extensively for domestic buildings. Flint farmhouses are to be seen in Kent, on the Isle of Thanet and along the coast, in Surrey from the ridge of the North Downs northwards and in Sussex in the chalk uplands and in that flat

coastal plain between the Downs and the sea. It was also to be found in
the chalk downs in Berkshire (Pigeonhouse Farmhouse, Eastbury,
dated 1620, and Brockhampton Farm, Lambourn) and in Wiltshire.
In Hampshire it was by far the most common stone, where the flints
were often polled and laid with brick in alternate courses. Similar
farmhouses can be seen on the eastern side of Dorset, such as Manor
Farm, Blandford St Mary.

This use of flint with other materials is one of its features. In general
it was restricted to the use of brickwork at quoins, window and door
openings, eaves and verges but there are farmhouses in Norfolk – Hall
Farmhouse, Hunworth (133), dated 1699 – and Kent – Stone Farm,
Broadstairs, dated 1710 – which have elaborate brick and flint shaped
gables. The use of flint with stone and brick has already been
mentioned in Norfolk, and in some parts of the North Downs flint was
also used in conjunction with chalkstone and brick. One of the most
pleasing examples is Alderstead Farm, Merstham, which is one of the
finest vernacular farms still remaining on the Surrey Downs. It is,
however, in Dorset and Wiltshire that the best effect of the combined
use of flint and stone can be found. In Wiltshire it was frequently
employed in combination with Greensand or limestone in a
chequerboard pattern (135), the stone forming the light squares and
the flints, which were polled to expose the dark interior, the black
ones. Similar houses can be found in Dorset but here the chequerboard
pattern is less common than the use of horizontal alternating bands of
stones and flints as at East Farm, Piddlehinton, East Cruxton
Farmhouse, Maiden Newton, and Quarleston Farm, Winterborne
Stickland.

Another material similar to flint is chert, and though like flint it is
formed of silica, it differs in appearance for whereas flint is black or
dark grey beneath its rind, chert is usually brown. Unlike flint, which
is to be found in the chalk formation, chert is to be found in a variety of
rock but usually Greensand. It was extensively used around Chard,
Somerset, as a walling material combined with Greensand quoins and
also in Devon in the Colyton–Axminster area. Chert was also used in
conjunction with flint, and there are a number of farmhouses built of
these materials and Beerstone along the coastal area from Otterton
eastwards to Beer.

Similar to flint in the way they are used in buildings, but not from
the geological standpoint, are pebbles and cobbles. These are derived
from a great variety of rocks, being fragments of broken rock which
have been transported by either glacial ice or water and which have in
the process been rounded. They can therefore be found in fields or
river beds or often along the beach. The only distinction between
pebbles and cobbles is one of size – pebbles being usually less than

135. Old Glebe Farmhouse, Winterbourne Stoke, Wiltshire. A chequerboard pattern formed of flint and stone extended with flints banded with stone.

three inches in diameter and cobbles varying between three inches and a foot across.

There are two main areas where these cobbles and pebbles were used as a building material. One is in Cumbria, along the coast and in the Lake District, but here they are generally restricted to field walls, barns and a few of the humbler cottages. The boulders are often built with alternative courses of slate and the interstice filled with small stones. The other area, and by far the most important, is in North Humberside in the alluvial plain of Holderness. The cobbles known as 'boulder stones' were either collected from the boulder clay or gathered from the beach and were at one time extensively used around Spurn Head and northwards along the coast. Because of the size of these stones – often a foot long and five to six inches thick – they could produce only a rough, irregular-looking wall which required a great deal of mortar, often with broken bricks forced into the gaps.

These then are the principal rocks used in building in this country.

There are many small pockets of differing stone not mentioned and even within each group the stone varies greatly in both texture and durability, in fact stone obtained from differing parts of the same quarry can often vary. It was therefore the character of the stone when quarried that largely determined how the wall was built.

CONSTRUCTION

Walls could be built either of rubble work, which comprised blocks of stone either undressed or comparatively roughly dressed with wide joints, or of ashlar, which comprised carefully dressed blocks of stone with fine joints. Ashlar, being extremely expensive, was generally restricted to important buildings although it can be found occasionally on vernacular buildings (136), normally as a facing to the front elevation. Most vernacular buildings, however, were built in rubble work, and indeed often there was little alternative, for many quarries yielded only small stones, and so rubble walling was employed to use every piece.

Basically two types of rubble work were employed, random rubble or squared rubble, depending largely on the type of stone available. In random rubble the stones were quarry-dressed and, not being of uniform size and shape, required great care and ingenuity in arranging so that the weight was spread over a maximum area and so that no long continuous vertical joints occurred. It was necessary to bond the wall both transversely – across the width of the wall – and longitudinally – along the face of the wall. The transverse bond was obtained by the use of 'headers', stones from each side of the wall which reached beyond the centre to overlap in the middle, and 'throughs', stones which extended the full thickness of the wall. When the impermeability of the stone was unsatisfactory, throughs were not used as moisture would be conducted through them to the inner face. To overcome this the throughs were replaced either with three-quarter headers or with the throughs extending to within one inch of the internal face and the end covered with slate bedded in mortar.

The cheapest and roughest form of random rubble is uncoursed (137A). The waller selected the stones more or less at random from the heap, knocking off any inconvenient corner or projection to assist in obtaining a bond. The larger stones were laid flat and packed and wedged with small pieces of stone, called 'spalls', with the resultant spaces being filled with small stones. The stones were arranged without any attempt to form horizontal or vertical joints, and the appearance varied greatly with the differing shapes and sizes of the stones. At the quoins and jambs larger stones, roughly squared with a walling hammer, were used, bonded into the wall to increase stability

136. Manor Farm, Middlemarsh, Dorset.

and also to improve the overall appearance. The other form of random rubble is built or 'brought' to course (137B) and is similar to the above except that it was roughly levelled to form courses. Large, roughly squared stones were again used at the quoins and jambs, and the rubble was built so that it roughly coursed in with them. The height of these courses varied according to the type of stone used and was anything from 12 to 18 inches high. Walls brought to course were stronger than the uncoursed type for the long continuous vertical joints were more readily avoided, although the horizontal joints sometimes detract a little from its appearance. The life of a random rubble wall depended as much on the skill of the waller in selecting and laying the stones as it did on the weathering qualities of the stone.

The stability of rubble walling improved if the stones were first squared before use, so that they could be bonded more accurately with thinner mortar joints than was practicable with random rubble walling. This could be achieved where the stones were found in thin

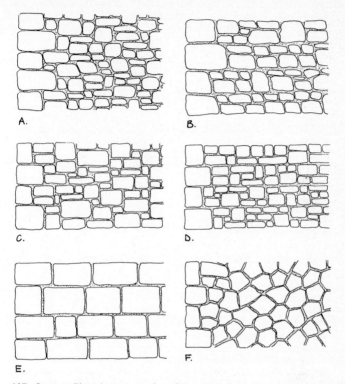

A.

B.

C.

D.

E.

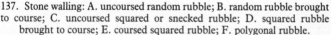

F.

137. Stone walling: A. uncoursed random rubble; B. random rubble brought to course; C. uncoursed squared or snecked rubble; D. squared rubble brought to course; E. coursed squared rubble; F. polygonal rubble.

beds or in thicker beds of laminated stone which could be readily split into smaller blocks and where comparatively little labour was required to form straight bed or side joints. This form of construction was known as squared rubble walling and as with random rubble, the type of squared rubble used depended on the ease with which the rubble could be squared, whether the stones could be matched for height without too much selection, and the skill of the mason. The simplest form employed was uncoursed squared rubble (137C), often known as square-snecked rubble, in which the stones, roughly squared, were available in various sizes and arranged on face to form several irregular patterns but without continuous horizontal courses. A pleasing effect was obtained when the wall comprised a combination of four stones – a large stone called a 'riser' or 'jumper', which was also generally a bonder, two thin stones called 'levellers' and a small stone called a 'sneck', a characteristic of this type of walling used to prevent long continuous vertical joints. Squared rubble could, like random rubble, be brought to course (137D). The stones were similar to those used for uncoursed squared rubble but were levelled up in courses of varying depth and, as with random rubble, larger stones were used at quoins and jambs. In some areas the stones could be quarried in more uniform sizes and were laid in what is known as coursed squared rubble (137E). The wall was built in courses of varying height, but the stones within any one course, unlike other rubble walling, were all of the same depth. Depending on the stone, these courses varied from 3 to 18 inches but were generally of about 9 inches and were 6 to 9 inches wide on bed. In certain areas where there was available a plentiful and convenient supply of hard stone with good weathering qualities, the face of the stones could be dressed to give a smooth finish, and they are sometimes referred to as 'rough ashlar'.

There are many varieties of walling which can be classified as rubble work but which, due to the character of the materials as well as the traditional forms of construction peculiar to any one locality, differ from both random and squared rubble walling. Perhaps the most common is what is known as polygonal rubble walling (137F), where the stone used, although strong, could be easily split but was difficult to dress. It was dressed to an irregular polygonal shape and was bedded in position to show the face joints in all directions. This type of walling is also known as Kentish rag after the limestone found in Kent and used fairly extensively for this purpose.

Another local variation can be found in Cumbria, in the Lake District, which is unique and required great skill by the wallers. The stone, which was found locally, varied in size from small pieces up to about two feet by three feet and was broken and dressed to the required size and shape by the waller as the work proceeded. Two forms of Lake District masonry, as it is known, are to be found: rough-faced random, where the stones are roughly dressed and irregular in shape, and best-faced random, which resembles square-snecked rubble, the stones being squared on face with a hammer. Rough-faced random was used for humbler work, and the blocks were tightly fitted together with the through stones forming a continuous course every two or three feet. The wallers worked in pairs, the more experienced man working on the outside and the other on the inside assisting in packing up the face stones with 'spalls'. The walls were built in three sections, the inner and outer skins with an intermediate 'hearting', and were built 'watershot', that is the stones tilted downwards towards the external face, with particular attention being given to the throughs. Both skins are nowadays partially bedded in mortar, kept back from the face some two or three inches, but were originally built dry with the hearting being dry-packed with small stones. This ensured that any water penetrating the outer skin would pass down the dry filling to the throughs below, which being watershot would carry the water to the outside. The thickness of these external walls varied from 21 to 30 inches. Like other random walling, quoins and jambs were formed of larger stones, usually limestone and often hammer dressed.

Flint is another material that because of its nature required special treatment. Flints, being easy to split, could either be 'polled' – snapped across to expose the inside – or 'knapped' – snapped across and then the split face dressed to give a face approximately four inches square. Both polled and knapped walling were generally reserved for the more pretentious buildings or for decoration and for vernacular buildings the flints were mainly undressed, built either uncoursed or, when small flints were used, roughly coursed. Because of the nature of the material a great deal of mortar was required and so the strength of the wall depended upon the type of mortar used. It was essential that the external face of each flint was completely ringed with mortar, and the excessive amount of mortar required restricted each rise to no more than a foot or two at any one time before it was to be left to dry out.

As the flints used were generally small and round, the wall always had a tendency to bulge out and, to overcome this, brick, or where available occasionally stone, was introduced to provide greater rigidity. This was achieved by two methods: first the quoins and jambs were built of brick or stone (138A), not only for greater strength but also because the nature of the material made it impracticable to build square corners, and secondly by the introduction of lacing courses (138C). These lacing courses comprised a continuous course of bricks or stones extending the full width of the wall every three to six feet. Where the flints were small and regular in size, the wall was often coursed, and to strengthen these walls brick bonders were introduced, replacing every fourth, sixth or eighth flint to give a chequered appearance (137D).

The appearance of flint can be rather drab but in some parts of Hampshire, Dorset and Wiltshire it was used in conjunction with other materials to good effect. The flints were nearly always polled to expose their dark interior and used with sandstone or limestone (138E and F) and brick to form decorative chequered patterns or horizontal courses (138B and G). The results can be quite striking.

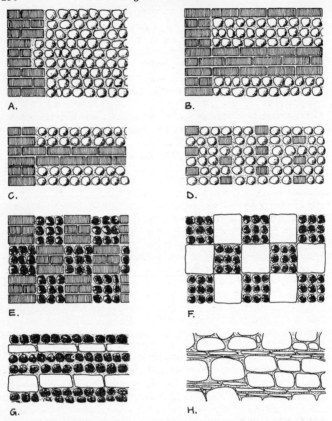

138. Flint, cobble and pebble: A. coursed sea-washed flints built with brick dressings; B. horizontal alternating bands on flint and brick; C. coursed flints with brick lacing course; D. brick and flint chequers; E. brick and polled flint chequerboard pattern; F. stone and polled flint chequerboard pattern; G. polled flints with bands of stone; H. cobble and slate built in alternate courses.

Brick

Although bricks have been used in this country since Roman times, it was not until the thirteenth century that the first English bricks were made, and it was not until the fifteenth century that their use gained popularity. Before this time bricks were referred to as 'waltyles', and it was not in fact until the fifteenth century that the word 'brick' entered the English vocabulary. The one building that perhaps did more than any other to popularize the use of brick was Hampton Court Palace, erected by Cardinal Wolsey at the beginning of the sixteenth century and later appropriated by Henry VIII.

During the sixteenth century the use of brick flourished and many grand houses, mainly on the eastern side of the country, were built. With such an impetus in the use of brick its use soon spread to the vernacular level and there are a number of farmhouses of Elizabethan or Jacobean date to be found in eastern England and the South-east. This is particularly true in those areas of East Anglia where there was a lack of good timber but where there was much admirable soil for brick making. One of the oldest is Ash Farm, Mutford, Suffolk, which is clearly of Elizabethan date with stepped gable ends and moulded and pedimented windows. Others of similar date in Suffolk are Hill Farmhouse, Weston, and Redhouse Farm, Witnesham, both with stepped gables, while in Norfolk there are Old Quaker Farm, Wramplingham, and Old Hall Farmhouse, Foulsham (140).

Brick-built farmhouses of late sixteenth- or early seventeenth-century date can also be found in the South-east, although probably less common than in East Anglia, the most notable being Brunger Farm, Tenterden, and Badsell Manor Farm, Capel, both in Kent, Hobbs Farm, Crowhurst, Sussex, and Brickhouse Farm, Eversley, and Grange Farm, Rowner, both in Hampshire.

Slowly the use of brick gained momentum for whilst the price of timber was rising, the price of bricks was falling. This increase in the popularity of the use of brick is clearly evident in the South-east and East Anglia. Many brick farmhouses are to be found in north-east Kent – Treasury Farm House, Ickham, dated 1663, Crixhall Farm, Goodnestone, Poplar Farm, Lower Goldstone, Perry Farm, Preston, and Vine Farm, Northbourne – all built in the second half of the seventeenth century. Houses of similar date can be found throughout

139. Hatchetts Farm, Nether Wallop, Hampshire. A small farmhouse built at three periods and of three materials all common in Hampshire. The furthest part is of cob, the middle part of banded brick and flint and the nearest part of brick, now all painted under a continuous thatched roof.

140. Old Hall Farm, Foulsham, Norfolk. A brick-built farmhouse with rounded and decorated chimneyshafts and stone finials. The house is inscribed with the date 1556.

the South-east: in Surrey one of the best is Fulvens Farm, Sutton, near Abinger; in Hampshire, there are Wyford Farm, Pamber End, Polhampton Farm, Overton, and Parker's Farmhouse, Basing, and in Sussex, Church Farm, Donnington, Buckholt Farm, Bexhill, Filsham Farm, Hastings, and Standard Hill Farmhouse, Ninfield.

Even more brick farmhouses, built in the second half of the seventeenth century, can be found in East Anglia and in particular in Norfolk where one can cite Pound Farm, Hevingham, dated 1675, Dakin's Farm, Aylsham, Church Farm, Foulsham, and Rookery Farm, Thurning. In Suffolk there are such houses as Manor Farm, Herringfleet, dated 1655, Grove Farm, Ufford, Stud Farm, Stratford St Andrew, and Redhouse Farmhouse, Knodishall. Cambridgeshire too has similar houses; Manor Farm, Sawtry, dated 1672, and Manor Farm, Comberton, dated 1687, are two excellent examples.

Apart from its continuing use in the South-east and eastern England during the seventeenth century, brick spread throughout all those areas either formerly dominated by timber-framed construction or where stone was not available. Brick farmhouses are not common but can be found in many areas for instance in Nottinghamshire – Top Farm, Rempstone, and Old Hall Farm, North Wheatley, dated 1673; in Warwickshire – Manor Farm, Muncetter, and in County Durham – Grange Farm, Stockton-on-Tees. Brick houses of seventeenth-century date can be found to the west of the limestone belt. The former county of Worcestershire is essentially a brick county, and there are many good brick-built farmhouses to be seen of late seventeenth-century date. Among the most notable are Mitton Farm House, Bredon, Manor Farmhouse, Longdon, Court Farm, Martin Hussingtree, and Green Farmhouse, Queenhill. Brick began to appear further north in the northern parts of Shropshire and Staffordshire and in Cheshire. Farmhouses of similar date – late seventeenth century – such as Leyland Farm, Hindley, dated 1671, Webster's Farm, Lathom, dated 1682, and Tan House Farm, Charnock Richard, dated 1695, are also to be found in Lancashire between the western edge of the Pennines and the coastal plain. In many of these areas brick had been virtually unknown prior to the seventeenth century.

By the eighteenth century the use of brick had become firmly established. It became the predominate building material in the low-lying counties of the East Midlands, and one of the features of Nottinghamshire is the number of large and lofty brick-built farmhouses to be seen in many of the villages. They are especially common in the south of the county in the villages around Rempstone – Elms Farm (141) – and Costock – Fulwell Farm. Similar farmhouses can be found further south across the border in Leicestershire and as far south as Great Dalby – Manor Farm – although to the west and south of the county they are much more modest. Three-storey houses similar to those in the East Midlands can be found in Warwickshire (142), between Over Whitacre and Astley, as well as in Shropshire – Farmcote House, Claverley – and Hereford and Worcester – Top Farm, Cleeve Prior.

The use of brick continued to flourish, ousting timber as the most popular material for walling, and soon brick began to encroach on areas that had formerly been solely stone, although the imposition of the Brick Tax in 1784 and its continuation until 1850 restricted its use in some areas. Finally in all but a few areas – the South-west, the Cotswolds and Cumbria – stone succumbed to the flood of mechanically produced cheap bricks during the nineteenth century.

Such was the social standing of brick in Elizabethan and Jacobean times that bricks were often used in conjunction with timber-framing. Brick chimneys within timber-framed farmhouses are common enough but in East Anglia, especially in north Suffolk and south Norfolk, there are many examples of its use in the construction of gable walls. In Norfolk they are of sixteenth- or early seventeenth-century date – Castell Farmhouse, Raveningham, Dairy Farm, Tacolneston, and Valley Farm, Fersfield – while in Suffolk there are Buck's Farmhouse, Cookley (143), Ash Farm, Chediston, Maypole Farmhouse, Buxhall, and Moor Farmhouse, Middleton Moor. Timber-framed houses with brick gables continued to be built throughout the seventeenth century not only in East Anglia but also in the South-east.

Early brick making was a highly localized trade; the bricks were made from any local earth, often from the site of the new building. During the winter the clay would be dug and left for the frost to break it up for use in the spring. It would then be wetted and trodden out by foot, on hay or straw strewn out on the ground to prevent sticking, until all pebbles and other foreign matter had been removed. The clay was then placed and pressed into wooden moulds and left to dry for about a month before being fired, probably for a week, in a kiln. As the clay was often dug on the site of a new building, it was necessary to build an improvised kiln, known as a 'clamp'. This comprised a large stack of dried bricks daubed on the outside with clay into which the fuel, often only brushwood, was placed. Consequently the kiln temperature was difficult to control, which resulted in the production of bricks of irregular size and shape and of differing colours. Although some attempt was made to standardize the dimensions of these early bricks – in 1590 it was legislated that bricks should be 10 by 5 by $2\frac{1}{2}$ inches – little was achieved and bricks continued to vary greatly in size. The average size of bricks at this time was about 8 by 4 by 2 inches, much smaller than those laid down.

141. Elms Farm, Rempstone, Nottinghamshire. A typical lofty brick-built farmhouse as found in many of the villages of southern Nottinghamshire.

142. Farmhouse near Astley, Warwickshire. There are many brick-built farmhouses of eighteenth-century date such as this to be found in the Midlands.

143. Buck's Farm, Cookley Street, Suffolk. A timber-framed farmhouse with brick crow-stepped gable.

During the seventeenth century small brickworks sprung up throughout the East, South-east and Midlands. The clay was still dug during the winter to be used in the 'making' time from March to October. The method of production improved at the end of the seventeenth century with the invention of a machine known as a 'pugmill'. The machine was powered by a horse, and for the first time the necessity was removed for men to tread out the earth with their bare feet. As the horse walked round and round, the clay was fed in at the top and the required amount of water added, and out of the bottom emerged the clay, free from all pebbles and impurities. When the pugging was complete, the extruded clay was loaded onto the maker's table. The ground clay was then scooped from the pile and, prior to being thrown and pressed into wooden moulds, was rolled in sand to assist in its removal. The bricks were then turned out, stacked outside in heaps between three and four feet high and placed on edge so that air could circulate around them. Each heap was then thatched or sometimes covered with tiles to protect the bricks from excessive heat or rain. This method of protecting the unburnt bricks was later replaced with long narrow sheds with open sides; the bricks were stacked on racks and placed in these sheds to dry. The bricks were left for at least two weeks before firing. The fuel was still often wood but at the beginning of the eighteenth century coal-fired kilns were introduced. These small brickworks flourished for over 150 years, producing bricks from local clay which harmonize so well with their surroundings.

In about 1850 the old method of manufacture was replaced by an improved process. The old pugmills were replaced by power-driven grinding machines, enabling clays which had hitherto been considered unsuitable to be used; the old hand method of making bricks was replaced by mechanical process, pressing the clay into metal moulds; hot-air dryers replaced the sun as a method of curing unbaked clay, and the improved kilns made it possible for them to burn continuously for the first time. The result of these improvements in manufacture was not only a considerable fall in the cost of production; it also became possible to make bricks of exactly the same size, colour and texture. Many of the small local brickworks could no longer compete, for these mass-produced bricks were transported to all parts of the country, and only a few isolated areas remained unaffected.

The most pleasing feature of English brickwork is its colour, which was determined mainly by the constitution of the clay and the materials contained within it. So where iron was present the bricks were of differing shades of red, depending on the amount of iron; lime produced the so-called 'white' bricks but which are, in fact, a dusty-looking yellow or even grey; brown bricks contain lime and a little iron. The colour was altered not only by these impurities in the clay but also by the process of firing. Changes in colour could be obtained by increasing the heat, and so those exposed to the greatest heat emerged the darkest; white bricks could be turned brown, while red bricks could be turned various shades of purple. Changes in phased in could also be obtained by different fuels. Flared h of the bricks so diaper work, were obtained by burning furze; the ends placed that they were in contact with the flames.

To obtain the maximum strength as well as giving the building a pleasing appearance, all brickwork required to be bonded. Much of the early brickwork was built with little regard to either pattern or bond, yet much of the charm of early brickwork was this haphazard use of headers and stretchers. When a bond was used, it was always English (144A) – alternate courses of headers and stretchers – and although it can be found on some farmhouses built in the seventeenth century, for instance Vine Farm, Northbourne, Kent, it had by this

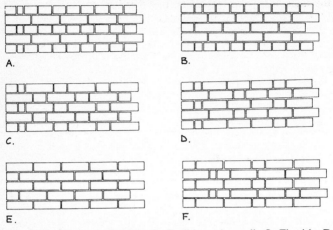

144. Brick bonds: A. English; B. English garden wall; C. Flemish; D. Flemish garden wall; E. Stretcher; F. Monk or Yorkshire.

time been generally replaced by Flemish bond (144C) – alternate headers and stretchers in the same course – which despite its name is seldom to be found in Flanders. Less strong than English bond, because of the increased number of straight joints, it is both more pleasing to the eye and more economical in its use of facing bricks. Stretcher bond (144E), so widely used today in the construction of cavity walls, consists of rows of stretchers, the only headers used being at quoins and jambs. Formerly not used in structural walls, its use was restricted to brick-nogging of timber-framed buildings or as a cladding to those constructed of timber, cob or clay-lump. There were many variations to both English and Flemish bonds. One is English garden wall bond (144B), which comprises three or five courses of stretchers to especially headers. This bond was commonly used in the North and such as Wo Lancashire where there are a number of old farmhouses odhouse Farm, Haydock, Tan House Farm, Charnock Richard, and Webster's Farm, Lathom, all built in either the late seventeenth or early eighteenth century. Houses built of this bond can also be found further south, like Church Farm, Oxton, Nottinghamshire. Another which is a variation of Flemish bond is Monk or Yorkshire bond (144F), where each course comprises two stretchers to one header. This bond is relatively rare outside northern England. Another variation is Flemish garden wall bond (144D), which incorporates three stretchers to each header in each course, with the header being placed one above the other. The use of this bond, also known as Sussex bond, is generally confined to the South-east. The use of other bonds, such as rat-trap and Dearne's, was generally confined to humble cottages or farm buildings, though they were sometimes used on farmhouses which were to be clad in tiles.

A. Pointing and jointing   B. Dentilations

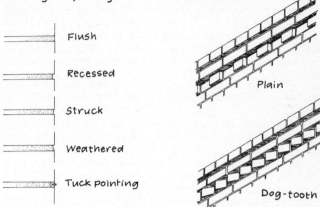

Flush

Recessed

Struck

Weathered

Tuck pointing

Plain

Dog-tooth

145. Brickwork details: pointing, jointing and dentilations.

The overall appearance of brickwork can be greatly enhanced or marred by the method of jointing and pointing (145A). With the irregular size of early bricks, wide joints were essential, resulting in a most pleasing visual effect over the face of the wall with the continual varying width of joints – seldom less than half an inch and often as much as one inch wide. In the seventeenth century, when bricks of a more regular size were produced, the overall thickness of these joints was greatly reduced. In the eighteenth century, when rubbed and cut bricks were introduced, even thinner joints were possible. Joints were generally pointed with a simple weathered or struck joint but sometimes the joints were raked out and pointed in a different-coloured mortar. In Georgian times 'tuck' pointing was introduced to give the illusion of a fine joint to ordinary brickwork. To achieve this the joints were raked out and repointed, flush to the face of the wall, with coloured mortar to match the colour of the brick. Grooves, between an eighth and a quarter of an inch wide, were subsequently scored along the joints into which were pressed flat narrow strips of chalk-lime putty, which were afterwards trimmed. As the process was laborious and expensive, its use was generally restricted to large houses.

One of the advantages of brickwork was the relatively easy way decorative effects could be achieved. Of these, surface patterns using differently coloured bricks was the most popular. This art of producing coloured patterns on the face of the wall originated in the latter part of the fifteenth century in northern France and soon spread to this country. By Tudor times this patterning had become widespread, and by the reign of Henry VIII few large buildings were erected in the southern and eastern counties without some form of patterning being incorporated. By far the most popular pattern in Tudor times was a diaper (146A) of diamonds, and as well as being found in most of the larger buildings built in the sixteenth century, it is also to be found on the occasional farmhouse of the period. In the eastern counties it can be found on the brick extension to the earlier timber-framed house at Redfant's Farm, Shalford, Essex, as well as at Redhouse Farm, Witnesham, Suffolk, and the gable wall of Castell Farm, Raveningham, Norfolk.

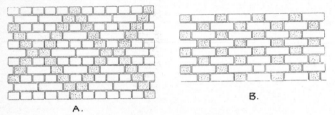

A.   B.

146. Brick patterns: A. diapered, B. chequered.

The use of the diamond pattern declined after the reign of Henry VIII and although it continued to be used especially in the East Midlands on many small houses during the eighteenth century – Old Hall Farm, East Leake, Nottinghamshire – it was not until Georgian times that it regained widespread popularity.

With the introduction of Flemish bond an all-over chequer pattern (146B) could be easily achieved and throughout the Georgian period was the most common form of polychrome patterning. Its use was not restricted, as in former times, to large houses but became, in some areas, a popular pattern on small houses and cottages. The main area where this chequer pattern is to be found is in the South-east and in particular the Weald. This chequered brickwork is rarely to be found in East Anglia and the West Midlands but can be found in the South Midlands and in particular in Buckinghamshire, where one can cite such houses as Manor Farm, Mursley. In Victorian times, although diapering continued to be used, on many buildings bricks of a different colour were introduced at quoins, jambs and arches or as band courses, two or three courses high, incorporated at first-floor level and on occasions at eaves level.

Raised decoration has also been a feature of English brickwork over the years and could be achieved in many instances without the necessity of producing special bricks. Projecting string courses, known as 'platbands', obtained by the use of two or three courses of ordinary bricks projecting from the face of the wall, were often employed at first-floor level on smaller buildings. Oversailing courses were also commonly used to break the transition from wall to roof. Often this oversailing course incorporated dentilations (145B) – a course of headers with every other one projecting – or a 'dog-tooth' pattern, obtained by laying each brick diagonally so as to produce a serrated edge. There were, however, many raised decorations, such as the imitation of classical forms, which required special bricks which could be obtained by moulding, cutting or rubbing. And so such architectural details as moulded transomes and mullions to windows, dripstones, string courses, cornices, corbels, plinths and pediments could all be achieved in brick. Much of this work was carried out with moulded bricks for, if there was a quantity of bricks of a similar section required, it was the least expensive. However, there was much elaborate work undertaken in the hundred years from 1660 to 1760 involving the careful cutting and rubbing of bricks.

It was perhaps the construction of brick chimneys that provided both the brickmaker and bricklayer with the greatest opportunity to express their craftsmanship. It was during the reign of Henry VIII that the most elaborate chimneys were built. In the larger houses the single stacks began to be grouped together. Set in a well-moulded base, these stacks could be square, hexagonal, octagonal, circular, fluted, reeded or even spiral with their surface enriched with a variety of raised designs. At the top a projecting ring, known as the necking, was usually provided; above this was the cap, which was always corbelled out. In East Anglia even in some ordinary farmhouses the elaborate chimney stack contrasts sharply with the simplicity of the rest of the building. This exuberance in chimney building was short-lived, and during the reign of Elizabeth I more restraint was exercised for although the chimneys were often of lofty and admirable proportions, moulded and carved bricks were seldom used. A great number of brick chimneys of this type were built during the sixteenth and seventeenth centuries, often within timber-framed houses of an earlier date. In the seventeenth century the chimney shafts were often set diagonally to their base.

Another area which afforded some decoration was the gable wall.

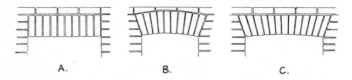

147. Brick arches: A. soldier arch; B. segmental arch; C. cambered arch with cut or rubbed bricks.

During the sixteenth century, when building in brick was flourishing, the builders were influenced by the Netherlands in their designs, and this was particularly true in regard to gables. One innovation was the crow-step gable in which the sloping projection of the wall beyond the roof level was in the form of steps, sometimes finished with specially made coping bricks. These gables belong to the sixteenth or early seventeenth century. They are to be found generally in East Anglia and the South-east. Notable examples in East Anglia are High Ash Farm, Ketteringham, Old Quaker Farm, Wramplingham, Buck's Farmhouse, Cookley, Dairy Farm, Tacolneston, Cottage Farm, North Cove, and Short's Farm, Thorndon, and in the South-east, Brunger Farm, Tenterden, Bax Farm, Tonge, and Toddington Farm, Littlehampton.

In the seventeenth century came the shaped gable and a little later the Dutch gable crowned by a pediment. These gables were of numerous designs and from the many dated examples in East Anglia and the South-east appear to have been popular in the second half of the seventeenth century (148 and 149). In the East they are to be found mainly in Norfolk – Pound Farm, Hevingham, dated 1675, College Farm, Denver, Dakin's Farm, Aylsham, Quaker Farm, Haveringland, Old Hall Farm, Bylaugh, Rookery Farm, Thurning, and perhaps the finest example Rookery Farm, Bedingham, which has no less than five shaped gables; in the north and eastern parts of Suffolk – Old Hall Farmhouse, Burgh Castle, Manor Farm, Herringfleet, dated 1655, Woodland Farm, Peasenhall, Stud Farm, Stratford St Andrew, Church Farm, Sudbourne, Packway Farm, Walpole, and the best of all Redhouse Farmhouse, Knodishall, dated 1678, which has three large Dutch gables. They are to be found elsewhere in eastern England, for instance at Manor Farm, Sawtry, Cambridgeshire, dated 1672, but they are far less common. In the South-east these shaped and Dutch gables are to be found in north-east Kent and in particular on and around the Isle of Thanet. Treasury Farm House, Ickham, dated 1663, Hode Farm, Patrixbourne, dated **1674, Crixhall Farm, Goodnestone, Poplar Farm, Lower Goldstone,**

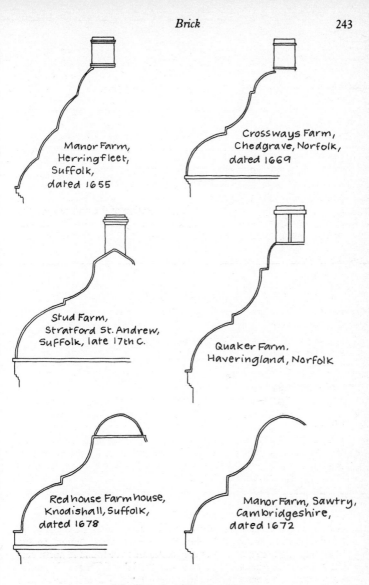

148. Shaped and Dutch gables – 1.

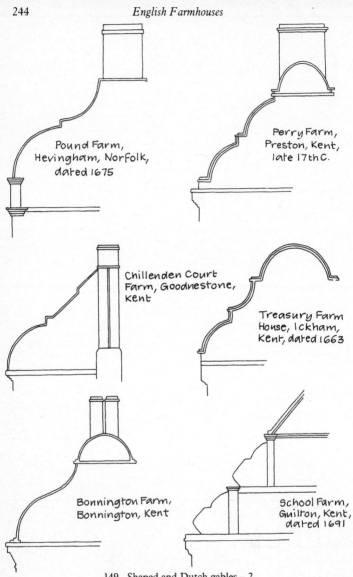

Pound Farm,
Hevingham, Norfolk,
dated 1675

Perry Farm,
Preston, Kent,
late 17th C.

Chillenden Court
Farm, Goodnestone,
Kent

Treasury Farm
House, Ickham,
Kent, dated 1663

Bonnington Farm,
Bonnington, Kent

School Farm,
Guilton, Kent,
dated 1691

149. Shaped and Dutch gables – 2.

150. Lower Farm, Bury Green, Hertfordshire. A late medieval house built of timber and extended with a brick wing dated 1665.

151. Old Farmhouse at East Claydon, Buckinghamshire with large brick-built gable chimney.

and Perry Farm, Preston, are some good examples. Unlike the stepped gable, which is rarely seen outside East Anglia and the South-east, shaped gables spread to other parts of the country. They are not as common as and are generally of a later date – late seventeenth or early eighteenth century – than most of those in the East and South-east. They are to be found mainly in those areas where brick was replacing timber as the principal building material, for instance in Hereford and Worcester – Bellend Farmhouse, Belbroughton, and Churchill Farm, Churchill – and in Cheshire – Bridge Farmhouse, Lower Kinnerton, dated 1685. The most unusual gable can be seen at Guilton, near Ash, Kent, where School Farm, dated 1691, has two Dutch *halsgevel* gables – stepped gables with volute scrolls on the steps.

While the crow-step and Dutch gables were used on larger buildings, on humbler dwellings another Dutch device, known as 'tumbling-in', was commonly employed to provide a straight gable which was both cheap and reliable. The bricks were laid diagonally, at right angles to the slope of the roof, to form a series of triangular wedges, thus producing a straight gable securely bonded to the wall. First introduced into this country in the seventeenth century, it remained popular on the eastern side of England until the end of the eighteenth century. Introduced to overcome a practical problem, it had the added advantage of providing a decorative finish to many small farmhouses and cottages.

Roof Coverings

We have seen previously that the roof is closely related to its walls. In cruck construction the roof is an intricate part of the structure as a whole, while in box-frame construction and in all mass-wall construction, whether of stone, brick or unbaked earth, it forms an independent structural unit. Obviously the main task of all these roofs was to support the roof structure and thence the roof coverings. It was these coverings, more than any other item, which determined the roof shape of our vernacular houses, for each material had its appropriate pitch and whereas thatch, plain tiles and limestone stone-slates could all incorporate hips, valleys and dormers, the slates, sandstone flags and pantiles were more appropriate to a simple roof without valleys or dormers. We will see later that generally the smaller the roofing unit, the steeper the pitch and the more intricate the roof. All these considerations have led to the use of two basic roof shapes (152), the hipped, in which all four sides slope, and the gabled, in which only the two opposite sides slope, with the other two finishing up to the gable walls which project above the eaves. Within these two main groups there are several variations.

There were in addition local traditions which also affected the roof shape. In the eastern counties gabled roofs were predominant with hipped ones being fairly rare, whereas in the South-east and in particular in Kent, Surrey and East Sussex, the situation was reversed, yet both were covered with plain tiles. The large, steeply pitched tiled roofs are a feature of Wealden houses of Kent and Sussex. Another feature widely used on the farmhouses of the South-east is the half-hipped roof which gives a part-gable at the end of the house, which often incorporated a window to light the roof space or attic. Again unlike in the East, dormers were not widely used, and most of those that exist today are almost certainly later insertions. Many of these half-hipped roofs of the South-east incorporate a small gablet at the ridge.

In some regions the use of gables to break up the roof slope is a feature, whether decorative or to provide attic accommodation. These secondary gables incorporating a window to light the upper rooms within the roof space are a feature of many farmhouses in the Cotswolds and are one of the details which give them their distinctive

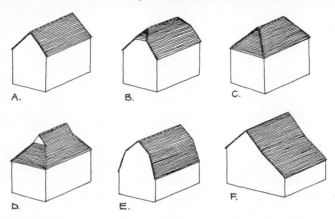

152. Roof shapes: A. gabled; B. half-hipped; C. hipped; D. gablet; E. mansard or gambrel; F. gabled with catslide extension.

character. Although far less common than in the Cotswolds, these secondary gables can be found elsewhere in the country. Examples such as Elms Farm, West Hanningfield, a farmhouse of sixteenth-century date remodelled in the seventeenth century, and a farmhouse at Manwood Green, Hatfield Broad Oak, can be found in Essex. In both these cases, unlike those in the Cotswolds, these were decorative features for they did not incorporate any windows. In some instances these secondary gables were added to an older house when the floor was inserted into the open hall, adding to the existing gables of the cross-wing, as at Fitzjohn's Farm, Great Waltham, Essex, These secondary gables can also be found in the West Midlands, where Moat Farm, Dormston, which has three gables to the front and one at each end, and Middle Beanhall Farm, Bradley, are two examples.

Some farmhouses have both a gabled and a hipped end, and this is particularly true of some of the smaller farmhouses of the South-east, particularly in the Weald. A similar type of roof was common on some of the smaller farmhouses built in Cornwall in the middle of the seventeenth century with hipped ends at the service end whilst being gabled at the other with the hipped service end usually pointing windward. Leaze, St Breward, is one such example.

THATCH
The old word 'thack' originally meant any kind of roof-covering, and as the materials employed in early days were invariably straw, heather,

153. Thatched farmhouse at Tidpit, Hampshire.

reed or other vegetable products the word 'thatch' has these days acquired its more limited connotation. Reed, straw and heather are the three principal materials used for thatching and of these reed is the best, for although the initial expense is more, it will last longer than any other – at least sixty and in some cases as long as one hundred years. It is laid in such a way that only the sharp butt-ends of the stalks are exposed, so shedding the rainwater from tip to tip on its way down the roof. However, over much of the country straw was the principal roof-thatching material; wheat, rye and to a lesser extent oats and barley were all used. Of these rye-straw was the best, for it was the longest and strongest, but the most commonly employed was and still is wheat. Known as 'long-straw', it has its own distinctive appearance, for the straw is applied lengthwise, giving a rather gentle, moulded appearance. Another form of thatch using wheat is 'wheat-reed', which botanically has no connection with true reed but which owes its name to the method of laying which is similar to true reed in that only the ends are exposed. In the moor and heathland regions where no corn was grown, heather was a useful alternative. It was cut in the autumn when in bloom and laid out to dry with its roots uppermost; to obtain a smooth finish it was cut with shears. Sedge was another material at one time used and is still in demand to form ridges. Other materials formerly used were flax, ferns, rushes and even broom.

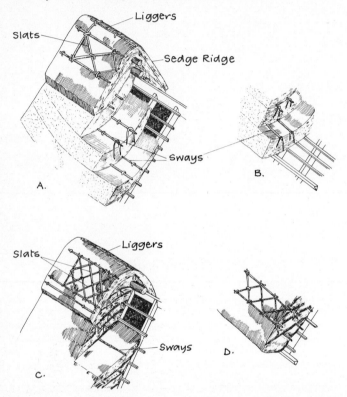

154. Roof coverings – 1. Thatch: A. detail of ridge in Norfolk reed; B. detail at eaves in Norfolk reed; C. detail of ridge in straw; D. detail at eaves in straw.

There were four methods of applying thatch: sewing the thatch to the rafters, pinning it down by a system of rods, working the thatch in layers of turfs or securing it by a series of weighted ropes passing over the surface. All these methods were used either individually or in a combination of two or more. Today the second is most commonly employed, the thatch being held down by horizontal rods, called 'sways', secured with 'spars'. The sways and spars, which were always of hazel, are these days being replaced with ones of mild steel. In modern roofs the thatch base is fixed to battens, but formerly a base – made of wattle or woven straw – was generally provided into which the hazel spars could be driven. Decorative effects can be obtained to the surface of the thatch by the use of hazel 'liggers' pegged to the ridge, eaves and gables. At the eaves and ridge they are generally arranged in two parallel lines with smaller rods, called 'slats' forming a lattice pattern between them. In addition many roofs, and in particular ones thatched with reed, are given a cap, the lower edges decorated with scallops and zigzags.

155. East Codford Farm, Codford, Wiltshire. A thatched farmhouse of eighteenth-century date.

Once the use of thatch was widespread in England even in those areas which today have none. In the eighteenth and early nineteenth century in such unlikely places as Lancashire, the Lake District and the Dales and Moors of North Yorkshire, slates and sandstone flags were only used by those who could afford them, with thatch being the most common roofing material. Today it is estimated that fifty thousand thatched buildings still survive, and of these a great number are cottages of one kind or another. There are, however, a number of thatched farmhouses still to be seen in eastern England, particularly in Suffolk, which according to one report has more thatched buildings than any other. Among the finest in the eastern counties are Low Farm, Elsworth, Cambridgeshire, Poplars Farm, Brettenham, Bridge Farm, Clopton, Oak Farm, Worlingworth and Whiting's Farm, Great Finborough, all in Suffolk, and in Norfolk, Dairy Farm, Tacolneston. In Essex and Hertfordshire thatched farmhouses are rare, as they are in the South-east where there was always a plentiful supply of good roofing tiles, and it is not until one reaches West Sussex and Hampshire that more are to be found.

The other major area where thatched farmhouses are to be found is in the South-west, and in particular in Dorset and in Devon where the widespread use of cob made it the most appropriate roof covering. One can cite numerous examples, among them Townsend, Stockland, where the medieval wattle to support the thatch still survives, Brown's Farm, Woodbury, Pitt Farm, Ottery St Mary, and Cadditon Farm, North Tawton. More unusual is the high concentration of thatched farmhouses on and around Dartmoor, Lower Tor Farm, Widecombe-in-the-Moor, and Collihole Farm, Chagford, are two good examples. Thatched farmhouses still survive elsewhere; Wiltshire has several as have Gloucestershire and Oxfordshire, as well as the West Midlands.

STONE-SLATES AND FLAGS

Both limestone and sandstone could, if they were suitably split, produce stone-slates, an unfortunate term for geologically they have nothing to do with slate. Of the two, limestone was perhaps the best, for it could be split into thinner slates to produce a lighter roof; even so the weight was considerable – a roof weighing almost a ton per square (a hundred square feet). They were rarely flat, almost always having a slight camber, so a steep pitch, usually between forty-five and fifty-five degrees, was required, producing a roof of considerable weight. Yet because they could be split easily and cut into relatively small slates, intricate-shaped roofs incorporating laced (156D) or swept valleys (156E), hips and dormers could all be achieved.

In contrast to limestone slates sandstone flags are thick, heavy roofing slabs which can be four feet wide and three inches thick and so heavy that two men can hardly lift them. They were rarely laid to a pitch in excess of thirty degrees, and their size made them suitable for only the simplest of roofs, with valleys and dormers only rarely incorporated.

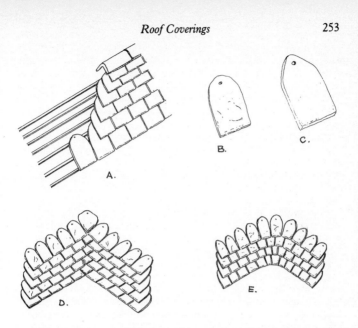

156. Roof coverings – 2. Stone-slates and flags: A. isometric view showing stone-slates in random width in diminishing courses; B. stone-slate; C. stone flag; D. stone-slates in laced valley; E. stone-slates in swept valley.

Limestone and sandstone slates were laid in a similar manner; each slate was fixed with an oak peg hooked over a batten which was in turn pegged or later nailed to the rafters. In both cases diminishing courses – the largest at the eaves and the smallest at the ridge – were used, but with limestone slates the graduations were less marked. The underside of the slates were either bedded in moss or other vegetable matter or later torched to prevent draughts and the penetration of rain or snow.

The best of these limestone roofs can be found in the Cotswolds, where steeply pitched golden-brown, honey-yellow stone-slated roofs, encrusted with moss and lichen, give a charm to many farmhouses. Because the tiles are relatively small, secondary gables, hipped dormers and swept valleys are a common feature and so provide roofs of various designs, each with their distinctive character. Further north, in the north-east corner of Northamptonshire, stone-slates comparable with those of the Cotswolds were quarried at Collyweston. Not perhaps so pleasing in appearance, being larger and more regular in both colour and texture than those of the Cotswolds, they had a great advantage in that they could be split thinner, so weighing about half of those of the Cotswolds. Collyweston stone-slate roofs can be seen on many of the older farmhouse roofs in the area spreading into the adjoining parts of Leicestershire, Cambridgeshire, Lincolnshire and Bedfordshire. Although the stone-slates of the Cotswolds and Collyweston produce the finest of the limestone roofs, many others are to be found all along the limestone belt from Dorset to Yorkshire. In contrast to most limestone stone-slates, which are relatively thin and small in size, those from Purbeck stone are very heavy and thick, producing a roof of considerable charm. Because of their weight the timbers supporting them tend to sag, leaving gaps under the large slabs which are then generally pointed in mortar to make the roof watertight.

Sandstone flags were much more widely distributed than limestone slates, and although aesthetically less pleasing than limestone they are, none the less, an equally appropriate roofing material for the somewhat austere farmhouses of northern England as well as for the timber-framed farmhouses of the Welsh border counties and the South-east. Their use was generally restricted to the highland zone but in much of Sussex and Surrey, south of the North Downs, and also to a lesser extent in the adjoining part of Kent, roofs of Horsham stone are fairly common on many of the older farmhouses. Laid at a steeper pitch than the flag roofs of the highland zone, they add a distinctive character to many of the older timber-framed farmhouses in the area such as Bell's Farm, Slaugham, Chennell's Brook Farm, Horsham, and Copsale Farm, Copsale, all in Sussex, and in Surrey, Brewerstreet Farmhouse, Bletchingley, and Aldhurst Farm and Misbrooks Farm, both in Capel.

In the highland zone these sandstone flags are from a variety of rock formations. In Hereford and Worcester they are from the Old Red Sandstone, in the Welsh border counties from the Ordovician and Silurian rocks, and from the Coal Measures and Millstone Grit in the North. From Derbyshire northwards, in the Peak District, on both sides of the Pennines, in the Yorkshire Dales, in Cumbria and in parts of Lancashire, these flags were for centuries the traditional roofing material and although many of these roofs have now been replaced with tiles and Welsh slates, many still survive, their rugged broad surface and sombre colours – usually dark brown or dark grey – blending happily not only with the comparatively simple rugged buildings of the North but also with the harsh moorland landscape in which they are to be seen.

SLATES

Most of the slate found in this country today is Welsh slate, a blue-grey

157. Idehurst Farm, near Wisborough, Sussex with Horsham slate roof.

slate which can be split into thin slabs of uniform thickness and size producing a roof which is smooth and precise and also uninteresting. Most of these roofs are products of the nineteenth century for with the improvement in transport during that century it was used in many parts of the country both on new buildings and as a replacement of old roof coverings, particularly thatch. Its advantage over other roofing materials was that, because it could be split into thin slabs, it produced a light roof – a roof of Welsh slates weighed only one-fifth that of one roofed in limestone or sandstone slates. In addition it would be laid at a very low pitch, seldom exceeding thirty degrees and sometimes as low as twenty-two degrees, producing therefore a considerable saving on the cost of the roof construction.

English slate, although restricted in its use, is altogether more attractive. It is found only in the South-west, in Leicestershire and in Cumbria. Unlike the Welsh slates which were always laid in regular courses, all these English slates were graded, with the largest at the eaves to the smallest at the ridge, which in the Lake District can vary from twenty-four to as little as six inches. This feature alone gives the roof a distinctive character which a Welsh-slate roof can never achieve.

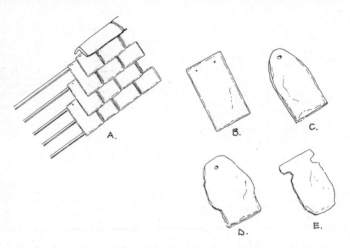

158. Roof coverings – 3. Slates: A. isometric view of slating; B. square slate with two nail-holes; C. rough slate found in the Lake District; D. 'rag slate' found in the South-west; E. 'wrestler' slate used in the Lake District to alleviate the use of stone ridge.

In Cornwall it was almost the universal roofing material up to the nineteenth century. Some old farmhouses (Methrose, near Luxulyan, and Trebarwith, Tintagel) covered with these heavy slates produce widely dipping and uneven roofs which are one of the unforgettable sights of Cornwall. Slate was also common in the South Hams of Devon; elsewhere in Devon there were several quarries which produced a good-quality slate. However, by the middle of the nineteenth century most of the quarries closed and slates from Cornwall, which were of a better quality, were used. The slates in the South-west are often referred to as 'peggies', a name derived from the method of hanging them on oak pegs over battens. These are small in comparison with the large, thick and rough 'rag slates' (158D) which were preferred in some parts, particularly in North Cornwall and North-west Devon. These slates were trimmed only on the parts that were exposed, the ragged edge being concealed beneath the slate above. A feature of some farmhouses in the exposed parts of Cornwall, particularly along the coast, is the application of a coat of cement slurry

159. Blea Tarn House, Cumbria. An isolated slate-roofed farmstead built on the edge of the moor.

over the slates to make the roof watertight against the Atlantic gales.

Whereas in the South-west the slates are dark grey, in Cumbria they are of a variety of colours – greys, greens and blues – and of numerous shades. They vary greatly too in texture, some being very rough while others are comparatively smooth. The slates are to be found on many farmhouses in the Lake District being laid to a shallow pitch between thirty and thirty-five degrees. The only other place in England where slate was quarried was at Swithland in the Charnwood Forest. Local slates were widely used in the area, prior to being replaced in the nineteenth century by Welsh slates, and add charm to many modest red-brick farmhouses which but for their roofs would be undistinguished.

PLAIN TILES

The manufacture of clay plain tiles (160) for use as a roof covering followed much the same development as brick making for they were generally made at brickworks, often fired within the same kiln. The

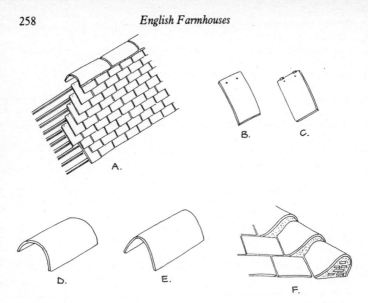

160. Roof coverings – 4. Plain tiles: A. isometric view showing tiles with each tile overlapping two others; B. peg tile with holes for oak pegs; C. later plain tile with nibs on underside for hanging over battens and with nail holes to secure each tile every third or fourth course; D. half-round ridge tile; E. saddle-back ridge tile; F. detail of bonnet tile hip.

size of these tiles was standardized in 1477 as 10½ × 6¼ inches, and this was reaffirmed again in 1725. Yet their size often varied. Plain tiles are double-lap tiles in which each tile overlaps two others forming a double thickness of tile over the entire roof, leaving only about four inches of each tile exposed. They are laid in regular courses – each tile not overlapping the neighbouring tile in the same course – and fixed to battens by means of small wooden pegs driven through two holes in the tiles and hooked over the batten. These are known as 'peg' tiles. Later in the nineteenth century nibs were cast on the back of each tile to hook over the batten, and in addition at every fifth course, or in exposed positions every third course, the tiles were nailed. The tiles were usually laid to a pitch of forty-five degrees or more and, like other roof coverings, before the use of bitumen roof felt, were generally torched. Hips and valleys, including laced and swept, were not difficult to form with the aid of special tiles, and so quite intricate roof shapes could be obtained.

Early tiles were hand-made with an exaggerated camber in both their length and breadth, and this, coupled with the slight variation on both size and shape, gives an aesthetic appearance with its shades of light and shadow that few Victorian or modern roofs of machine-made plain tiles can match. These undulations may not always be due entirely to the irregularity in the tiles but also to the sagging of battens and rafters or the settlement of the walls. Some of the best and earliest tiles are to be seen on the farmhouses of the South-east and eastern England particularly in Kent and parts of Sussex and Essex where they replaced thatch long ago.

As with bricks, the colour of clay tiles depends upon the clays used. Reds, of various shades, predominate, with the red and terracotta tiles of Kent perhaps being the most pleasing. In Cambridgeshire, the Gault produces tiles of a dull yellow, while around Elsworth and Eltisley and in the neighbouring part of Suffolk roofs of variegated colours – yellows, browns, pinks, greys and reds – arranged in a haphazard fashion can be seen. In east Staffordshire and the adjoining parts of Derbyshire the tiles are of an unusual dark purply colour, with a slightly shiny surface, and are a distinctive feature of many of the farmhouses in this area, contrasting in many cases with the pale limestone walls.

PANTILES

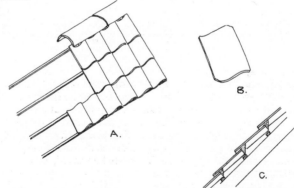

161. Roof coverings – 5. Pantiles: A. isometric view showing widely spaced battens; B. detail of pantile; C. detail of roofing showing torching.

Although similar to the plain tile in material and manufacture, the 'S'-shaped pantiles (161) differed from them in size (13½ × 9½ × ½ inches), shape and appearance, making them more suitable for simple gabled roofs, for both hips and valleys were difficult to form and dormers awkward to incorporate. They were single-lap tiles, each tile lapping the one underneath, but in addition the S-shape of the tile made it possible for each tile to form a sideways lap with the adjacent tile and could be laid at a low pitch, thirty-five degrees or even slightly less if the tiles were torched. Using a single-lap tile, a pantile roof was light, requiring a light structure, and this coupled with the low pitch produced an economical roof. First imported from Holland in the seventeenth century, pantiles soon became popular in eastern England, and in the early part of the eighteenth century the supply was supplemented by the first English-made pantiles.

Pantiles are to be found generally in the coastal areas on the eastern side of England from Essex northwards to Northumberland and spreading westwards in Cambridgeshire, Hertfordshire, Nottinghamshire and Leicestershire. In Essex and central-southern Suffolk their use was almost entirely restricted to the roofs of cottages and farm buildings, and it was not until they moved further north in Suffolk and along the coast that they gained popularity for farmhouses. However, by the time one reaches Norfolk and in particular north Norfolk one finds most buildings – farmhouses, cottages and farm buildings – roofed in this material. In Humberside, Lincolnshire, South and North Yorkshire, Durham and Northumberland too, it is almost universally used. The colour of these pantiles varies in East Anglia; they are generally of a reddish-orange, although in Cambridgeshire they are often a dull yellow or of variegated colours, but further north they are a strong red getting darker the further north one travels until they become a bright red. A feature occasionally met with in Norfolk and Suffolk are black glazed pantiles, their gleaming black surfaces, such as those at Church Farm, Southerton, and Cottage Farm, North Cove, both in Suffolk, reflecting the light of the vast East Anglian skies. Apart from eastern England, the only place in England where pantiles occurred was in Avon and Somerset, where Bridgwater was one of the principal areas of production. These pantiles, which are generally laid to a steeper pitch than those in the East, are brown or a subdued red and are an attractive feature of many farmhouses and cottages, contrasting well with the grey stones from the Lias.

Architectural Details
and Features

Until now the structural elements of the farmhouse have been largely discussed but there are, however, many details and features both externally and internally which add considerably to the overall character of many old farmhouses.

SMOKE BAYS, FIREHOODS, CHIMNEYS AND FIREPLACES

It was not until the second half of the sixteenth century that chimneys constructed of brick began to be introduced into the farmhouses of the South-east and eastern England, and it was not until well into the following century that it became common practice. As open-hall houses with open hearths had in these areas been generally abandoned by the end of the fifteenth century to be replaced with houses of two storeys throughout, it became necessary during the period of transition from open hearths to brick chimneys to introduce other methods of channelling the smoke from the ground floor to the roof. This was achieved by the use of timber and plastered structures.

From the evidence so far collected it seems that the method generally adopted in timber-framed houses was to introduce smoke bays which comprised a bay some four or five feet in length which ran the full height of the house. The hearth was located in the centre of this bay and was plastered from first floor to ridge level. In many cases these were housed in the former open hall, for when the floors were inserted, the hearth would extend over only one bay with the second bay being turned into a smoke bay. Most of these conversions seem to be from about 1500, and it was not long before this improvement was adopted for new houses built with two storeys throughout. Smoke bays continued to be in general use for at least another hundred years and it seems that, despite the increased production of cheap bricks that accelerated the introduction of brick chimneys, some at least continued in use until about 1700. There is now much evidence of the widespread use of smoke bays in timber-framed buildings not only in South-east and eastern England where many are to be seen but also in the West Midlands.

An alternative to the smoke bay was the smoke hood, a chimney made of timber with a wattle-and-daub infilling and usually plastered internally to protect the timbers. The structure itself, which tapered to an outlet in the roof, was built against a timber-framed partition usually with two return walls and was supported at the front by the mantel beam above the fireplace. Such were the fire-resistant properties of these structures that several still survive and in a few cases have remained in use until recent years. The smoke hood was probably first introduced at the end of the fifteenth century when it was often inserted into the open hall, usually prior to the insertion of the first floor, and probably continued to be built in many of the smaller houses until the beginning of the eighteenth century.

A variation of the smoke hood was the firehood, a feature widely used in the North. The open hearth was rarely employed even in the earliest timber-framed open halls to be found in the North and instead, built against a stone reredos at the lower end of the hall, there was a timber and plastered firehood. In later houses in the North the adoption of the firehood became universal, and it was the equivalent of the brick chimney in the South. The firehood was built against a stone wall and supported at each end by stone return walls. In later years, especially in the stone-bearing parts of Cumbria and Yorkshire, the hearth beneath the hood increased considerably in size, extending in some parts of Cumbria to almost the complete width of the hall and from a quarter to a third of the length of the hall. The firehood was built against a stone wall, usually the wall backing onto the cross-passage or the gable, and was supported at the front by a stout timber beam which spanned from the external wall to a short screen wall, known as the 'heck', which sheltered the hearth from the entrance. In the external wall was a fire window which lit the hearth. Such was the size of these hearths that during the winter months benches and chairs would be drawn up and placed beneath the hood and around the fire. Today few of the timber and plastered firehoods survive, nearly all being replaced by stone-built chimneys.

As previously stated, brick chimneys and fireplaces began to appear in the second half of the sixteenth century not only in new timber-framed houses but also in many of the medieval former open-hall houses. The process of modernizing these open halls was carried out over a considerable period, the majority being undertaken in the sixteenth century, and it was not until the following century that the conversion was complete. Obviously in most of these later examples these new brick stacks replaced earlier smoke bays or smoke hoods. There is much evidence that these stacks were often built within a former smoke bay. One of the last farmhouses to have a brick chimney inserted is at Chodd's Farm, Handcross, Sussex, which is dated 1693.

Chimneys of brick were undoubtedly the most common in much of the lowland zone but in the stone-bearing areas of the country stone was generally used, although in some districts brick was still preferred for it was less affected by heat. The decorative brick chimneys of Tudor times have previously been described and are more common in the East than elsewhere. This is true of the South-east where they are squarer, decorated perhaps with recessed vertical bands and oversailing courses at the top. Later brick stacks, not only in eastern England and the South-east but elsewhere, became much smaller, decorated only with oversailing courses. Because the quality of building stone differed considerably from region to region, the design of stone chimneys varied greatly. The finest are undoubtedly those of the limestone belt from the Cotswolds northwards into Lincolnshire, where because of the quality of the stone the stack could be capped with finely ashlared stone and delicately moulded cornices. In most areas rubble stone was used which was often less suitable. In many of the older farmhouses of the Lake District – Fell Foot Farm, Little Langdale, and Glencoyne Farm, Patterdale – the chimneys terminated in round, slightly tapered stacks, so built because of the difficulty in forming corners out of the slatey stone of the area. Similar stacks are also to be found in the South-west, in northern Devon – Town Farm, Countisbury – and in Somerset where a similar slatey building stone occurs.

The width of early fireplaces provided in the average farmhouse was often from eight to twelve feet, while in the chambers above they were probably only three feet wide. They also varied in appearance depending on their position and use. Those in the kitchen were generally spanned by a large oak beam probably only decorated with a stop chamfer although there are examples, especially the earlier ones, which have a flat four-centred arch with a carved pattern in the spandrels. Elsewhere in the house they were often constructed of either brick or stone with a four-centred arch over. Within the hearth the log fire was supported on iron dogs to improve the draught, and at the rear of the fire a cast-iron fireback was provided to reflect the heat of the fire and also to protect the rear of the fireplace from excessive heat.

To one side or to the back of the hearth in the kitchen an oven for bread making was often constructed. This was a domed structure two feet or so in diameter internally, provided with an opening but no flue. The interior of the oven was heated by burning wood, furze or bracken, and when hot the ash was raked out, the bread inserted and the opening sealed. In the South-west, the Cotswolds and the West Midlands where the stacks were usually provided on an outside wall, these ovens were generally placed at the rear of the fireplace protruding from the wall and housed under a pyramidal or lean-to roof. In the flue itself above the fire, irons were often built in to enable bacon and hams to be cured in the smoke from the log fire. In Devon a smoking chamber was sometimes provided to cure the bacon and ham. This comprised a chamber to the side of the flue with an opening at low level and a corbelled flue at the top leading back to the main flue.

Later fireplace openings were reduced in width, and towards the end of the seventeenth and eighteenth centuries these openings were lined with a chimney-piece of stone or more usually in smaller houses of timber. The shouldered architrave was a common feature and continued so during the first part of the Georgian period when the surround merged with consoles under a cornice. Later a keystone or tablet was introduced above the surround to break up the entablature. The mantel shelf as we know it today was not yet a feature. These fireplaces still retained the open hearth of either brick or stone but the iron dogs were replaced by a basket grate. These grates were open containers usually constructed of iron bars and were designed to burn sea coal as well as logs.

With the gradual introduction of coal as a fuel instead of wood, there came a need for smaller grates and hearths and consequently smaller flues and chimney stacks. In the second half of the eighteenth century the open hearth began to be abandoned, with the basket grate being replaced by a fixed grate generally with bowed bars to the front. In bedrooms and smaller living-rooms the hob grate in which the fire was enclosed and which was designed to fit between the returns of the fireplace was generally preferred. These hob grates were generally constructed with a cast-iron front with wrought-iron bars with relief decoration on the side panels. A popular design was a double semi-circular front, the so-called duck's nest grate. The fireplace surround was retained, often of timber, but of more classical design than previously, with more refined and delicate mouldings. The shouldered architrave with a carved frieze often with a central plaque was one popular pattern. As these fixed grates were designed to fit into the fireplace, the opening had to be reduced. This was achieved by bricking in the opening and facing it in stone, usually marble. Later this stone was replaced with glazed tiles. Towards the end of the eighteenth century and the beginning of the nineteenth century many of the large open-hearth fireplaces of the preceding centuries were reduced in size to accommodate the new type of coal-burning grates. In the kitchen too, changes appeared from the end of the eighteenth century; the new cast-iron cooking range began to replace the pot crane, pot hangers and other cooking aids which had for almost four hundred years been in common use in the farmhouse kitchen.

DOORWAYS AND DOORS

The two features of the medieval doorway were the frameless door – all doors were hung directly to the jambs whether of stone or timber – and the overall shape of the opening. In the fourteenth and early part of the fifteenth century doorways were constructed of a simple two-centred equilateral arch (162A and B), those in timber being formed by two solid pieces shaped to form the arch and door jambs all in one, while the doorway in stone had a simple moulded jamb.

The two-centred arch in stone is rare at the vernacular level, for few vernacular stone houses survive before 1600, by which time this arch form had long been abandoned. They do survive, however, in a few farmhouses which were undoubtedly of manorial status when first built. At Grange Farm, Haversham, Buckinghamshire, a house built in the late fourteenth century, there is a good example with a continuous moulded jamb. Further examples are at Manor Farm, Little Chesterford, Essex, which has two doorways between the earlier stone block and the later aisled hall.

In timber, two-centred arches are far more common. At Ringer's Farm, Terling, Essex, a fourteenth-century house, the entrance to the screens-passage has a two-centred arch with quatrefoil spandrels, and although the door is not original, it has an original iron escutcheon plate with four pierced quatrefoils. The screens-passage at Middle Farm, Harwell, Oxfordshire, contains four two-centred arches of about 1350 date, two into the service wing and one at each end of the passage. Another example can be found at Hawkenbury Farm, Staplehurst, Kent.

Towards the end of the fifteenth century the four-centred arch appeared (162E and F), developing into the depressed pointed arch which became popular in the late Tudor and Jacobean times, particularly in timber-framed buildings, where a false timber arch usually with sunk spandrels was let into the head of the frame. Examples of this doorway in both timber and stone can be found in many parts of the country, particularly in the South-east, eastern England and the limestone belt.

Less common is the ogee-arch (162C) which dates from the fourteenth century (Swanstone Court, Dilwyn, and Wellbrook Manor, Peterchurch, both in Hereford and Worcester) until the sixteenth century (Hines Farm, Stonham Earl, Suffolk). Shouldered-arches (162D) are typical of the late fifteenth and early sixteenth centuries. They are to be found in many parts of the country, particularly in the South-west around Dartmoor. Old Farmhouse, Higher Stiniel, and Old Farmhouse, Higher Sigford, each contain such doorways. By the seventeenth century the plain square frame was widely used, occasionally on better-class work with some sort of moulding.

In the stone-bearing region of the Pennines and elsewhere in parts of the North the decorated lintel to the main entrance was the main

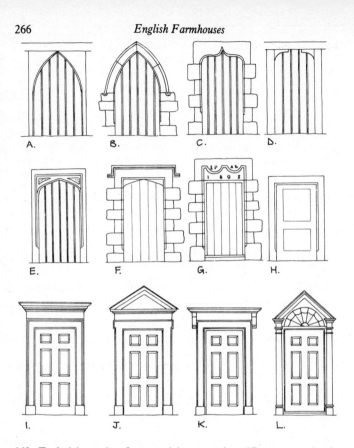

162. Typical doors, door frames and doorcases: A. and B. two-centred arch – fourteenth-early fifteenth century; C. ogee arch – late fourteenth-sixteenth century; D. shouldered arch – late fifteenth-early sixteenth century; E. and F. four-centred arch – late fifteenth-seventeenth century; G. square with decorative lintel – late seventeenth-early eighteenth century; H. square frame – late seventeenth-early eighteenth century; I.–L. typical eighteenth-century doorcases and panelled doors.

characteristic of the late seventeenth century, extending in some areas into the eighteenth century (162G). No two lintels were the same but all were moulded on the face and incorporated both the initials of the owner and the date of construction. During the eighteenth century the main entrance doorway became the focal-point of the front elevation. It was moved into the centre to conform with symmetrical Renaissance planning, and the great deal of attention it received bears testimony to the importance attached to it by many people.

Often the doorway was flanked by pilasters supporting a frieze or cornice above. In some instances this cornice projected to form a hood which could be either curved or flat supported by large carved brackets known as 'consoles' (162K). Indicative of the late seventeenth and early eighteenth centuries is the use of the pilaster on pedestals and the shell hood which can occasionally be found in farmhouses like Rectory Farm, Kemerton, Hereford and Worcester. Also of early eighteenth-century date is the use of the pediment both triangular and segmental (162J and K). In the second half of the century broken pediments often with a fanlight over the door gained popularity, the fanlight later becoming a highly ornamental feature. Also a feature of the late eighteenth century and early nineteenth century was the fluted pilaster with the entablature over resting directly on the abaci of the caps of the pilasters. Although many Renaissance features can be found on some of the larger farmhouses, they are more common on many town and village houses of the period, for the doorcases and doors to most ordinary farmhouses remained unassuming in character.

The earliest entrance doors were ledged ones, the simplest consisting of vertical boards secured at the back by horizontal battens or ledges and, when the door was wide, with additional diagonal braces to prevent the door from sagging. A stronger and more elaborate form was one in which the inner face was constructed of a continuous series of horizontal battens. The boards were either butt jointed, half lapped or occasionally tongued and grooved at each joint and fixed to the batten by either wooden pegs or nail studs with the gap between the boards covered with a moulded cover strip.

These early doors, although still to be found on many churches, are rarely to be found on domestic buildings. One outstanding example is the main door to Middle Farm, Harwell, which retains not only its original fourteenth-century ledged and studded door but also its original hinges.

Towards the end of the sixteenth century there appeared another type of battened door, the so-called 'creased' door which had vertical mouldings so designed to create a shadow. The door comprised three vertical boards, the two outer ones wider than the central one, with the outer ones splayed, moulded and rebated to fit over the twice-splayed central one. In the earlier examples framing was applied to the face of the door. Two doors of this type still survive at Doe's Farmhouse, Toothill, Essex, one of lighter construction, probably an interior door, and the one of heavier construction being formerly an exterior door.

The creased door remained a feature of many farmhouses during the seventeenth century, but towards the end and particularly in the following century with the improved techniques in joinery, the battened door, in whichever form, had generally been replaced, particularly for the front entrance door, by the panelled door with raised and fielded panels and bolection moulds. However, in many farmhouses the old battened door was still used on the rear or kitchen doors and other doors of little significance. A form of battened door which remained popular on many farmhouse kitchen doors was the heck-door, a door divided horizontally into two parts, enabling the upper part to be opened to admit light and air while the lower part remained closed.

Internal doors followed much the same development as external doors. They were generally of lighter construction, those of battened construction seldom having the moulded cover strip found on external doors while the panelled doors were often plain with no moulding around the panel. Like the external battened door, by the eighteenth century the internal battened door was used only in doorways of little significance although the use of panelled doors was in many smaller farmhouses restricted to the parlour.

As previously mentioned, medieval doors had no frame and were hung directly to the opening either on 'harr-hinges' or on wrought-iron 'strap and hook hinges'. Harr-hinges were a simple arrangement in which the vertical board on the hanging side of the door was increased in thickness – the harr-tree, the ends extending beyond the door at top and bottom and shaped to form dowels which fitted and rotated in holes in the lintel and sill. Strap and hook hinges were largely restricted to important buildings during the medieval period but because of the width and weight of many batten doors they continued to be used throughout the Tudor and Stuart period. In many cases the strap fitted around both sides of the door, and the end of the external face of the strap was frequently shaped, usually in the fleur-de-lis, and the hook also known as the 'ride' was fixed directly to the stone or timber jamb. It would not have been until the sixteenth century that in the South-east iron strap hinges and the familiar 'cockshead' hinges began to be used in smaller houses, the harr-hinge probably continuing to be used, especially in the North and West, until cheaper iron became more readily available in the eighteenth century. Towards the end of the seventeenth century, when the lighter panelled doors became fashionable, doors were hung on H-hinges or L-hinges fixed to the face of the frame and door.

Like hinges, metal door furniture was usually restricted to larger buildings. Handles normally comprised a ring with a spindle passing through the centre of a decorative iron cover plate and operating a latch on the inner face of the door. Heavy iron bolts were also provided to external doors, together with the 'stock-lock' – a lock within a wooden case. However, in most farmhouses, all door fittings, with the exception of hinges, would have continued to be made of wood until the eighteenth century, and even then the iron fitments would be restricted to doors of important rooms. Wooden latches, precursors of the later iron thumb latch, were a common feature. They could be worked from the outside by a string tied to the latch and passing through a hole in the door or by a wooden peg attached to the latch and passing through a slot to the outside. These latches were made secure by the insertion of a peg or the like into the staple, thus preventing the latch being raised. Wooden bars placed across the inside of the door and wooden bolts were also common features to enable the door to be secured from the inside.

WINDOWS

Early windows were unglazed even in superior houses and they remained so in all but the largest houses until the end of the sixteenth century when for the first time glass became more widespread, but even then in many small farmhouses, particularly those in the North and West, it was probably the following century before it was universally used. Oiled paper, oiled cloth and the horn of cattle, as well as lattices of wood, wickerwork and reeds, were all employed as a substitute for glass. Consequently, prior to the use of glass, windows, being a source of draught, were generally kept to a minimum. From the evidence of the two reconstructed farmhouses – Winkhurst and Pendean – at the Weald and Downland Open Air Museum, at Singleton, West Sussex, windows were generally situated away from the prevailing winds. In most cases these early unglazed windows were fitted with some form of battened wooden shutters to afford some protection from the elements and to provide some security. Hinged shutters, fitted either externally or internally, were frequently used on larger houses especially on the large windows to the open hall but it seems that horizontal sliding shutters, fitted internally, were most commonly provided in smaller houses, obviating the necessity of expensive iron hinges. At Green Tye Farmhouse, Green Tye, Hertfordshire, there survives an original timber shutter to a five-light wooden window. At other places remains of these shutters can still be found on occasions; at Blue Gates Farm, Great Bromley, Essex, as at many other farmhouses, there survive the shutter grooves to several of the windows. However, in most cases, as the whole complex was easily removed, little evidence remains apart from the nail holes by which the grooved runners were fixed to the framing. In the reconstructed

Bayleaf Farmhouse at the Weald and Downland Open Air Museum, three differing forms of shutters were used including an unusual form in which the shutter slides vertically up and down in vertical grooves. These vertical sliding shutters occur in the solar wing of the house, which seems to have been added at a later date.

In Tudor times windows of the larger houses had some form of tracery, often of Gothic design, in their heads. Later, with the increased use of glass, the pierced tracery was replaced by a small depressed arch which was usually plain except for a hollow chamfer. On occasions the spandrels were sunk or pierced and cusped. These windows still survive in some farmhouses; Selby's Farm, Hildenborough, Kent, has an example with a window with a cinquefoil head.

However, in most timber-framed farmhouses the window would have been square-headed and was usually situated at high level either beneath the first-floor bressummer or at eaves level. Unglazed windows were divided by plain square mullions set diagonally about six inches or slightly wider apart, with each light usually sub-divided vertically by a slender intermediate bar (163A and B). These early unglazed windows with the mullions set diagonally can still be found in many timber-framed farmhouses although in nearly all cases they have been blocked in. Notable examples are Cross Farm, Betchton, Cheshire, Great Barwick Farm, Hertfordshire, and Dales Farm, Barton, Cambridgeshire, which has two mullioned windows each of four lights, one with the square mullions set diagonally and unglazed and the other one with ovolo-moulded mullions with intermediate vertical bars. They can perhaps be best seen at the three reconstructed farmhouses at the Weald and Downland Open Air Museum.

When glass was introduced, the mullions were no longer placed diagonally, being rectangular in shape, and were generally set wider apart than before. Although the mullions on occasions remained square in section, they were often moulded. At first the mullions and jambs were splayed; later they were hollow-chamfered, although this had been widely used in many of the unglazed traced windows of the fifteenth century. Early in the seventeenth century the hollow-chamfered mullion was replaced almost universally by the simple ovolo-moulded one which, because of the side fillets, enabled easier fixing of the glazing. Stone mullioned windows followed much the same transition; generally one can say that hollow-chamfered mullions were superseded by ovolo-moulded ones by the second quarter of the seventeenth century. These mullioned windows, whether in timber or stone, were seldom of any great height, the characteristic feature being long, horizontal runs of narrow-mullioned lights ranging from, in timber, between two and eight lights and, in stone, from between two

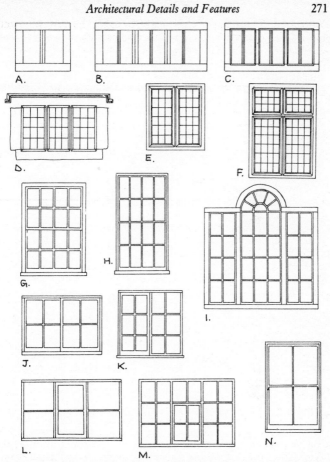

163. Typical window types: A. medieval two-light timber window; B. medieval three-light timber window; C. late sixteenth-century timber window rebated for glazing; D. seventeenth-century three-light stone-mullioned window; E. seventeenth-century two-light timber-mullioned window; F. late seventeenth-century cross window; G. late seventeenth-early eighteenth-century sash window; H. late eighteenth-century double hung sash window; I. Venetian window; J. Yorkshire sliding sash window; K. eighteenth-century casement window; L. nineteenth-century casement window; M. casement window common in Suffolk; N. Victorian sliding sash window with horns to the upper sash and large panes of glass.

to sixteen lights, although these long ranges were usually sub-divided into three or four lights by king-mullions. Above these stone windows there was usually provided a moulded hood-mould or drip-stone to carry the rain-water running down the face of the wall away from the window. This was superseded by a continuous string course although throughout the seventeenth century a compromise was frequently struck whereby two or more windows shared a single hood-mould.

164.　Pendean Farmhouse. A late sixteenth-century farmhouse formerly built near Midhurst and rebuilt at the Weald and Downland Open Air Museum, Singleton, West Sussex, clearly showing the unglazed mullioned windows.

Because of the manufacturing process of early glass – the glass was blown in cylinders or muffs which, when split along their length, gradually opened up and flattened as they cooled – the panes or 'quarries' were by necessity small. In order therefore to make a window of reasonable size, these panes were set in lead cames which in turn were joined together to form a lattice known as a 'leaded light'. Because of the expense the panes were diamond-shaped, thus allowing even the smallest pieces to be used at the edges. Later, in the middle of the seventeenth century, when glass manufacture became more widespread and a little cheaper, square panes were preferred. When fixed, these leaded lights were stiffened by horizontal saddle bars set inside the glazing and housed into the mullions and jambs, the leaded lights being secured to them with lead tapes or later with wire. Opening lights which were kept to a minimum were formed of wrought-iron casements and comprised little more than an iron frame with saddle bars fixed to it onto which the leaded light could be fixed in the usual way. The casement was then hung on hinges and provided with a stay and fastener. These were widely used in many of the farmhouses in the seventeenth century, and many of them still survive, often complete with their original fasteners.

Only in the open hall would the window be over one light high for here the window was tall, sub-divided by a transom. These windows would have at first been unglazed, as at Bayleaf Farmhouse, with separate shutters to the upper and lower lights. The shutters would be either of the hinged type which could be fixed externally or internally or of the sliding variety and fixed internally. It was also normal to place these large windows on opposite sides of the hall so those on the windward side could be closed. Later these windows would have been glazed but few now survive for they would have had to be removed or altered when the floor was later inserted into the open hall. One good example is at Corner Farm, Langley, Kent, where the intruding floor has been removed and the full height, four-plus-four-light windows with a transom, has been restored.

Full-height bay windows, usually square-cornered, were also used in the open halls of the larger farmhouses and built off a brick base. Brewerstreet Farmhouse, Bletchingley, Surrey, is an excellent example of this type of window. At Old Bell Farm, Harrietsham, Kent, the bay window has cant returns and although it is now glazed only on the ground floor, the projection continues the full height of the former open hall and was probably at one time fully glazed. Often these bay windows were of the oriel form which was a feature of many Wealden-type houses in Kent and Sussex. However, they seem to be a vulnerable feature; many were undoubtedly altered when the upper floor was inserted into the open hall, and as a result survivals are now not too numerous. Yet they clearly indicate the high level of these houses when they possessed bay windows which were obviously intended to be glazed from the start at a time when many other farmhouses were being built with unglazed windows. Bay and oriel windows are commonly found on jettied buildings often situated beneath the jetty, the underside of the oversailing forming the top of the window. Old Harrow Farm, Egerton, Kent, a continuous jettied house, has oriel windows on brackets above and bay windows on a brick plinth below.

In the latter half of the seventeenth century the long, horizontal

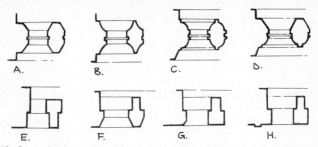

165. Stone jambs and mullions: A. splayed – fifteenth-late seventeenth century; B. hollow chamfered or cavetto – sixteenth-seventeenth century; C. ovolo – late sixteenth-late seventeenth; D. ovolo/splayed – early seventeenth century; E. square-cut – late seventeenth–early nineteenth century; F. square-splayed – eighteenth century; G. square-splayed adapted for inside glazing – eighteenth-early nineteenth century; H. as G. but with architrave to surround – early eighteenth-late nineteenth century.

ranges of mullioned windows began to give way in the larger houses to taller windows. They were divided horizontally by a transom and could be, although at the vernacular level this was rare, up to six lights wide. They were often only two lights wide divided by a single mullion and were often divided horizontally by a transom so placed that the light above the transom was smaller than that below, so forming a 'cross' (163F). The two-light mullioned window is a feature of many farmhouses built in the late seventeenth and earlier eighteenth centuries in the stone-bearing regions of England. The windows were still glazed with leaded lights with iron casements although the rectangular panes had become universal and were more suited to these taller windows. However, in the eighteenth century with the improved quality of glass and the influx of imported softwood, glazing bars of wood, being cheaper and more rigid than lead cames, came into general use.

Towards the end of the seventeenth century the vertical sliding sash window made of softwood was first introduced, each sash divided into small panes by glazing bars which were often rectangular in section and heavy in appearance (163G). At first the upper sashes were fixed, only the lower ones sliding in grooves and held open by means of a wedge or hook. It was not, in fact, until the end of the eighteenth century that the now familiar double-hung counterbalanced sash replaced this older system. Venetian windows – a window with three lights, the central one arched and wider than the other two – also became a feature of many stone and brick-built farmhouses in the eighteenth century (163I). Circular windows too can also be seen on many farmhouses and were a typical feature in about 1675 (Filsham Farm, Hastings, East Sussex, dated 1683).

A cheap alternative to the vertical sliding sash was the horizontal sliding sash or so-called 'Yorkshire' sliding sash (163J), in which one light was fixed and the other sliding. It was first introduced at the beginning of the eighteenth century (Moss Farm, Moss, near Doncaster, dated 1705) and became extremely popular in many small farmhouses and cottages throughout the country for it was particularly suited to houses with low ceilings.

The panes to all these windows remained small, for although the cylinder glass had been replaced by crown glass, the size obtainable still remained small. The glass was blown too, not into muffs but by the use of a glass-blower's pontil into a disc some three to four feet in diameter, called a 'table'. The disc was always thicker towards the centre, culminating in the 'bull's eye' in the middle where the glass was attached to the pontil. The bull's eye was normally discarded in all but the poorest buildings. With the general improvement in the glass the glazing bars were reduced in size and moulded and by the beginning of the nineteenth century were often no wider than half an inch (163H). It was in about 1840 that good-quality sheet glass was first manufactured, and so for the first time large panes could be used. It led almost immediately to the omission or reduction in the number of glazing bars; sashes with one large centre pane with a border of narrower panes, and sashes divided into two panes with a central glazing bar, are typical of the Victorian period (163N). Because of the increased weight of this heavy glass it was necessary to strengthen the sash, and one of the features of this period is the introduction of the moulded horn to the stiles of the upper sash, strengthening the tenons of the meeting rails which now carried the complete weight of the glass.

In many timber-framed farmhouses built before the end of the seventeenth century sash windows replaced the earlier mullioned windows, and in many cases they would have been the first glazed windows these farmhouses received. It was a comparatively easy process to cut a new opening in the studwork and to block in the existing windows, and it is not uncommon to see these earlier blocked windows alongside later sash ones. This can clearly be seen at Lower Dairy Farm, Little Horkesley, where each floor has a pair of original mullioned windows of three or four lights, now blocked, alongside later sash windows. In East Anglia these old mullioned windows were often plastered over, and in recent years these have been rediscovered beneath the plaster, many almost intact. There are many notable examples to be found in eastern England and in the South-east. There are a few old timber-framed farmhouses which still retain the original glazed mullioned windows such as Lane Farmhouse, Feckenham, Hereford and Worcester.

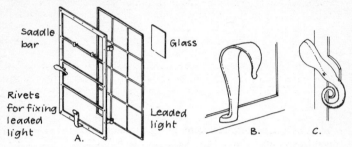

166. Wrought-iron casements: A. typical detail; B. tulip-leaf design pull; C. pigs-tail turnbuckle.

Sash windows were not universally adopted. From about 1800 and particularly after 1833 casement windows reappeared although now made from cast iron instead of wrought iron. They were cheap to manufacture and soon widely used. In many parts of the highland zone where stone mullioned windows were common, these cast-iron windows divided into small panes with opening casements were preferred, and in fact in many of the farmhouses with narrow lights between the stone mullions they were the only practicable solution when replacing many earlier wrought-iron ones. Throughout the country timber casements were also used, from the eighteenth century onwards, in many of the smaller farmhouses where the low ceilings made the tall vertical sliding sash impracticable. There are also local variations; in Suffolk the windows are often divided into small panes with only the central and lower panes formed into a casement (163M), while in Cumbria, particularly in the Lake District, the window was divided into two, the top half pivoting with the bottom half fixed.

To overcome this difficulty of low ceilings some farmhouses have vertical sliding sashes with the sashes of unequal height, the upper one being smaller than the lower one. This alters the overall proportion of the window from a vertical one to a horizontal one. In some cases this horizontal window shape, which is perhaps more suited to many of the long, low farmhouses, is obtained by the use of narrow false sashes to either side of the main sliding sash.

PORCHES

Porches of either timber, stone or brick are a feature of many farmhouses throughout England, their original purpose being to reduce draughts through the main entrance doorway and so increase the general comfort of those using the hall. At the vernacular level they came into favour towards the end of the sixteenth century and were at first nearly always of two storeys or more. There are, however, some single-storey porches of similar or early date, such as the medieval porch at Middle Farm, Harwell, Oxfordshire, but the majority are of the seventeenth and eighteenth century.

Timber-framed porches of sixteenth- and seventeenth-century date, although not common, are not by any means rare. Occasionally one finds a single-storey porch but the majority are of two storeys or more in height and often jettied as at Jenkin's Farm, Wormingford, Essex (167), Nether Hall Farmhouse, Cavendish, Suffolk, and Puddleford Farmhouse, Eastham, Hereford and Worcester. Some porches have open balustraded sides, as at Valley Farm, Stowmarket, and Holly Farm, Bramfield, both in Suffolk, Hope Farm, Edvin Loach, and Parsonage Farm, Much Cowarne, both in Hereford and Worcester, while Woundale Farm, Claverley (168), Shropshire, has a delightful porch with not only open balustraded sides on the ground floor but fully balustraded sides and front to the first floor. Perhaps the most unusual is the three-storeyed porch at Dairy Farm, Tacolneston, Norfolk (169), in which the first and second storeys are set back from the one below, each with its own gable.

The single-storeyed stone porch protecting the entrance is a common feature of many of the farmhouses in the mountainous and moorland districts of the highland zone. Most are of gabled construction containing a stone bench to either side and are often additions to the house. On and around Dartmoor one finds many farmhouses with a simple lean-to porch as at Sanders, Lettaford, and Jordon, Ponsworthy, but it is the more prestigious two-storeyed porch, which began to appear towards the end of the seventeenth century, that is the principal feature of many of the larger farmhouses. On and around Dartmoor these porches are of granite, and nearly all are dated and initialled – Lake, Poundgate, dated 1661, Lower Tor, Widecombe, dated 1707, and Hole, Chagford, added to the existing house in 1668 – but such was the social standing of these porches that outside Dartmoor they were of timber-framed construction – a technique unique in rural Devon. Similar porches constructed of timber and clad in slates can be found in the Lake District. Outside the harsher areas of the highland zone and in particular the limestone belt two- or three-storeyed stone porches are fairly common and are nearly all seventeenth century.

Brick-built porches of Elizabethan or Jacobean date are to be found in many parts of eastern England particularly in parts of Norfolk

167. Jenkin's Farm, Wormingford, Essex. A timber-framed farmhouse built in 1583.

where, due to the lack of good building timber, brick was introduced earlier than most areas. Most, such as Hall Farm, Colkirk, are of two storeys but Old Hall Farmhouse, Burlingham St Edmund, has a fine three-storey red-brick porch with polygonal angle shafts and rounded

168. Woundale House Farm, Woundale, Claverley, Shropshire with a delightful porch with open sides on the ground and first floor.

169. Dairy
Farmhouse,
Tacolneston, Norfolk.

170. Fell Foot Farm, Little Langdale, Cumbria.

brick finials, while North Farmhouse, Hoveton, has a four-storeyed porch with a stepped gable. Seventeenth-century porches with shaped or Dutch gables are more common, two good examples being Church Farm, Carleton Forehoe, Norfolk, and Redhouse Farmhouse, Knodishall, Suffolk. Early brick porches can also be found in Kent, among the earliest being one at Brunger Farm, Tenterden.

Although the single-storey porch protected the entrance, those of two or more storeys provided additional accommodation, although there are some, such as Woundale Farm, which were open on the first floor. At Lower Marsh Farm, Dunster, Somerset, a fifteenth-century house, the two-storeyed porch contains a chapel on the upper storey.

Occasionally one finds a porch which contains stairs to the floors above, enabling access to the upper rooms without entering the house. Examples can be seen at Tomson Farm, Winterborne Tomson, Dorset, where the stone newel staircase leads directly to the two rooms occupying the entire upper floor, and Tardebigge Farm, Stoke Prior, Hereford and Worcester, which has a two-storeyed porch with stairs leading directly to the attic.

FLOORS

The ground floor in most farmhouses prior to the end of the sixteenth century would have been little more than compacted earth, perhaps treated with ox-blood and ashes which hardened sufficiently to prevent dusting and wear and which could also be polished. In most cases the earth for these floors was dug and raked to a fine tilth, and water was added until it was the consistency of mortar. It was then spread in position and when the surplus water dried and the earth began to harden, it was compacted by treading and ramming with a heavy wooden rammer until a hard true surface was achieved. Other materials were also added to help the earth bind together, of which horse dung was perhaps the most popular admix. Where lime and gypsum were available, these too were used.

The use of these solid floors continued in some areas into the nineteenth century but generally in most of the larger farmhouses they began to be replaced with floors of a more substantial nature by the seventeenth century. In those areas where brick production was gaining popularity, bricks of similar size to those in wall construction began to be used, laid either directly onto the earth or onto a bed of sand. In eastern England and in particular Suffolk clay tiles, known as 'pammetts', again laid directly onto the earth, were commonly employed. Where stone was readily available, stone flags were used. However, in districts where there was little brick manufacture or where the stones were unsuitable for use as paving, earth floors and floors made with lime and gypsum remained in constant use.

These solid floors no matter of what material were cold and damp for they relied almost solely on the impervious nature of the floor for rarely was any form of damp-proof membrane introduced. It was not until the eighteenth century that the boarded ground floor on joists began to be introduced into the average farmhouse, and even then it was almost entirely restricted to the parlour, the hall-cum-kitchen and service rooms still retaining the old solid floors. In many farmhouses these boarded hollow floors, which undoubtedly provided a warmer and more comfortable floor, did not appear until well into the eighteenth or nineteenth century.

The upper floors in the early farmhouses were in nearly all cases of

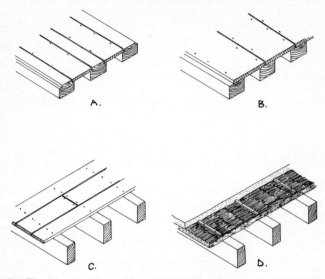

171. Flooring: A. joist and boarded; B. close-boarded with boards fixed parallel to joists; C. close-boarded with boards fixed across joists; D. plaster on layer of reed or straw.

boarded construction, being regarded as superior to other types of flooring. In the days of closely placed joists the boards ran parallel to them, being either fitted into rebates, with the joists forming part of the floor (171A), or more commonly laid over them (171B). Later, when the joists were set wider apart, the floor boards were fixed across and not parallel to them in order to distribute the weight (171C). This type of flooring enabled, for the first time, boards of varying widths to be used and in some buildings the width of these boards varied between one and three feet, as at Manor Farm, Little Chesterford, Essex. Few, if any, boards would span the whole room, and the carpenter's main aim was to fill in the area and produce a sound floor with the boards available. Oak, as always, was the carpenter's first choice for flooring, but in the sixteenth century elm competed with it and in the eighteenth century softwood replaced it.

Not all upper floors were boarded and where lime and gypsum were available, a well-tempered plaster was often used in place of boards (171D). In the East Midlands – Lincolnshire, Nottinghamshire and the adjacent part of Leicestershire and Derbyshire – and further west in the Cotswolds, from the sixteenth to the nineteenth century this form of flooring was in common use for every class of house from the manor house to the smallest cottage. Generally a layer of reed or straw was placed over the floor joists and secured by a batten but sometimes either sawn timber laths or wattle were fixed across or between the joists. Onto this base was spread a layer of plaster two or three inches thick, trowelled smooth and allowed to dry slowly to prevent cracking. When lime and gypsum were not available, for instance in Lincolnshire, earth, mixed with horse dung and ashes, was sometimes used.

CEILINGS

The joists and beams of the upper floors were left exposed and the floor upon them, whether of timber or plaster, constituted the ceiling of the room below. In the medieval farmhouses with the open hall, the only upper floor would be over the parlour and perhaps over the service room as well. In these rooms the beams would be rarely moulded. In fact the rude square joists of the parlour ceiling in particular are a common feature of many medieval houses. It was not until the sixteenth century in some of the more pretentious farmhouses that the exposed joists and beams became richly moulded and in some cases carved. In the main, however, from the sixteenth century onwards the decoration was generally restricted in the average farmhouse to a chamfer or ovolo mould to the edge of the timber. These decorations were usually stopped near the end of the timber with a variety of designs. Even so, in many small farmhouses only the principal timbers would receive any form of decoration, the joists between remaining plain.

As previously stated, the flooring upon the joists and beams formed the ceiling of the room below. When boards were used, these were at first left exposed and the ceiling completed by the whitewashing of the underside. The fashion of plastering between the joists first occurred in the sixteenth century. In some districts a layer of reed or straw was placed over the joists and secured in position by the floor boards to provide a base for the plaster. In other areas straw or reed was secured to the underside of the boards by short strips of timber lath fixed between the joists and the plaster applied to this. Later the reed and straw were replaced with timber laths fixed directly to the underside of the boards as a key for the plaster.

The ceilings of exposed beams with plaster between remained and still remain in many farmhouses but from the end of the seventeenth century onwards there came an increasing desire in both new and old houses for the ceiling to be 'underdrawn' in plaster. In many of the older houses the deeper main beams remained exposed. Laths were generally but not universally used as a backing for the plaster for in parts of South Yorkshire and the East Midlands they were replaced with thick-stemmed reed-grass fixed to the underside of the joists and secured to them with battens.

The plastered ceiling of most farmhouses remained plain with little or no decoration but by the end of the seventeenth century in many of the more pretentious farmhouses ornamental moulded plasterwork became fashionable. Moulded ceilings first appeared in the principal rooms of the great houses during the sixteenth century, and those of the Elizabethan period are usually characterized by small moulded ribs applied in geometrical patterns. At the intersection of the ribs are often ornamental bosses, and between the ribs there is a somewhat restrained use of decorative motifs which are usually restricted to heraldic bosses, shields, sprigs of foliage, the Tudor rose and the fleur-de-lis. In the larger houses many of the ceilings were of the pendant type where the moulded ribs descended into pendants with bosses or other forms of decoration at the junction. Moulded ceilings of the Jacobean period are far more ornate, divided into panels by moulded trabeations – wide ribs in high relief – providing greater space on the soffit for running ornamentation, usually comprising flowers and foliage. The panels are more freely filled with motifs than earlier ceilings; pendants of fruits, heraldic devices, wreaths of leaves and berries and cherubs are all typical. Later moulded ceilings became more dignified and restrained, with simpler patterns employed. A centre-piece became a common feature. First, in the second half of the seventeenth century, it was in high relief and richly decorated but later, towards the end of the century, although the centre-piece was retained, the mouldings were often plain and in low relief. The centre-piece remained a feature in the eighteenth century, again in low relief and often connected to the moulded cornice by a delicate moulding. In most instances in both these early ceilings and later ones, the protruding main ceiling beam would be cased in plaster and finished with a continuous moulded cornice which ran around the beam and the adjoining wall. However, by the beginning of the eighteenth century beams projecting below the ceiling line were avoided, with sometimes separate ceiling joists framed into the main beams and independent of the floor joists above.

STAIRCASES

Although many of the larger medieval houses with a first-floor hall had an external staircase, with the general adoption of the ground-floor open hall, with its two-storeyed solar and service bays at either end, an internal stair became essential. These early stairs were either a simple ladder or at its best the more elaborate companion way – a straight flight of steps comprising solid triangular timbers housed into the strings and so situated that the foot was placed beneath the slope of the step above. Later there were the stairs with solid steps constructed in either stone or, more surprisingly, timber. In all stone-bearing regions the stone newel stair, allied to the centuries-old spiral stairs of castles and church towers, was almost universal, with the inner end of each step forming a circular section of the newel. These stone newel stairs were generally housed in projecting turrets at the rear of the building, although there are examples of straight flights of solid stone steps of seventeenth-century date built between two bearing walls. In timber-framed buildings both newel and straight stairs of solid steps were used, the newel being preferred to the straight stairs for they occupied less room and would conveniently be placed in many small farmhouses beside the axial stack, so taking up little room.

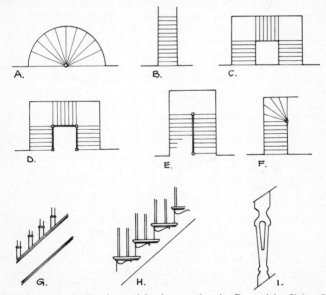

172. Staircase details: A. semicircular newel stair; B. straight flight; C. staircase rising round a solid core; D. open-well staircase; E. dog-leg staircase; F. winder staircase; G. detail of closed-string; H. detail of cut string; I. splat baluster.

The solid steps were housed into a newel post – a large circular post – which went from floor to ceiling and sometimes, as at Bower

Farmhouse, Hammerwood, Sussex, the full height of the house. Although solid stone steps are relatively common and continued to be used until the end of the seventeenth century, those of solid timber have largely been destroyed and replaced with boarded stairs. Some, however, still remain; Fitzjohn's Farm, Great Waltham, Redfant's Farm, Shalford, Blue Gates Farm, Great Bromley, all in Essex, Old Bell Farm, Harrietsham, Kent, and Lane Farmhouse, Feckenham, Hereford and Worcester, all retain solid timber step stairs of sixteenth-century date or earlier.

The newel stairs remained the most popular in nearly all small farmhouses up until the eighteenth century, although where space was less restricted straight flights were also frequently used. By this time, however, the solid steps had been replaced by the framed stairs with separate strings, treads and risers. In larger farmhouses, framed stairs had been used from the end of the sixteenth century; the dog-legged staircase was particularly common in smaller houses in the seventeenth century as was the open-well staircase, from the middle of the seventeenth century, in many of the larger houses. The late Elizabethan and Jacobean staircases were of heavier construction than the more delicate ones of the following century. Generally they had heavy square newels which projected above the handrail, finished with a carved or moulded cap and below the strings the end finished with a similar-fashioned pendant. Wide moulded handrails and closed strings with the balusters housed into the string and handrail were also characteristic features of the period. The early splat balusters, flat balusters either shaped or tapered and occasionally pierced, are fairly common. These were superseded by the more elaborate turned baluster towards the end of the seventeenth century. The twisted baluster was also a feature of many staircases constructed after the Restoration. Towards the end of the eighteenth century, with improved joinery techniques, the more delicate cut-string stair constructed of softwood developed. The strings were cut to the profile of the treads and risers and the tread extended beyond it, the nosing of the tread being returned at the end. The balusters were now lighter in section framed into the tread and handrail, which was generally of mahogany and extended over the newel and was often finished in a scroll. The bottom step was frequently curtailed and the space beneath the stairs filled in with panelling. However, in most small farmhouses the closed-string staircase, being easier to construct, continued to be used.

With the introduction of the two-storeyed hall block and with the chambering-over of many open halls, only one staircase was necessary to serve the upper floor, and although in many farmhouses the stairs were situated alongside the newly built chimney stack, in some cases, especially those of the dog-legged type, it required more space. Generally they were situated in the hall itself, but occasionally the staircase was accommodated in a projecting annexe at the rear of the building, usually with access from the hall. Some of the notable examples of these projecting staircase wings are Doe's Farmhouse, Toothill, and Warren's Farm, Great Easton, both in Essex, Dawes Farm, Bolney, Sussex, Low Farm, Elsworth, Cambridgeshire, Warren's Farm, Stanton, Gloucestershire, and Hookstone Farm, Chobham, Surrey.

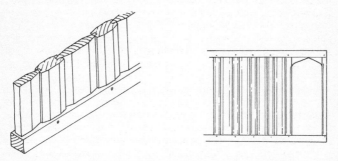

173. Typical sixteenth-century plank and muntin partition.

INTERNAL PARTITIONS

In most farmhouses, from the fifteenth century onwards, the private rooms were separated from the main living-rooms by partitions. These were usually non-structural and could, no matter what the material of the main house, be built in timber. The most common type was the so-called 'plank-and-muntin' partition (173), which consisted of alternate vertical boards or planks housed into the edges of the muntins, which in turn were framed into the sill and ceiling beam. The muntins were often only chamfered, but on better-class work they were sometimes moulded on the living-room side, while the planks might be given a simplified type of linenfold pattern. The partition generally incorporated a doorway and sometimes a built-in bench with pew-like shaped ends. There are many surviving examples of this type of partition from the end of the fifteenth century until the end of the seventeenth century. From about the middle of the seventeenth century the framed partition began to appear in vernacular buildings; here horizontal rails were framed into the muntins to form square panels which were filled in with thin timber housed on all edges to the muntins and rails. Both the muntins and the rails were moulded. During the latter part of the seventeenth century built-in cupboards became popular in farmhouses, and these were sometimes incorporated in the timber partitions.

PANELLING

Wall panelling was first introduced into houses in the late fifteenth century, when it was referred to as 'sealing'. This early form of panelling comprised little more than vertical oak boards, with the edges either simply overlapping or crudely grooved into each other. This form of sealing or wainscoting, as it was later known, was followed by panelling comprising thin boards set into grooves in heavy muntins with these uprights framed into a sill and head. In some instances a horizontal middle rail was introduced. This type of panelling was obviously a development of the plank-and-muntin screens and partitions previously described.

These early forms of wall panelling soon established panelling as a method of adding comfort to rooms. Because panelling had no structural importance, the heavy sections previously used were progressively reduced in thickness until by about 1550 the panelling was often only one inch thick. At the same time the muntins were set closer together, with horizontal rails being introduced in the Elizabethan period to form small, nearly square panels.

In Tudor and Jacobean panelling the horizontal rails were usually one continuous length framed at the end into styles, with the panels formed by muntins pegged and morticed and tenoned between them. The mouldings were 'out of the solid'; at first only the muntins were moulded, with the rails left square with a scratched bead above and below each panel (174A). Later the top edges of the rails were chamfered either continuous with the muntin scribed over the chamfer or the chamfer stopped on either side of the muntin (174B and D). As the mouldings were wrought out of the solid, when the edges of the rails were moulded, as well as the muntins and styles, this caused a problem at the junction of the two. This was overcome either by the introduction of a mason's mitre (174I), in which the muntins were butted square with the rails, and the mouldings of the rails returned to meet those on the muntins, or occasionally the muntins were scribed over the mouldings or the rails (174E). The true joiner's mitre in which the mouldings were cut at forty-five degrees did not come into common use until the beginning of the seventeenth century (174F). It was not until well into the seventeenth century that applied mouldings cut and mitred at the corners were adopted. This method proved to be a great advance, being both quicker and cheaper, and it had the added advantage of being less wasteful.

The panels too were often decorated, and in the early Tudor period the linenfold pattern was the characteristic embellishment, in which

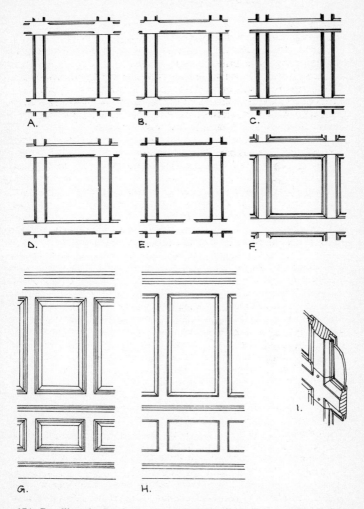

174. Panelling: A., B., C., D., E. and F. sixteenth- and seventeenth-century panelling; G. late seventeenth-early eighteenth-century panelling; H. late eighteenth-century panelling; I. detail of mason's mitre.

the panels were carved with vertical grooves to resemble the folded linen. This form of decoration is not a common feature in farmhouses though there are good examples, such as Moat Farm, Shadingfield, Suffolk. There were other motifs, with the most ornate treatment being attained in the reign of Henry VIII, when the subjects included carved animals, shields and bunches of grapes twined between ribbed patterns. Another popular design was the use of Renaissance-type heads in profile carved in round medallions, as at Hatches Farm, Little Burstead, Essex, and Home Farm, Fen Ditton, Cambridgeshire. A feature of some Jacobean panelling is its division into bays with pilasters supporting a rudimentary frieze, the whole connected with strapwork and arabesques. In some cases the panels are large, being overlaid with moulded strips of wood to form diamond or other shapes. In the second quarter of the seventeenth century the size of the panels increased, and the use of bolection mouldings was freely adopted.

The use of panelling declined in the second half of the seventeenth century, and it was not until the beginning of the following century that it regained popularity. Whereas in the preceding centuries the panelling had been of oak, the timber now was invariably pine. The feature of early Georgian panelling was the raised and fielded panels framed in bolection mouldings with large panels above a dado rail and squat ones of the same width below (174G). Later in the eighteenth century in many unpretentious farmhouses the panels became plain with the bolection mouldings replaced by a simple moulding run out of the solid (174H). Georgian panelling is fairly common in farmhouses and was used not only in new buildings of the period but in many older timber-framed buildings when modernization took place in the eighteenth century. Often later wall panelling was taken up only to dado height.

INTERIOR WALL DECORATIONS

The plastering of internal walls to render the interior of houses less austere was first undertaken in the Middle Ages. Stone walls, previously left bare or simply whitewashed, were given a thin coat of plaster onto which patterns and scenes were painted, though from the fourteenth century the walls in the chief apartments were usually draped with tapestry. The use of both mural decorations and tapestry remained the vogue in the larger houses, but during the fifteenth century the desire for some form of wall decoration penetrated down the social scale into houses of yeoman farmers. This new kind of wall decoration was a painted hanging of cloth or canvas, as a cheap substitute for tapestry. That they became extremely common during the sixteenth century is evident from the domestic inventories of the period which abound in references to 'painted cloths' and 'painted hangings' for walls.

It was about the middle of the sixteenth century that wall paintings, that is to say decorative designs painted directly onto the face of the plaster, first emerged in the domestic house. These early paintings were generally executed in colours in which the pigments were diluted with glue or alternatively mixed with the white of eggs to form a distemper. The earliest form of these paintings was pictorial, often of a religious nature. A fine example is to be found at Faulkners End Farm, Harpenden, Hertfordshire, a sixteenth-century farmhouse, which has a late sixteenth-century wall painting which includes figures and a landscape. More common and perhaps later in date are ones of a floral or geometrical pattern, sometimes in an all-over design but more frequently of a repetitive nature in panels or bands often contained within a decorative border. Strapwork was another popular design in Tudor times – Brook Farm, Stratford St Mary, Suffolk, and Church Farm House, Howell, Hertfordshire – as were running floral designs such as the one at Bradfield's Farm, Toppesfield, Essex, in which the running design is of leaves and flowers outlined in black or white paint and coloured with red and blue. Although many of these patterns were of a repetitive nature, most repeats appear to have been undertaken free-hand, and it was not until after the Reformation that stencilling became widely accepted.

Decorative wall paintings were used not only on plasterwork but on many occasions timber partitions and doors were similarly treated. At Bradfield's Farm, Toppesfield, a flower design similar to that already described for the walls was applied to the face of the door in the same room, while at Hoestreet Farm, Roxwell, Essex, the painted strapwork of early seventeenth-century date is taken across the adjoining door. In stud walls too, where the timbers were exposed, it was common for the studs to be whitened and the wall painting continued across.

Of the numerous wall paintings which must have once existed, relatively few now survive; most have been destroyed with old plaster or obliterated by successive coats of whitewash. In recent years the stripping of old wallpaper and the removal of old whitewash has revealed many remnants of these paintings. Most are seldom fit for preservation but many good examples of all types still remain.

Wall painting continued throughout the eighteenth century, and surviving examples are all of a repetitive nature, almost certainly undertaken with the aid of stencils. In design, they followed much the same pattern as the early wallpapers. Although wallpaper in England had been known since Tudor times, it was not until the early part of the eighteenth century that it began to gain popularity. The designs were usually block printed on sheets of rectangular paper which, though small in size were the largest capable of being produced by the hand methods then employed. Colour was added to the design either by hand painting or more commonly with the aid of a stencil. It was not until the beginning of the nineteenth century, with the improved methods of paper manufacture, that wallpaper began to gain popularity in the average farmhouse, and it was not until the 1840s, when an effective machine was produced, that machine-printed paper began to replace the hand-printed ones. Such was the demand for this new wall covering that its mass production was soon established.

Bibliography

Of the great number of books, booklets and articles which have all contributed to the writing of this book, it is possible to mention here only those that have proved most valuable.

GENERAL BOOKS

ADDY, S. O., *The Evolution of the English House* (Allen & Unwin, 1898; revised 1933)
ALCOCK, N. W., *A Catalogue of Cruck Buildings* (Phillimore, 1973)
AYRES, James, *The Shell Book of The Home in Britain* (Faber & Faber, 1981)
BARLEY, M. W., *The English Farmhouse and Cottage* (Routledge & Paul, 1961); *The House and Home* (Vista Books, 1963)
BERESFORD, M. & HURST, J. G., *Deserted Medieval Villages* (Lutterworth Press, 1971)
BRAUN, H., *The Story of the English House* (Batsford, 1940); *Old English Houses* (Faber & Faber, 1962)
BRIGGS, M. S., *The English Farmhouse* (Batsford, 1953)
BRUNSKILL, R. W., *Illustrated Handbook of Vernacular Architecture* (Faber & Faber, 1971; new edition 1978); *Traditional Buildings of Britain* (Gollancz, 1981)
BRUNSKILL, R. W. & CLIFTON-TAYLOR, A., *English Brickwork* (Ward Lock, 1977)
CAVE, Lyndon, F., *The Smaller English House – Its History and Development* (Hale, 1981)
CLIFTON-TAYLOR, Alex, *The Pattern of English Building* (Batsford, 1962; new edition Faber & Faber, 1972)
COOK, Olive and SMITH, Edwin, *Old English Cottages and Farmhouses* (Thames & Hudson, 1954)
CROSSLEY, F. H., *Timber Building in England* (Batsford, 1951)
CUNNINGTON, Pamela, *How Old is Your House?* (Alphabooks, 1980)
HARRIS, Richard, *Discovering Timber-Framed Buildings* (Shire Publications, 1978)
HEWETT, C. A., *English Historic Carpentry* (Phillimore, 1980)
HOSKINS, W. G., *Provincial England* (Macmillan, 1964)
INNOCENT, C. F., *The Development of English Building Construction* (Cambridge University Press, 1916)
JONES, S. R., *The Village Homes of England* (The Studio, 1912); *English Village Homes and Country Buildings* (Batsford, 1936)
MASON, R. T., *Framed Buildings of England* (Coach Publishing House)
MERCER, Eric, *English Vernacular Houses* (Royal Commission on Historical Monuments, HMSO, 1975)
PENOYRE, John & Jane, *Houses in the Landscape* (Faber & Faber, 1978)
PRIZEMAN, J., *Your House – the Outside View* (Hutchinson, 1975)
REID, Richard, *The Shell Book of Cottages* (Joseph, 1977)
SALZMAN, L. F., *Building in England Down to 1540* (Oxford, 1952)
WARREN, C. Henry, *English Cottages and Farmhouses* (Collins, 1948)
WEST, T., *The Timber-framed House in England* (David & Charles, 1971)
WOOD, M. E., *The English Medieval House* (Phoenix, 1965)

REGIONAL BOOKS

BRUNSKILL, R. W., *Vernacular Architecture of the Lake Counties* (Faber & Faber, 1974)

CHESHER, V. M. & F. J., *The Cornishman's House* (Bradford Barton, Truro, 1968)

DAVIE, W. G. & CURTIS GREEN, W., *Old Cottages and Farmhouses in Surrey* (Batsford, 1908)

DAVIE, W. G. & DAWBER, E. G., *Old Cottages and Farmhouses in Kent & Sussex* (Batsford, 1906); *Farmhouses and other Buildings in the Cotswold District* (Batsford, 1905)

FORRESTER, Harry, *The Timber-framed Houses of Essex; A Short Review of the Types and Details, Fourteenth to Eighteenth Centuries* (Tindall Press, 1959)

GRAVETT, Kenneth, *Timber and Brick Building in Kent* (Phillimore)

HEWETT, C. A., *The Development of English Carpentry 1200–1700: An Essex Study* (David & Charles, 1969)

HOSKINS, W. G., *Old Devon* (David & Charles, 1966)

MASON, R. T., *Framed Building of the Weald* (Privately published, 1964; revised edition, 1969)

NAIRN, Ian & PEVSNER, Nikolaus, *The Buildings of England – Surrey* (Penguin, 1962); *The Buildings of England – Sussex* (Penguin, 1965)

NEVILL, R., *Old Cottages and Domestic Architecture in South-west Surrey* (Billing & Son, Guildford, 1889)

NEWMAN, John, *The Buildings of England – North East and East Kent* (Penguin, 1969); *The Buildings of England – West Kent and the Weald* (Penguin, 1969)

OLIVER, Basil, *Old Houses and Village Buildings in East Anglia* (Batsford, 1912)

PARKINSON, J. & OULD, E. A., *Old Cottages and Farmhouses in Shropshire, Herefordshire and Cheshire* (Batsford, 1904)

PEVSNER, Nikolaus & LLOYD, David, *The Buildings of England – Hampshire and the Isle of Wight* (Penguin, 1967)

PEVSNER, Nikolaus, *The Buildings of England – Derbyshire* (Penguin, 1953 revised 1978 by Elizabeth Williamson); *The Buildings of England – Essex* (Penguin, 1959, revised 1965 by Enid Radcliffe); *The Buildings of England – Hertfordshire* (Penguin, 1953, revised 1977 by Bridget Cherry); *The Buildings of England – N.E. Norfolk and Norwich* (Penguin, 1962); *The Buildings of England – N.W. and South Norfolk* (Penguin, 1962); *The Buildings of England – Suffolk* (Penguin, 1961); *The Buildings of England – Worcestershire* (Penguin, 1968)

RAISTRICK, Arthur, *Buildings of the Yorkshire Dales* (Dalesman Books, 1976)

RAMM, H. G., McDOWALL, R. W. & MERCER, Eric, *Shielings and Bastles* (Royal Commission on Historical Monuments, 1970)

ROLLINSON, William, *Life and Traditions in the Lake District* (Dent, 1974)

ROYAL COMMISSION ON HISTORICAL MONUMENTS, *Buckinghamshire; Volumes I & II* (1912–13); *Cambridgeshire; Volumes I & II* (1968–72); *Dorset; Volumes I–V* (1952–78); *Essex; Volumes I–IV* (1916–23); *Herefordshire; Volumes I–III* (1931–4); *Huntingdonshire* (1926); *Westmorland* (1936)

SANDON, Eric, *Suffolk Houses* (Baron Publishing, 1977)

WALTON, J, *Homesteads of the Yorkshire Dales* (Dalesman, 1947)

WOOD-JONES, R. B., *Traditional Domestic Architecture of the Banbury Region* (Manchester University Press, 1963)

WORTH, R. H., *Dartmoor* (Reprinted David & Charles, 1967)

ARTICLES *etc*

ALCOCK, N. W., 'Devon Farmhouses I' (*Transactions of the Devonshire Association*, 100, 1968, pages 13–28); 'Devon Farmhouses II' (*Ibid*, 101, 1969, pages 83–106)

ALCOCK, N. W. & HULLAND, C., 'Devon Farmhouses IV' (*Transactions of the Devonshire Association*, 104, 1972, pages 35–57)

ALCOCK, N. W., CHILD, P. C. & LAITHWAITE, J. M. W., 'Sanders, Lettaford – A Devon Long House' (*Proceedings of the Devon Archaeological Society*, 30, 1972, pages 227–33)

BAGGS, A. P., 'Hook Farm, Lower Woodcut, Hampshire' (*Transactions of the Newbury District Field Club*, 11, No. 4, 1967, pages 27–8)

BARLEY, M. W., Chapter X in Joan Thirsk (ed.) *The Agrarian History of England and Wales 1500–1640* (Cambridge University Press, 1967)

BEREFORD, G. T. M., 'Northend Farm House, Long Crendon' (*Record of Buckinghamshire*, 18, ii, 1967, pages 125–35)

BRUNSKILL, R. W., 'The development of the small house in the Eden Valley from 1650 to 1840' (*Transactions of the Cumberland and Westmorland Antiquarian and Archaeological Society*, 53, 1953, pages 160–89); 'The clay houses of Cumberland' (*Transactions of the Ancient Monuments Society*, NS 10, 1962, pages 57–80)

CHARLES, F. W. B., 'Medieval Cruck-Building and its Derivatives' (*Society for Medieval Archaeology*, Monograph Series, No. 2, 1967)

CHILD, P. C. & LAITHWAITE, J. M. W. 'Little Rull – A late Medieval House near Cullompton' (*Proceedings of the Devon Archaeological Society*, 33, 1975, pages 303–10)

COLMAN, J. G. & S. J., 'A Thirteenth Century Aisled House: Purton Green Farm, Stansfield, Suffolk' (*Proceedings of the Suffolk Institute of Archaeology*, 30, ii, 1965, 149–65)

FLETCHER, J. M., 'Three Medieval Farmhouses in Harwell' (*Berkshire Archaeological Journal*, 62, 1965–6, pages 45–69); 'Crucks in the West Berkshire and Oxford Region' (*Oxoniensia*, 33, 1968, pages 71–88)

GLENDINNING, S. E., 'Manor Farm, Pulham Market' (*Norfolk Archaeology*, 30, iii, 1951, pages 223–5)

HARTLEY, M. & INGILBY, J., 'Farm Houses of the Yorkshire Dales' (*Country Life*, 147, 1970, pages 442–3)

HEWETT, C. A., 'Structural Carpentry in Medieval Essex' (*Medieval Archaeology*, 6–7, 1962–3, pages 240–70); 'Jettying and Floor Framing in Medieval Essex' (*Ibid*, 1966, pages 89–112); 'Some East Anglian Prototypes for early Timber Houses in America' (*Post Medieval Archaeology*, 3, 1969, pages 100–21); 'Seventeenth Century Carpentry in Essex' (*Ibid*, 5, 1971, pages 77–87); 'The Development of the Post-Medieval House' (*Ibid*, 7, 1973, pages 60–78); 'Structural Carpentry in the Medieval House' (*Transactions of Association for Studies in the Conservation of Historic Buildings*, Vol. 1, 1973); 'The Smaller Medieval House in Essex' (*Archaeology Journal*, 130, 1973, pages 172–81); 'Aisled Timber Halls and Related Buildings, Chiefly in Essex' (*Ancient Monuments Society's Transaction*, 1976, pages 45–99)

JONES, S. R., 'Shelfield Lodge Farm, Aldridge' (*Transactions of the South Staffordshire Archaeological History Society*, 10, 1968–9, pages 63–9); 'Devon Farmhouses III – Moorland and Non-Moorland Long Houses' (*Transactions of the Devonshire Association*, 103, pages 35–76)

JONES, S. R., & SMITH, J. T., 'Manor House, Wasperton' (*Transactions of the Proceedings of the Birmingham Archaeological Society*, 76, 1958, pages 19–28)

JONES, T. L. & FIELD, C. M., 'The Melkridge Bastle, Northumberland' (*Archaeological Aeliana*, 45, 34, 1956, pages 138–41)

JOHNSON; I. & FENEY, P., 'Grange Farm, Widmer End' (*Record of Buckinghamshire*, 19, 1974, pages 449–56)

JOPE, E. M., 'Cornish houses 1400–1700' (*Studies in Building History*, 1961, pages 192–222).

MASON, R. T., 'Tickeridge a 14th Century Farmhouse' (*Sussex Archaeological Collection*, 82, 1941, pages 65–72); 'Bell's Farm, Slaugham' (*Ibid*, 88, 1949, pages 15–21); 'Hurter's Farm, East Chiltington' (*Sussex Notes and Queries*, 15, No. 6, 1960, pages 203–4); 'Pond Farm, Southwater' (*Ibid*, 16, No. 2, 1963, pages 43–5)

MASON, R. T. & PACKER, G. A., 'Chennell's Brook Farm, Horsham' (*Sussex Archaeological Collections*, 101, 1963, pages 40–7)

MASON, R. T. & WOOD, R. H., 'Winkhurst Farm, Bough Beech' (*Archaeologia Cantiana*, 83, 1968, pages 33–7)

McDOWALL, R. W., 'The Westmorland Vernacular' (*Studies in Architectural History*, 1956, pages 125–43)

OGLE, H., 'Yew Tree Farm, Samlesbury' (*Transactions of the Historical Society of Lancashire and Cheshire*, 100, 1948, pages 45–54)

PANTIN, W. A., 'Medieval Priests' Houses in south-west England' (*Medieval Archaeology*, I, 1957, pages 118–46); 'Chantry Priests' Houses and Medieval Lodgings' (*Ibid*, III, 1959, pages 216–58)

RAISTRICK, A., 'Dales Building of the 16th and 17th centuries – V. Farms' (*Yorkshire Dalesman*, 10, 1942)

RIGOLD, S. E., 'The timber-framed buildings of Steventon (Berkshire) and their regional significance' (*Transactions of the Newbury District Field Club*, 10, No. 4, 1958, pages 4–13); 'Fourteenth century halls in the East Weald' (*Archaeologia Cantiana*, 82, 1967, pages 246–56)

SINGLETON, W. A., 'Traditional dwellings in the Cheshire countryside' (*Cheshire History* I, 1951, pages 4–12); 'House types in rural Lancashire and Cheshire' (*Transactions of the Historical Society of Lancashire and Cheshire*, 104, 1952, pages 75–91); 'Traditional domestic architecture in Lancashire and Cheshire' (*Transactions of the Lancashire and Cheshire Antiquarian Society*, 65, 1955, pages 33–47).

SMITH, J. T., 'A 14th century aisled house; Edgar's Farm, Stowmarket' (*Proceedings of the Suffolk Institute of Archaeology*, 28, i, 1958, pages 54–61); 'Medieval roofs: a classification' (*Archaeological Journal*, 115, 1958, pages 111–49), 'Timber-framed Building in England; Its Development and Regional Differences' (*Ibid*, 122, 1965, pages 133–58).

SMITH, P., 'The Longhouse and the Laithe-house' (*Culture and Environment Essays in Honour of Sir Cyril Fox*, 1963, Chapter 17, pages 415–38)

STELL, C. F., 'Pennine Houses; an introduction' (*Folk Life*, 3, 1965, pages 5–24); 'Hill Farm, Chalfont St. Peter' (*Record of Buckinghamshire*, 18, i, 1966, pages 73–7)

SUMMERS, N., 'Old Hall Farm, Kneesall' (*Thoroton Society Transactions*, 76, 1972, pages 17–25)

THORPE, J., 'Some Old Devon Farmhouses' (*Country Life*, 96, 1944, pages 546–8)

TONKIN, J. W., 'An Old House at Staunton-on-Wye, Herefordshire' (*Woolhope Club Transactions*, 37, iii, 1963, pages 327–9); 'An Introduction to the Houses of Herefordshire' (*Ibid*, 39, ii, 1968, pages 186–97)

WATSON, R. C., 'Traditional Fylde Houses' (*Transactions of the Historical Society of Lancashire and Cheshire*, 109, 1957, pages 61–6); 'Some Fylde Longhouses' (*Post-Medieval Archaeology*, 6, 1972); 'Parlours with External Entrances' (*Vernacular Architecture*, 6, 1975, pages 28–30)

WELFORD, A., 'The Restoration of a 16th century farmhouse in Suffolk' (*Proceedings of the Suffolk Institute of Archaeology*, 24, i, 1946, pages 1–19)

WILLIAMS, E. H. D. 'Poltimore Farmhouse, Farway' (*Transactions of the Devonshire Association*, 106, 1974, pages 215–29)

WILLIAMS, W. M., 'Farmhouses of South-west Cumberland: a preliminary survey' (*Transactions of the Cumberland and Westmorland Antiquarian and Archaeological Society*, 54, 1954, pages 248–64)

Index of Farmhouses

Page numbers in *italics* refer to illustration

General Index

Page numbers in *italics* refer to illustrations